I0038818

Continuous Improvement

DIRECTIONS IN DEVELOPMENT
Human Development

Continuous Improvement

*Strengthening Georgia's Targeted
Social Assistance Program*

Tinatin Baum, Anastasia Mshvidobadze, and Josefina Posadas

WORLD BANK GROUP

© 2016 International Bank for Reconstruction and Development / The World Bank
1818 H Street NW, Washington, DC 20433
Telephone: 202-473-1000; Internet: www.worldbank.org

Some rights reserved

1 2 3 4 19 18 17 16

This work is a product of the staff of The World Bank with external contributions. The findings, interpretations, and conclusions expressed in this work do not necessarily reflect the views of The World Bank, its Board of Executive Directors, or the governments they represent. The World Bank does not guarantee the accuracy of the data included in this work. The boundaries, colors, denominations, and other information shown on any map in this work do not imply any judgment on the part of The World Bank concerning the legal status of any territory or the endorsement or acceptance of such boundaries.

Nothing herein shall constitute or be considered to be a limitation upon or waiver of the privileges and immunities of The World Bank, all of which are specifically reserved.

Rights and Permissions

This work is available under the Creative Commons Attribution 3.0 IGO license (CC BY 3.0 IGO) http://creativecommons.org/licenses/by/3.0/igo. Under the Creative Commons Attribution license, you are free to copy, distribute, transmit, and adapt this work, including for commercial purposes, under the following conditions:

Attribution—Please cite the work as follows: Baum, Tinatin, Anastasia Mshvidobadze, and Josefina Posadas. 2016. *Continuous Improvement: Strengthening Georgia's Targeted Social Assistance Program.* Directions in Development. Washington, DC: World Bank. doi:10.1596/978-1-4648-0900-2. License: Creative Commons Attribution CC BY 3.0 IGO

Translations—If you create a translation of this work, please add the following disclaimer along with the attribution: *This translation was not created by The World Bank and should not be considered an official World Bank translation. The World Bank shall not be liable for any content or error in this translation.*

Adaptations—If you create an adaptation of this work, please add the following disclaimer along with the attribution: *This is an adaptation of an original work by The World Bank. Views and opinions expressed in the adaptation are the sole responsibility of the author or authors of the adaptation and are not endorsed by The World Bank.*

Third-party content—The World Bank does not necessarily own each component of the content contained within the work. The World Bank therefore does not warrant that the use of any third-party–owned individual component or part contained in the work will not infringe on the rights of those third parties. The risk of claims resulting from such infringement rests solely with you. If you wish to reuse a component of the work, it is your responsibility to determine whether permission is needed for that reuse and to obtain permission from the copyright owner. Examples of components can include, but are not limited to, tables, figures, or images.

All queries on rights and licenses should be addressed to World Bank Publications, The World Bank Group, 1818 H Street NW, Washington, DC 20433, USA; fax: 202-522-2625; e-mail: pubrights@worldbank.org.

ISBN (paper): 978-1-4648-0900-2
ISBN (electronic): 978-1-4648-0901-9
DOI: 10.1596/978-1-4648-0900-2

Cover photo: © UNICEF/Geo-2015/Khetaguri. Used with the permission of UNICEF. Further permission required for reuse.
Cover design: Debra Naylor, Naylor Design, Inc.

Library of Congress Cataloging-in-Publication data has been requested.

Contents

Boxes

Figures

Maps

Tables

Acknowledgments

This publication is a joint venture between the United Nations Children's Fund (UNICEF) and the World Bank Group (WBG). It is part of a common effort to support the government of Georgia in reforming the Targeted Social Assistance (TSA) program.

The task was led by Tinatin Baum, Anastasia Mshvidobadze (UNICEF), and Josefina Posadas (WBG). The full team also comprises George Berulava, Lasha Bokuchava, Tamar Chelidze, David Gzirishvili, Varlam Kvantaliani, Nikoloz Pkhakadze, and Vasil Tsakadze from UNICEF, as well as Cesar Cancho, Silvia Guallar Artal, Denis Nikitin, and Julieth Santamaria from the WBG.

This work was undertaken in response to a request from the Ministry of Labor, Health, and Social Affairs, and the Social Services Agency of Georgia. The collaboration was initiated in 2013 with a memorandum of understanding signed between the ministry, the agency, and UNICEF. In 2014, when this reform was identified as a trigger candidate for a WBG Inclusive Growth Development Policy Operation, the WBG joined to provide further technical assistance. During the process, there has been close collaboration with Tengiz Tsekvava, George Kalakashvili, Temur Paksashvili, and Tata Gulua from the National Statistics Office of Georgia; Zaza Sopromadze, Nutsi Odisharia, Tatia Gvaramadze, Dimitri Chkheidze, Sargis Tsikhelashvili, Tengiz Abazadze, Gia Gvazava, Avtandil Vasadze in the government of Georgia; and David Lomidze, Gaioz Talakvadze, Gia Kakachia, Akaki Danelia, and Gela Chiviashvili. General guidance has come from Minister David Sergeenko.

The team is grateful for the input and comments of Sudhanshu Handa, Philippe Leite, Kathy Lindert, and Ruslan Yemtsov (peer reviewers) and the overall guidance of Dandan Chen, Andrew Mason, and Manuel Salazar from the WBG, and Sasha Graumann and Jennifer Yablonski from UNICEF. Additional guidance was provided by Kathy Lindert (global lead on Systems in the Social Protection and Labor Global Practice, WBG) and Ruslan Yemtsov (global lead on Social Safety Nets in the Social Protection and Labor Global Practice, WBG). The team is also grateful to Veronica Silva and the team in the Latin American Social Protection and Labor Unit of the WBG for sharing their analytic framework for the social protection and labor system.

About the Authors

Tinatin Baum, a social policy specialist at UNICEF Georgia, focuses on policy analysis and research on topics such as inequality, welfare, poverty analysis, child poverty, social safety nets and social protection, gender, and public policy. Baum coauthored the child poverty discussion paper series and the simulation models developed by UNICEF Georgia on cash benefits for reducing child poverty and refining the social protection system. Earlier, Baum worked as head of the Analytical Department at the Ministry of Reintegration of Georgia. She has worked as a senior analyst in the Georgian Ministry of Internal Affairs as well as in organizations such as the Organization for Security and Co-operation in Europe and CARE International in the Caucasus. She holds a master's degree in public policy analysis from Pepperdine University, School of Public Policy, California, and a master's degree in international and regional conflicts from the Georgian Technical University.

Anastasia Mshvidobadze is a data analysis consultant at UNICEF Georgia. She assists in designing quantitative studies, monitors data quality, conducts secondary analysis of data, and contributes to report writing. Her main interests are social statistics and poverty reduction strategies. She is the lead author of the simulation models developed by UNICEF Georgia on cash benefits for reducing child poverty. Previously she worked at the National Bank and the Ministry of Agriculture of Georgia. Mshvidobadze holds a master's degree in economics from McGill University and in mathematics from the University of Nebraska–Lincoln, where she trained extensively in quantitative methods and modelling, including econometrics and population dynamics.

Josefina Posadas is a senior economist in the Social Protection and Labor Global Practice of the World Bank Group. Her area of expertise is labor economics, and since joining the World Bank in 2008 she has worked on issues related to labor markets, entrepreneurship, gender equality, and poverty. Between 1996 and 2002, she worked at the Universidad Nacional de La Plata (UNLP) in Argentina, where she reached the position of associate professor in 1999. During those years, Posadas also advised different government offices of

Argentina, at both the local and national levels, on employment, trade, and fiscal federalism matters, and taught several classes in master's programs in the UNLP and the Torcuato Di Tella University. She holds a PhD in economics from Boston University and a master's in economics from the Instituto Torcuato Di Tella in Argentina.

Executive Summary

Laying the Groundwork

At the end of 2013, the government of Georgia (GoG) began a technical review of its main social assistance program, Targeted Social Assistance (TSA). When the current administration took office in 2012, it promised to pay more attention to social issues in the country. At the same time, the GoG needed to be convinced of the efficiency and transparency of the TSA as a last-resort social assistance program and to present it to its constituency. The government was concerned that too many poor people would not be covered by the TSA and, conversely, that too many others would benefit from it, and therefore drain resources. Members of the government were also worried that the inclusion in the eligibility formula of subjective assessment of the social agents and of goods that could be concealed left room for abuses of the system. During the first years of government, the new administration took several steps to address these concerns. First, the technical features of the TSA were reviewed. Second, the administrative and business processes of program implementation were improved. Third, new legislation was passed that modified the targeting formula and benefits scheme of the TSA and adopted a new targeted program: the Child Benefit Program (CBP). Finally, implementation started in June 2015, and compensation measures were adopted in August 2015.

This report assesses the policies taken concerning the TSA in 2015 and provides an initial and basic set of recommendations for building a comprehensive and efficient social protection and labor system. The various policy actions were supported by sound technical work that is presented and evaluated in this report. The study comprises the estimation of the formula to determine eligibility to the program, the analysis of the expected distributional impact of the policies undertaken, and a brief discussion on the pretesting of the implementation of the changes and the compensation measures adopted soon after initiating implementation.

The report does not delve into the revision of the administrative and business processes of the program. It includes only a brief description of them in order to provide a context for the technical work and recommendations about how to continue improving them. In this way, the report also aims to set the agenda for future policy actions and to build institutional memory. The latter is of particular importance given the high turnover of officials (technical staff and decision makers) working with the TSA since 2013. In addition, the report provides guidance about next steps in light of its findings and the political actions taken by the government.

The technical work is a joint effort of UNICEF and the World Bank Group (WBG) in collaboration with the Ministry of Labor, Health, and Social Affairs (MoLHSA) and the Social Services Agency (SSA) of Georgia. UNICEF initiated the collaboration with the government late in 2013, and thus took the lead in the technical work behind the revision of the eligibility formula (chapters 3 and 4), while the WBG came on board later and took the lead on the analysis of the distributional impact of the policy actions (chapters 6 and 7). The pretesting of the TSA (chapter 8) was also led by UNICEF, with input from the WBG. All of the outputs were discussed with the government throughout their development, and the GoG in turn made policy decisions based on the analysis and on its political objectives. This report was written by UNICEF and the WBG and reflects the technical opinion of these teams.

Spending on the TSA program, the government's main instrument to support consumption by the extreme poor, is low by regional and global standards. The TSA budget is the third largest expenditure item within total social spending in Georgia, after social pensions and education. In 2014, 14 percent of total social spending went to this program. It is the main vehicle to alleviate poverty in a country that spends relatively low amounts by international standards on social protection and labor, although it is not much less than the average spending for social protection among the other countries in the region. Georgia spends 1.2 percent of its gross domestic product in social assistance, excluding social pensions, while the average for Eastern Europe and Central Asia is 1.8 percent.[1] This level of spending provides coverage for 13 percent of the population and lifts 6 percent of the population out of extreme poverty; in the absence of the TSA program, extreme poverty incidence would be 9.7 instead of the observed 3.9 percent.

The TSA program targets the poor using a proxy means testing (PMT) formula. Introduced in 2006, the TSA and the PMT were means of increasing efficiency of social assistance spending. The idea of PMT formulas is to approximate household well-being based on household assets as opposed to income. The PMT mechanism was chosen suitable for Georgia because income from formal sources was—and still is—a less accurate indicator than assets of household welfare. Employers and employees simply do not declare employment, or they declare wages below the negotiated amount. In response to these concerns, in 2014 the government introduced a nontaxable minimum income. However, the Ministry of Finance issued a statement annulling this privilege starting in 2016. The TSA has also gradually replaced other categorical benefits that have been phased out. For example, the allowance for internally displaced persons (IDPs) cannot be received jointly with TSA.

Compared to other social assistance programs in Europe and Central Asia, Georgia's TSA is one of the best if targeting and coverage, or poverty and coverage, are assessed jointly. In 2013, the poverty rate in Georgia was still high for the region. Twenty-five and 36 percent of the population was living on less than US$2.50 per day, according to UNICEF's and WBG's estimates, respectively.[2] In 2013, the TSA covered 12 percent of Georgia's households. Coverage of the bottom quintile was 48 percent, and of the bottom decile, 71 percent. Benefit incidence was 53 percent. In general, it is easier to achieve good targeting in relatively small programs, and easier to achieve higher coverage of the poor by tolerating weaker targeting accuracy. Figure ES.1 shows that for the level of poverty, coverage, and targeting accuracy, the TSA performs relatively better than social assistance programs in other countries in the region.

In spite of the good overall performance of the program by international standards, the government still had issues related to performance. The government was concerned about "outdated" information, as the status quo methodology was based on 2006 survey data. There were important concerns related to households from upper levels of the welfare distribution receiving benefits, the transparency of the subjective component of the formula, and households concealing goods such as mobile phones, TVs, and even refrigerators or stoves, based on the anecdotes and reports of the social agents. It was believed that some people may have been able to manipulate the program and the program may thus have included persons who did not deserve the benefit. There were also concerns about work disincentives, which were studied by the WBG as part of a regional effort based on four case studies.[3] This enabled the GoG to focus on the former set of issues (manipulation and effective targeting) and on strengthening implementation processes.

Since the inception of the TSA, there has been continuous improvement on process but no comprehensive technical evaluation. Various complementary and

Figure ES.1 Poverty Incidence and Benefit Incidence, Coverage in the Bottom Quintile, Georgia and Regional Comparators

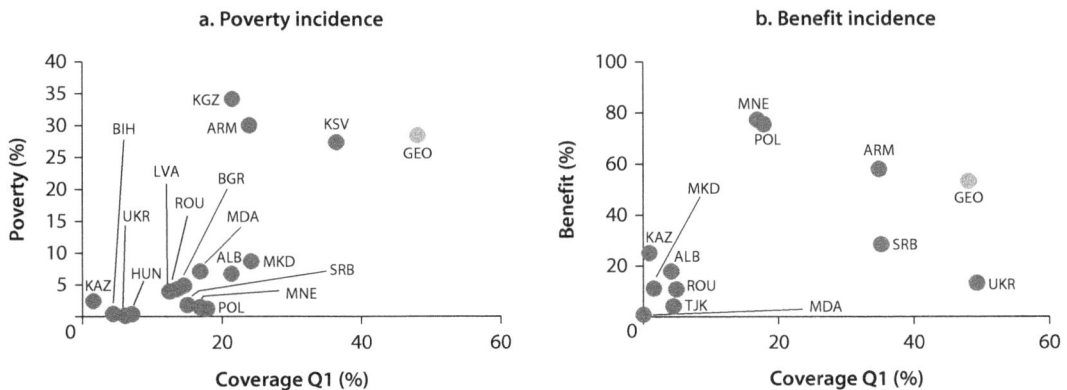

Source: Europe and Central Asia Social Protection Expenditure and Evaluation Database (SPEED), latest year available.
Note: Q1 = bottom quintile; the country-years in the graphs are ALB/Albania (2012); ARM/Armenia (2012); BGR/Bulgaria (2008); BIH/Bosnia and Herzegovina (2007); GEO/Georgia (2013); HUN/Hungary (2007); KAZ/Kazakhstan (2010); KGZ/Kyrgyz Republic (2007); KSV/Kosovo (2011); LVA/Latvia (2010); MDA/Moldova (2011); MKD/Macedonia, FYR (2010); MNE/Montenegro (2011); POL/Poland (2011); ROU/Romania (2011); SRB/Serbia (2010); TJK/Tajikistan (2009); UKR/Ukraine (2010).

practical measures have been taken over time to maintain the efficiency of the PMT. These range from updating software, networks, and hardware for business processes; rehabilitating offices; and simplifying procedures, to adjusting the level of benefits. For the technical design, it is good practice to revisit the validity of PMT formulas about every five years, because the patterns of consumption change and readjustments are usually needed. The PMT was updated only once, in 2010, but this update was not based on survey data. Other elements of the program were never reassessed. Thus, besides the concerns of the new government in the administration, it was time to pay attention to the technical aspects of the program.

The maximum potential in terms of performance can be achieved only by a combination of sound formula and well-functioning management processes. In 2010, UNICEF and the GoG performed an assessment of the access to social services, including the TSA program, for the bottom quintile of the population in terms of poverty. The assessment revealed that 96 percent of the quintile was aware of the TSA. This was interpreted as meaning that public information about the program was not a problem. Yet 24 percent of this quintile never applied to it (UNICEF and USAID 2011). When asked about the reasons for not applying, respondents expressed negative perceptions of the application system: 48 percent stated fear of an inaccurate assessment, 34 percent believed they would not receive benefits anyway,[4] and 22 percent had negative examples related to their neighbors who applied and did not receive benefits. This was interpreted as a need to ensure more transparency in the process and to work harder to avoid potential abuses of the system. The same survey revealed that 76 percent of families who never applied to the TSA did not even know what was required for registration. Additional measures need to be taken to improve communication mechanisms for the TSA and more broadly about social programs.

Even if these results were outdated, they still suggested the need to increase transparency, facilitate registration, and improve communication in order to increase outreach and eliminate negative perceptions about the program. Although the technical aspects of the TSA can achieve only so much in terms of targeting, the government believed that it was the cornerstone of the program. At this juncture, however, the government could only continue working on the implementation processes, creating an identity for the program—or for social assistance in general—and working on integrating the program into the social protection system.

Goal and Expected Impact of the Technical Assessment of the TSA

With this context in mind, the GoG decided to embark on assessing the technical aspects of the TSA. The overarching objective was to assess and improve the effectiveness of the program. In particular, the GoG wanted to (1) minimize inclusion and exclusion errors associated with the program, given the changing economy; (2) remove from the PMT formula easily concealable durable goods, as social agents were reporting that households had adopted the practice of concealing assets;

(3) include new, easily verifiable potential income-generating items; (4) reduce the total number of variables used in the PMT formula to simplify it (while maintaining targeting efficiency); and (5) remove from the PMT formula the subjective assessment of the social agents.

This technical work led to a reform of the TSA program and the introduction of the CBP. This reform comprised five elements: (1) update of the PMT formula that leads to the consumption index; (2) update and simplification of the needs index; (3) establishment of a new benefit structure that varies with the vulnerability score; (4) revision of the determination of the size of the household transfer depending on household demographic composition; and (5) introduction of an associated program—the CBP. In the rest of this report, elements 1–4 will be referred to as the *TSA reform*, and elements 1–5 as the *reform package*, or TSA+CBP. Box ES.1 summarizes them, and box ES.2 describes the main technical features of the TSA, including the definition of the consumption and the needs indexes. The timeline of technical work and policy actions is described in figure ES.2.

This reform package, TSA+CBP, is expected to contribute to a further reduction of extreme poverty, and in particular of child poverty. Although it is difficult to have efficiency gains with a program like the TSA that is already well targeted, there is always scope for improvement. At a minimum, the revision of the PMT of the TSA is expected to help maintain the targeting performance of the TSA. Marginal gains are also expected, especially in the second decile—partially covered by the TSA—leading to a reduction in poverty incidence. In addition, poor families without children were more likely to be in the TSA than families with children, and this revision of the PMT was an opportunity to address this bias and reduce child poverty. According to the module tailored to this analysis of the Integrated Household Survey (IHS 2013), 7.1 percent of the child population lived under extreme poverty (58 percent higher than the total population showing an extreme poverty rate of 4.5 percent). By introducing the new

---

Box ES.1 Elements of the TSA Reform and Introduction of the CBP

The five elements of the TSA+CBP (Targeted Social Assistance + Child Benefit Program) reform are:

1. Update of the proxy means test (PMT) and thus the coefficients of the formula that leads to the consumption index

2. Update and simplification of the needs index

} Change in the vulnerability score

3. Establishment of a new benefit structure that varies with the vulnerability score

4. Revision of the calculation of total household transfer depending on household demographic composition; and

5. Introduction of an associated program: the CBP.

} Change in the TSA

Box ES.2 Main Technical Features of the TSA's PMT

- The *household welfare index* or *vulnerability score* is calculated as a ratio of the consumption index and the needs index.
- The *consumption index*
  - is estimated in a conventional way for proxy means test (PMT) formulas, using ordinary least squares (OLS) regression;
  - uses monthly household consumption as the proxy of welfare; and
  - uses a large set of traditional predictors such as sociodemographic and location variables, ownership of durable goods, productive assets, and self-reported income.
- The *needs index*
  - is a normalization to account for differentiated needs of different persons, and
  - sets coefficients for different groups based on their gender, age, physical status, and social status compared to the needs of a healthy male adult (30–39).
- The final *vulnerability score* is rounded and rescaled.
- Households with vulnerability scores below 65,000 (after the PMT revision) are eligible for the Targeted Social Assistance (TSA) program.
- The 65,000 eligibility threshold is equivalent to the prereform eligibility threshold of 57,000, which leaves the coverage constant around 12 percent.

---

methodology, the extreme poverty rates are estimated to fall to 4.4 and 3.7 percent for children and the overall population, respectively. The way to equalize the extreme child poverty rate with the general population poverty rate is to introduce a well-targeted child benefit (according to the model, even GEL (Georgian lari) 10 per child per month can reduce both rates to 3.2 percent).

As a by-product, this revision of the PMT formula could enable other gains that facilitate the administration of the program, its transparency, and its evaluation. For example, simplifying some of the variables that enter the PMT formula could help to add transparency to the implementation and eliminate some of the beliefs about its level of effectiveness. Also, the original formula included the subjective evaluation by the social agent that, although this was well intentioned when introduced, it was not clear how effective it was in improving the targeting efficiency.

The Reform of the TSA and the Introduction of the CBP

Early in 2014, the GoG started to work intensively on the technical assessment of the TSA and its translation into policy actions. Since then, UNICEF and the WBG have been providing technical and financial assistance to the MoLHSA and the SSA.[5] Most of the technical assistance consisted of analyses that enabled the technical teams and high-level government officials to make decisions about

Figure ES.2 Timeline of TSA Technical Work and Policy Actions

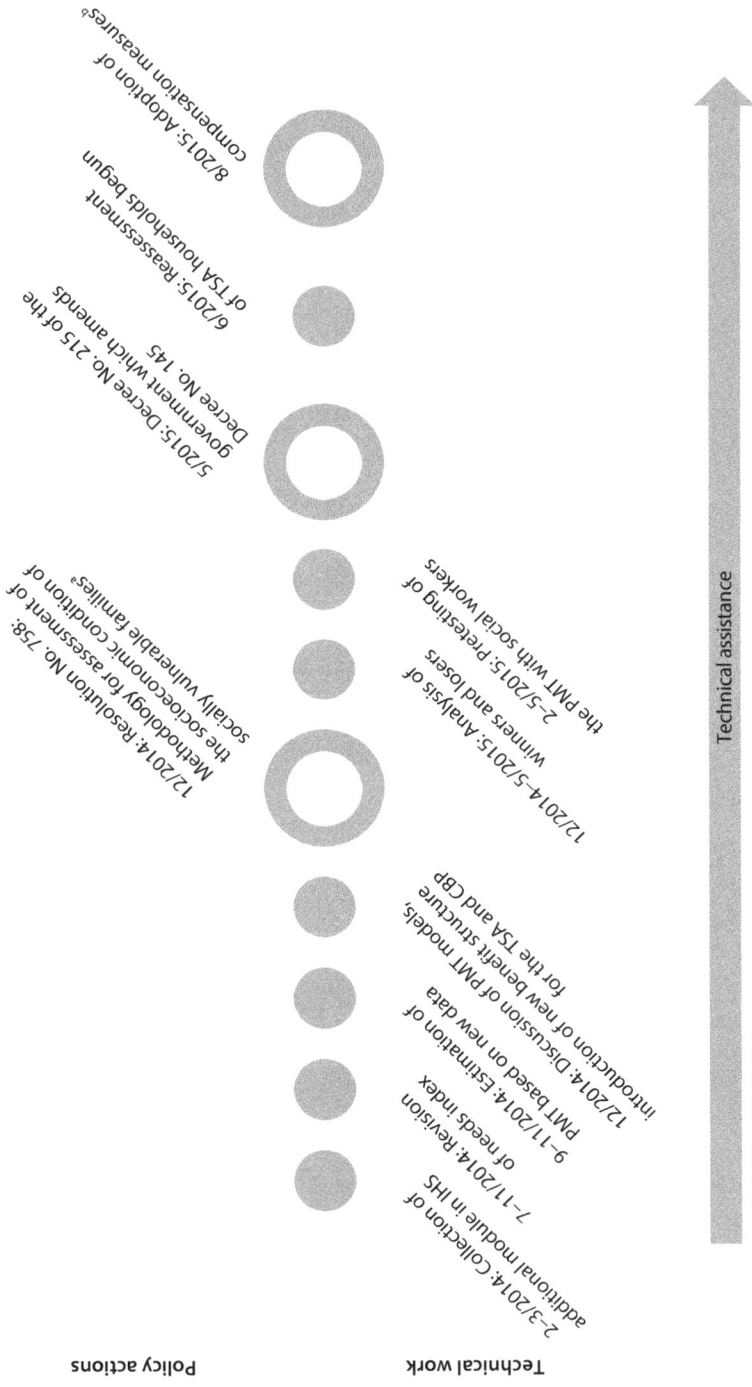

Policy actions

8/2015: Adoption of compensation measures[b]

6/2015: Reassessment of TSA households begun

5/2015: Decree No. 215 of the government which amends Decree No. 145

12/2014: Resolution No. 758: Methodology for assessment of the socioeconomic condition of socially vulnerable families[a]

Technical work

2–5/2015: Pretesting of the PMT with social workers

12/2014–5/2015: Analysis of winners and losers

12/2014: Discussion of PMT models; introduction of new benefit structure for the TSA and CBP

9–11/2014: Estimation of PMT based on new data

7–11/2014: Revision of needs index

2–3/2014: Collection of additional module in IHS

Technical assistance

Note: Large hollow circles represent legislation (or equivalent), and small solid circles relate to technical work or other agreements. CBP = Child Benefit Program; IHS = Integrated Household Survey; PMT = proxy means test; TSA = Targeted Social Assistance; WBG = World Bank Group.

a. Prior action to WBG Inclusive Growth Development Policy Operation.

b. Potential policy action to be counted as trigger for year 2 of WBG Inclusive Growth Development Policy Operation.

the design of the TSA and the introduction of the CBP. Figure ES.2 summarizes the milestones of the policy dialog among the institutions and how the GoG used the technical outputs to design and implement the five elements of the reform mentioned in box ES.1. By the end of 2015, the GoG had completed the technical revision, adopted compensation measures, and initiated implementation. The plan of the SSA is to reassess about one-twelfth of the registry each month and to complete the process in a year's time. The following paragraphs describe the salient messages coming from each piece of the technical work and how the technical work fed the policy actions.

Using newly collected household survey data, the revised eligibility formula was estimated. The TSA formula is the ratio of a consumption index, calculated via a PMT, and a needs index. The PMT is estimated in a conventional way: it uses linear regression and a rich set of predictors comprising sociodemographic and location variables, ownership of durables, and productive assets. New PMT models were estimated in this review following best practices in this area (see box ES.3). The estimated targeting efficiency of the PMT models was comparable to that of studies for other countries. The results showed that the objectives could be achieved and the targeting efficiency of the TSA could be improved—even if marginally—relative to the status quo. The main difference with respect to PMTs of other countries is that it predicts monthly household consumption—rather than per capita or per adult equivalent consumption—and it uses the needs index

---

Box ES.3 Good Practices Followed by the Estimation of the PMT and Indicators of Performance of the PMT

The estimation of the proxy means test (PMT) was carried out using standard practices:

- Work with two samples (one to estimate the PMT and another to validate the results).
- Work with various econometric models (ordinary least squares [OLS], probit, logit, and quantile regressions).
- Estimate several basic specifications.
- Refine specifications later based on goodness of fit and feedback from the government of Georgia (stepwise approach).

The PMT was evaluated using the following performance indicators:

- *Goodness of fit (R-squared):* models compared to minimize the unexplained errors in the regression, measured by the R-squared statistic.
- *Undercoverage:* defined as the number of poor households incorrectly excluded by the formula (*"exclusion"* or *type 1 error*) divided by the total number of poor households in the sample, where poor households are defined as being below the 15th consumption percentile.
- *Leakage:* defined as the number of eligible households incorrectly included by the formula divided by total number of eligible households (*"inclusion"* or *type 2 error*), where incorrectly included households are those above the 15th consumption percentile.

---

to adjust for the needs of special groups in the household. The formula is normalized and rescaled so the final score—called the *household-rating score* or *vulnerability score*—can be interpreted as the fraction of the needs met by the predicted household consumption. Hence, a vulnerability score of 100,000 is equivalent to achieving exactly the minimum consumption subsistence level.

The selected model performed better than the status quo in achieving the goals. The targeting efficiency of the selected model was equal to or better than the other runner-up models, including the status quo. More important, this was achieved by eliminating the subjective assessment variable as well as those that were associated with concealable goods. The chosen model was simple: it was estimated by OLS, eliminated variables, and used "number of adult household members of working age" as opposed to "share of salaried workers" among the regressors to avoid generating other distortions in reporting employment status. The estimated PMT model also performed well in terms of goodness of fit and targeting efficiency (undercoverage and leakage) when tested in the validation sample.

The efficiency gains were estimated to come from improvements in coverage in the second decile of the welfare distribution curve. Estimates based on household data predicted increments in coverage in the bottom quintile of the welfare distribution curve (from 47 to 53 percent), with marginal improvements in the bottom decile (from 71 to 73 percent). The reader should bear in mind that these survey predictions might overestimate the actual results because implementation issues usually decrease targeting efficiency. Moreover, under the new PMT, the distribution of benefits was estimated to remain equally pro-poor for almost all groups, and to become even more pro-poor for a few of them, such as seriously ill persons or single elderly persons. These two groups at the same time are the ones more exposed to changes in eligibility status due to the revision of the TSA. See figure ES.3.

Figure ES.3 Efficiency Gains Come from the Bottom and Second Deciles

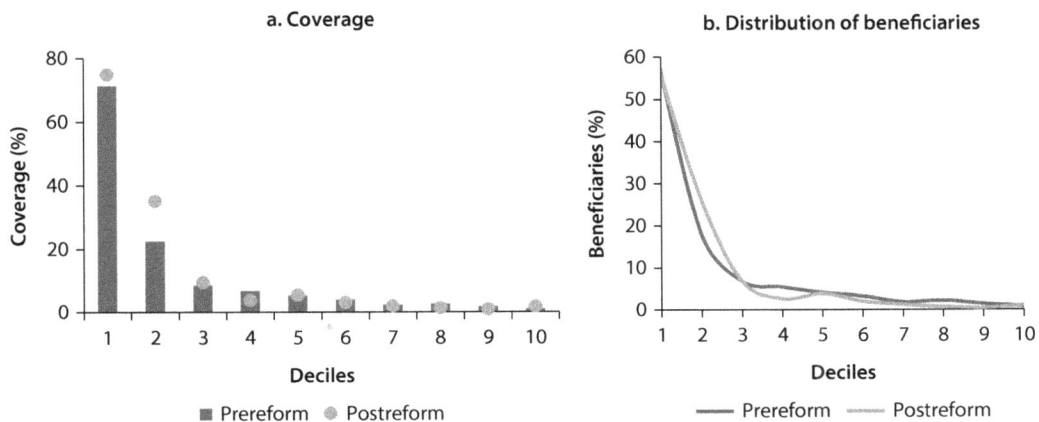

Source: Calculations based on Integrated Household Survey (IHS) 2013 estimation sample (additional module data).
Note: Deciles are computed using pre-TSA transfer consumption per adult equivalent (PAE). TSA = Targeted Social Assistance.

The update of the targeting formula was expected to cause a reshuffling of beneficiaries. Because coverage by design remained constant, the revision of the targeting formula generated almost equal numbers of newly eligible and newly ineligible households of the TSA program—sometimes called "winners" and "losers." This balance was broken with the introduction of the compensation measures: the number of newly eligible becomes larger than the number of newly ineligible.

It should be noted that losers of the TSA program may be gaining from transfers coming from other programs and services, and that this thus is a partial assessment of the total welfare change. Survey estimates indicated that 146,550 persons in TSA-recipient households before the reform were expected to gain eligibility and 119,003 persons were expected to exit the TSA program by the end of the implementation period around June 2016 and in the absence of compensation measures. After the compensation measures, there will be more entrants (155,939) and fewer newly ineligible persons (91,037). Given the efficiency gains, most of the newly eligible households were estimated to come from the bottom and second deciles of the welfare distribution curve.

Newly eligible beneficiaries are more likely to be families with children, while newly ineligible beneficiaries are more likely to be single nonworking pensioner households. Although the objective of the revision of the eligibility formula was not to generate this reshuffling of beneficiaries, this result was not totally unexpected, because the TSA funds before the revision of the eligibility formula were more likely to be directed to poor families without children than to poor families with children. Moreover, single nonworking elderly people receive transfers from the Old Age Pensions, which have been increased in recent years, reducing their eligibility to the program. In 2015 the Old Age Pension was GEL 160, which is GEL 10 above the minimum subsistence level used by the TSA formula.[6] Thus, this reshuffling of beneficiaries was in a way fixing a distortion present in the program, as the newly ineligible—although a vulnerable population—are mainly coming from the relatively wealthier groups of population. As figure ES.4 shows, more than 60 percent of newly ineligible households come from the third and higher wealth deciles, whereas around 75 percent of newly eligible households come from the first quintile. The analysis of the winners and losers expected from the targeting reform—based on the distributional analysis of household survey data—was also used to inform the design of the pretesting and to design compensation measures for the newly ineligible to the TSA.

Because these two groups—families with children and the single nonworking elderly—also benefit from other transfers, further analysis in terms of total transfers received should be done before cataloguing them as winners or losers. To understand if these groups are really winners or losers, the government needs to examine the total transfers received, the needs (access to and costs of services) of these groups, and their opportunities. Simply looking at whether they gain or lose eligibility to a single program such as the TSA is not enough to assess whether the group is improving its well-being. For example, during the past couple of years the Old Age Pension has increased and many of the medicine expenses of the elderly have been covered by the government since the introduction of universal

Figure ES.4 The TSA's Reshuffling of Beneficiaries

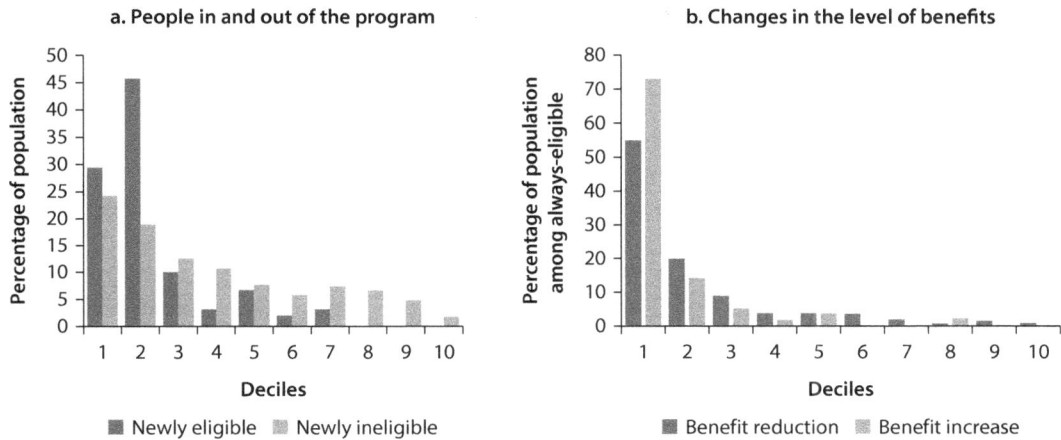

a. People in and out of the program

b. Changes in the level of benefits

Newly eligible   Newly ineligible

Benefit reduction   Benefit increase

Source: Calculations based on IHS 2013 estimation sample (additional module data).
Note: Deciles are computed using pre-TSA transfer consumption PAE. Population estimated based on number of household members of TSA-eligible households. Newly eligible and newly ineligible estimated based on revised eligibility formula before introducing compensation measures. See figures 9.2 and 9.3 for the result after compensation measures. PAE = per adult equivalent; TSA = Targeted Social Assistance.

Box ES.4 Child Benefit Program (CBP) Overview

- Benefits are for children under the age of 16.
- Households with a vulnerability score up to 100,000 are eligible. Households with scores of 65,000–100,000 receive solely CBP.
- The transfer is GEL (Georgian lari) 10 per child, payable every month.

Source: Decree No. 215 of the Government of May 18, 2015, which amends decree No.145.

---

health care in 2014. Thus, the question that needs to be answered is whether these other welfare-increasing changes have been larger (or not) than the TSA transfer for newly ineligible single pensioners.

The government also introduced the CBP to provide additional support to vulnerable families with children. From early on, part of UNICEF's dialog with the MoLHSA and the SSA revolved around the idea of introducing an associated program that gives an additional transfer for children. In May 2015, another decree was passed introducing the CBP. This new program covers about 24 percent of the poorest families with children and costs about GEL 2.6 million, or about 10 percent of total TSA budget. These resources were expected to halve extreme poverty among children, from around 7.1 to 3.23 percent based on UNICEF's measure of child poverty. Further details on the CBP can be found in box ES.4.

Jointly with the revision of the eligibility formula, a scheme of benefits for the TSA was introduced. On the one hand, the transfer is now calculated giving an equal amount for each adult household member. In the past, the transfer differentiated between the head and other household members. This change sought to address the concern of the government that two adult members belonging to one household could apply separately to the TSA to increase the value of the transfer. On the other hand, there was always the idea of introducing a scheme of benefits determined by the distance of the vulnerability score to 100,000.[7] However, the implementation of such a "continuous" scheme faced several challenges. The first one was technical. Even if the PMT does an excellent job in targeting the poor, the accuracy of the targeting is never good enough to sort households with such precision as to differentiate them by narrowly defined brackets of the score. The second challenge was financial, because the total budget needed to execute this scheme of benefits considerably exceeded available funds. The third was that the political economy of the transition from the pre-reform to the postreform score required that the nominal value of the transfer associated to the prereform eligibility threshold (at 57,000) was not reduced for any household, because it would add another layer of complexity to the implementation process.

After assessing all these challenges, the government decided to develop a four-tier benefit scheme. The first two tiers either provide higher transfers or maintain the level of transfers for those households that remained below the same eligibility score of 57,000, which is associated with a lower level of welfare in the new score from the eligibility formula. The next two tiers have narrow brackets up to a score of 65,000, at which point the coverage reaches the prereform level (before the introduction of compensation measures). The lowest transfer is equivalent to that of year 2013. Thus, how much families gain from this scheme of benefits depends on the score (or tier where the household lands) and the demographic composition of the household. Figure ES.5 shows the amount of transfers that result from the four-tier benefit scheme (or five-tier if the CBP is included) for a family with two adults and two children. Table ES.1 shows that households' welfare in the tiers are statistically different even if the third tier is somewhat narrow.

An alternative approach is to work with programs that are well articulated and tackle specific needs of households. The introduction of the CBP could be perceived as a first step in this direction. Based on a unique targeting system, different types and levels of benefits could be allocated to households based on their needs. For example, households with children could receive additional support given the additional expenses during this stage of life, or households in mountainous areas could receive a temporary supplement to deal with a shock.[8] This approach is further discussed later, since one of the recommended actions for Georgia is to move the attention from the main social assistance program to a comprehensive and efficient *system* of social protection.

The differentiated level of transfers resulting from the scheme of benefits of the TSA created another layer of winners and losers.[9] Among TSA always-eligible households, some of them will receive higher transfers—especially if the CBP is topped up—while others will receive a lower transfer. Without taking into account the CBP transfer, there are about an equal number of persons in

Figure ES.5 Structure of Benefits Comparing Current and New Programs

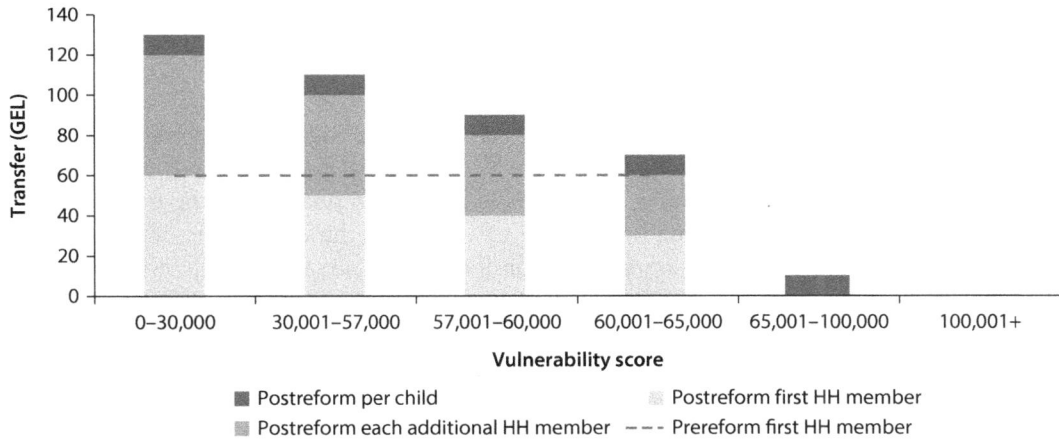

Note: GEL = Georgian lari; HH = household. The figure shows the transfers pre- and postreform for a household with two adults and two children. As can be seen in more detail in table 5.2 (chapter 5), no household in tier 1 will lose benefits, and in tier 2 (below the 57,000 prereform eligibility score) only households with two adults will lose benefits, and in that case only a tiny part.

Table ES.1 Household Income and Consumption, by Tiers (PAE)

Score range	Number of HHs in tier	Pre-TSA average HH income (in GEL)	Pre-TSA average HH income PAE (in GEL)	Pre-TSA average HH expenditure PAE (in GEL)
<30,000	22,485	163	47	25
30,001–57,000	59,971	175	69	100
57,001–60,000	11,870	302	99	102
60,001–65,000	17,173	244	116	112
65,001–100,000	147,642	307	126	176
Above 100,000	763,075	731	317	341

Source: Calculations based on IHS 2013 estimation sample (additional module data).
Note: Estimations based on postreform precompensation eligibility formula. GEL = Georgian lari; HH = household; PAE = per adult equivalent; TSA = Targeted Social Assistance.

households where transfers will be cut than in households where transfers will be augmented. However, most of the gains are concentrated around 20 percent, while most of the losses are of less than 10 percent. There is nevertheless a small but not negligible group of households that still are estimated to face losses of 50 percent or more.

The pretesting confirmed most of the predicted results of the distributional analysis and brought further attention to IDPs as potential winners of TSA transfers. The pretesting was conducted using the revised household declaration and carried out by social agents. A representative sample was selected from the households registered in the database. During the analysis, eight different groups of the TSA-registered population were specifically highlighted. The pretesting exercise uncovered IDPs as another group of potential winners, with an increase in total beneficiaries of this group of 8 percent (equivalent to families with children). It is not surprising that this result was not identified in the analysis based on the household survey, as IDPs were a small group in that sample.

The Compensation Measures

A typical policy recommendation when implementing reforms rendering winners and losers is to accompany them with transitional measures that help losers to adjust to their new status. Policies could range from phasing out the transfer over a short period, designing a trajectory of change of the coefficients of the formula (or the score itself) to smooth the transition, introducing changes in other programs, or introducing new programs. These measures are usually called *compensation measures*, because they aim to deal with the unavoidable unintended effects of a reform.

As expected, the government passed compensation measures to reduce the number of newly ineligible persons, in particular among the single nonworking pensioner households. One compensation measure consisted of increasing the coefficient of the needs index for the pensioners from 1.18 for men (1.12 for women) to 1.80 for both men and women. Notice that this increment for this group sets the needs coefficient at a higher value than before the revision of the needs index described in chapter 4.[10] The coefficient of the needs index for single pensioners above 60 is 38 (men) and 47 (women) percent higher than the prereform value. In this way the government is overcompensating pensioners as many of them may become ineligible not due to the revision of the eligibility formula but due to the simultaneous increase in Old Age Pensions. The other compensation measure consisted in altering the value of the utility consumption in the consumption index. Due to the increase in the cost of electricity per unit, the total consumption in utilities of poor families also went up. However, the out-of-pocket expenditure in utilities decreased due to the new electricity subsidy. Because spending in utilities is an important determinant of the PMT, this increase in consumption would also lead to additional TSA newly ineligibles, that is, losers. Thus, the government decided to use in the PMT formula the out-of-pocket cost of utilities. The compensation measures will increase the spending in the TSA 7.4 percent (or GEL 1.77 million or 68 percent of the cost of the CBP).

Other compensation measures could have been adopted by the government. Clearly the menu of options is large, and without doubt the group that needed to be compensated was the single elderly pensioners. The government could have considered (1) further investigating the needs of single pensioners based on their age, to focus the assistance to those that really need the support of the TSA on top of the Old Age Pension; (2) creating a similar program to CBP but for the single elderly within the TSA framework; and/or (3) leaving current single pensioners in the TSA but using the revised formula for newly registered to avoid biasing the targeting in the future. In any case, it is important to communicate to the population that the changes in other programs are appropriate and part of an overall reform and to inform them about the total transfers (from all programs) to losers' groups and not just those from the TSA.

Given the adopted compensation measures, it is recommended that the GoG reconsider (1) the level of the coefficient for single pensioners in the needs index as it seems to be too high for the objective and the prereform level; (2) the way the energy subsidy is treated in the eligibility formula (for example, consumption could be measured in watts, or the value of the subsidy could be added to observed cost); and (3) regularly updating the value of the minimum subsistence income in the PMT formula.

The Way Forward

The two next steps for Georgia are to (1) continue to revise the TSA for further efficiency gains, in particular by aligning the compensation measures with the objectives of the reform, and (2) move toward a comprehensive and efficient system of social protection and labor. Once implementation is completed, this revision of the TSA is expected to generate efficiency gains. It is always a good practice to continue improving the management processes and the monitoring of the program. In parallel, it is recommended that the government begin to think of social protection as a *system* of programs and services and improve the coordination (and design) of the TSA and other social programs and services within this system. Later, once public employment services are fully developed and job creation picks up in Georgia, further coordination between social assistance and employment services should also be introduced. For example, most European countries use the "rights and responsibility" approach, in which beneficiaries of social assistance actively seek jobs and/or participate in retraining programs with the objective of graduating from social assistance. Figure ES.6 shows the main recommendations along these two parallel tracks.

Continuing to Improve the TSA

The immediate need for the TSA is to reconsider the design of the compensation measures. The recently adopted compensation measures have achieved the objective of reducing the number of single, nonworking pensioners who would have been newly ineligible, at a cost of GEL 1.77 million. However, these measures have introduced distortions from the results of the economic analysis. For example, if the government is interested in supporting single, nonworking pensioners on top of the Old Age Pensions, a different program could be introduced associated with the TSA. Alternatively, the Old Age Pensions could be modified, introducing a scheme of benefits associated with age cutoffs. In addition, the bias associated with the measure of consumption of subsidized utilities needs to be adjusted.

In the medium term, the TSA should continue its commitment to periodically revise the formula, for which data collection needs to be regularized. To embark on the current reform of the TSA, an additional, tailored module needed to be introduced to the IHS. This module collected the variables of the TSA declaration form that are not part of the core household survey. In the future, it would be valuable if this additional module is collected regularly, even every two years, to ensure that the monitoring of the targeting formula becomes routine.

Continuous Improvement • http://dx.doi.org/10.1596/978-1-4648-0900-2

Figure ES.6 Parallel Tracks to Continue Improving the TSA and to Build a Social Protection and Labor System

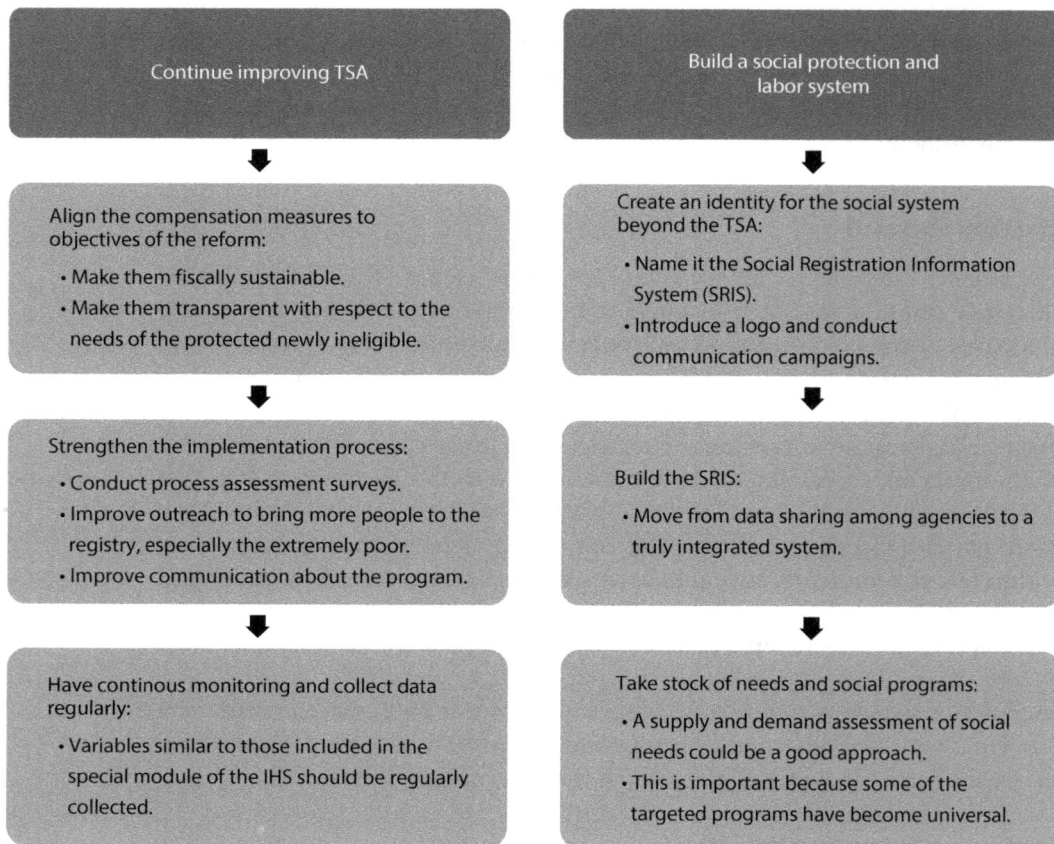

Continue improving TSA	Build a social protection and labor system
Align the compensation measures to objectives of the reform: • Make them fiscally sustainable. • Make them transparent with respect to the needs of the protected newly ineligible.	**Create an identity for the social system beyond the TSA:** • Name it the Social Registration Information System (SRIS). • Introduce a logo and conduct communication campaigns.
Strengthen the implementation process: • Conduct process assessment surveys. • Improve outreach to bring more people to the registry, especially the extremely poor. • Improve communication about the program.	**Build the SRIS:** • Move from data sharing among agencies to a truly integrated system.
Have continous monitoring and collect data regularly: • Variables similar to those included in the special module of the IHS should be regularly collected.	**Take stock of needs and social programs:** • A supply and demand assessment of social needs could be a good approach. • This is important because some of the targeted programs have become universal.

Note: IHS = Integrated Household Survey; TSA = Targeted Social Assistance.

Recent innovations in poverty measurement could be tested in the PMT formula to increase its fit. One of these is the use of small-area estimation models. To overcome the shortfalls in poverty measurement coming from incomplete and unreliable time series on consumption and price deflators, researchers in the field have been working to estimate poverty predictions based on poverty correlates. The methods that use small-area estimation techniques have produced poverty estimates that matched observed data very well, when employing either non-staple-food or nonfood expenditures or a full set of assets as predictors (Christiaensen et al. 2012). In principle, it seems reasonable to think that these techniques could be applied to the estimation of PMT formulas with equal success. Moreover, these estimates could help to better measure the higher costs of living in mountainous regions in a more accurate way, and could help to dissuade the GoG from discontinuing the recently passed subsidy for residents of those areas.

Another active area in poverty measurement looks at *multidimensional poverty* and might eventually be linked to targeting social assistance. Many countries are introducing multidimensional measures to track poverty (for example, Mexico) and to articulate the policy dialog among several line ministries (Colombia). This practice arises from the recognition that monetary poverty measures do not always capture all the deprivations that households face (Alkire and Foster 2011). In spite of consumption theory predictions (Ravallion 2011), deprivations in housing, health, education, and other fundamental aspects of life seem not to fully be captured by the poverty head count nor the estimation of the PMT. The multidimensional approach would require identifying verifiable measures that could be associated with these dimensions of deprivations. Currently Mexico is tackling this problem by developing a multidimensional measure of the PMT. Although applying multidimensional poverty concepts to PMTs will not increase targeting efficiency, it might be instrumental in linking various programs to one targeting instrument, as will be discussed further. In the context of Georgia, this could be worth exploring as some services (for example, health insurance and free childcare) have become universal. It is critical to understand if the poor population will have equal access to and use of these services, and if not, what prevents them from benefiting. In this new environment, we wonder if the TSA may have an additional role to play in improving targeting and coordination of services and programs.

Finally, but not least, Georgia needs to continue work on improving management processes. Outreach is very good; only 7 percent of households in the bottom decile (and 19 percent of households in the second decile) are not registered with the TSA. But communication about the aims of the program should be better explained to the population to create adequate expectations from the society. This could also increase the trust in the program. Once the implementation of the new formula is completed, it would be beneficial to repeat a satisfaction survey among the poor similar to the one run by UNICEF in 2010. The reform process envisaged revision of the administrative procedures and instructions and introduced a number of changes to the legal framework. Yet certain issues were identified as requiring further work: lack of the human resources and capacity in the departments responsible for overall monitoring and analysis of the program performance, outdated classification of diseases, and special needs of the population living near the border area, in particular those near conflict-affected regions.

From a Social Assistance Program to a System of Social Protection

Going forward, Georgia could shift focus from an efficient social assistance *program* to a comprehensive and efficient social protection *system*. Today, Georgia covers its bottom 12 percent of the population with the TSA. However, half of the population are registered in the TSA because other programs use the TSA vulnerability score to target their beneficiaries. This raises many questions: Are all these other programs reaching out to their intended beneficiaries by using the vulnerability score of the TSA? Is there any coordination among them? Do they jointly satisfy the needs of the population that the social protection system aims to address? Is this the result of high mobility in and out of the program? Is there a better way to support families that move in and out of the TSA? These among other questions still need to be tackled in Georgia.

Social protection systems can be an efficient tool with which to fight poverty and inequality. Social protection systems provide a coordinated set of programs and services that aim to maximize the impact in poverty alleviation and more generally provide equal opportunities for all. The advantage of thinking of *social protection* as a *system* is that it allows one to identify and reduce the vulnerabilities across the life cycle.

A system approach helps to exploit coordination and synergies as much as possible in order to have efficiency gains coming both from targeting and administration. In most countries, social protection programs are often fragmented and uncoordinated. Fragmentation can create significant inefficiencies, undermining the potential impact of social protection on building resilience and contributing to human development. Isolated programs may be effective in addressing a particular issue but may lead to duplication or contradictory results if not coordinated with other interventions in related sectors. More important, uncoordinated programs usually result in overlapping objectives or parallel structures serving a similar purpose. Initiatives not integrated into national structures and/or strategies result in inefficient allocation of resources and have limited capacity to benefit from economies of scale and be financially and politically sustainable in the long term.

Moreover, fragmentation has implications in terms of limited and scattered coverage, with high inclusion and exclusion errors, where those hardest to reach, the poorest and most excluded, are not covered. In many instances, although programs may have similar eligibility requirements for accessing benefits, limited coordination of administrative and information systems (for example, shared data of beneficiary lists and multiple targeting systems) reduce the likelihood of beneficiaries being able to access available services. Weak referral systems and limited awareness among staff about other programs and benefits become key obstacles to children's, families', and communities' access to essential benefits and services.

However, the benefits need to be weighed against the risks, challenges, and costs. First, there are risks of excessive centralization. A flaw of integrated systems is that errors can quickly propagate across programs. For example, if there is a single registry of beneficiaries for all programs and an individual is not included in that registry, he or she may not have access to any benefit. This can serve to exacerbate exclusion or segregation. Centralization can also limit entities' ability to adapt effectively to the needs of particular regions or groups. Systems can be less flexible in their ability to adapt to changing economic circumstances and to react rapidly to crises. Second, there are costs of coordination, such as transaction costs, given the involvement of various agencies or line ministries. Last, there are the challenges arising from complex political economy issues.

UNICEF and the WBG have a common understanding of the key steps to operationalizing a system approach to social protection. Rawlings, Murthy, and Winder (2013) describe in detail how the social protection strategies of UNICEF and the World Bank are based on common ground. First, the movement toward a more integrated system needs to be gradual and accompanied by sound analytic work and relevant data to monitor progress. Second, the operationalization must occur at different levels: policy, programs, and administration. At the policy level, a government needs to define a long-term vision that aligns the social protection system to broader political and economic goals of the country. This is usually reflected in the national social protection strategy that defines goals and priorities for the country, given the fiscal space and the socioeconomic context. At the program level, the strategy focuses on integrating, harmonizing, and coordinating programs to eliminate duplications, maximize synergies, and exploit interactions. At this level, the coordination could and must go beyond programs delivered by a single ministry or agency. Finally, at the administrative level, efforts should facilitate the functioning of programs and services. For example, they should focus on whether there has to be a single, unique social assistance registry, maybe with a common targeting tool and a developed identity. A common identity not only facilitates the administration but is fundamental for communication, for building transparency, and for reducing information asymmetries. Monitoring and evaluation of programs can also be coordinated to simplify the administration and the measurement of interactions.

Georgia has programs and services associated with the TSA targeting formula, and thus a nascent system is already in place. Some of these programs and services are provided at the national level, such as pro bono legal services; others are provided by subnational governments, such as the services run by the municipality of Tbilisi. Some have been made universal, such as the Medical Insurance Program, preschool, and the provision of school books. However, the system is not really developed. There are no consultative processes or coordination among ministries, let alone with the civil society. One example of the lack of coordination of programs is the recently adopted Law on High Mountainous Regions that delivers additional transfers (in various forms) to residents of such areas.

In Georgia there has not been, to our knowledge, a technical assessment of the system of social protection and labor. While much is known about the TSA program, less is known about the effectiveness of other social protection and labor spending efforts to fight poverty and build human capital. Besides the TSA, the rest of the social protection and labor spending (that constitutes 86 percent of total social spending) goes to categorical programs.[11] There are other subnational programs that also use the TSA vulnerability score to target beneficiaries (see the example of the municipality of Tbilisi in chapter 1). However, there is no systematic information about them. As a result, Georgia's spending in targeted programs appears low relative to the region. In 2013, Georgia's known spending in targeted programs was 14 percent, while the average for the region was 35 percent.[12]

One option to tackle this problem is to structure the analysis using a supply-and-demand of benefits and programs framework. The analysis of the demand of services should start with a characterization of the target population of the system. This includes creating a basic description of the risks and vulnerabilities for different socioeconomic groups, in order to understand what the target population is. This is

followed by the identification of specific risks and how they interact and an examination of common factors associated with specific risks, as well as their interactions.
The analysis of the supply starts by taking stock of programs and program features
existent in the country and investigating how they interact: what are the duplications and the complementarities? Once this is thoroughly done, policy makers can
design packages and add-ons (or layers) of programs to maximize efficiency.

Georgia has made strides with its TSA program and is now confronted with
the challenge of achieving the same level of success of this program in the social
protection and labor system to better serve the needs and aspirations of the
population. Georgia could start with various actions at the same time. On the
one hand we recommend that they consider developing a separate identity for
the social registration to be used by the system. This will help with budgetary
management, as the TSA currently does much more than what it has been
designed for. Several countries have moved toward building this identity by providing a name to the social registry, creating a logo, having information campaigns, as already noted in figure ES.6. This identity also helps with the efforts to
maintain and further modernize one-stop shops where all social services are
provided. In addition to these very important process actions, and as with the
TSA, more analysis is needed in order to make evidence-based decisions.

Continuous improvement is praiseworthy, but a challenge resides in balancing
costs and benefits. Going forward, Georgia will benefit the most by tackling those
improvements that offer the biggest payoff. This report aims to help policy makers understand how much and where effort needs to be placed in continuing to
improve the TSA and in building a system of social protection.

Notes

1. Based on the Social Protection Expenditure and Evaluation Database (SPEED) for
   Europe and Central Asia. Average calculated over 23 countries of Eastern Europe and
   Central Asia. The countries are selected based on their data availability.

2. Chapter 2 discusses the various poverty measures of the GoG, UNICEF, and the
   WBG.

3. Using a regression discontinuity econometric model, the authors compare the labor
   market engagement of household members around the eligibility threshold of the
   TSA. The results showed the presence of work disincentives for women. Women just
   below the eligibility threshold were 7 to 11 percentage points less likely to work than
   women just above it, in 2011. The reader interested in comparing performances across
   countries can consult the multicountry report (World Bank 2015b). The details of the
   analysis for Georgia are discussed in a background paper (World Bank 2015a).

4. Given the level of coverage (12 percent), it is correct to expect that about 8 percent
   of those interviewed will not qualify for the program, and this is what was observed
   in the survey ($0.20 \times 0.96 \times 0.34 = 0.065$).

5. The reform of the TSA that reviews the PMT formula has been included as a prior
   action of the WBG Inclusive Growth Development Policy Operation.

6. In 2012 the Old Age Pension benefit ranged between GEL 110 and GEL 125,
   depending on the age of the pensioner. In April 2013 it was leveled at GEL 125,

independent of age. In September 2013 it rose to GEL 150 and in September 2015 to GEL 160. Notice that since the inflation rate between 2013 and 2015 was 9 percent, the increase of 2015 in the Old Age Pension was not enough to catch up with prices. Nevertheless, a transfer of GEL 160 is above the minimum subsistence level estimated by GeoStat at GEL 150 and used as a reference point in the estimation of the vulnerability score of the TSA.

7. The vulnerability score is normalized so a score of 100,000 corresponds to the subsistence level for a healthy man of age 30–39 years.

8. As further discussed in chapter 3, the PMT formula is computed for four different regions, taking care of the differential cost of living in these areas. Thus, no additional support would be needed for residents of these areas, as they are more likely already to qualify for the TSA program.

9. "Winners" and "losers" refer to the narrow definition that involves only the TSA program.

10. The coefficient of the needs index before the revision was 1.3 for men and 1.22 for women. The reduction of the needs coefficient for pensioners (not only single pensioners) reflects the changes in prices of medicines with the introduction of universal health care.

11. Of total social spending, 7.4 percent went to the Targeted Medical Insurance Program (TMIP) that is no longer in place in the country.

12. Average calculated using SPEED data and based on 23 Eastern European and Central Asian countries.

References

Alkire, Sabina, and James Foster. 2011. "Counting and Multidimensional Poverty Measurement." *Journal of Public Economics* 95 (7): 476–87.

Christiaensen, Luc, Peter Lanjouw, Jill Luoto, and David Stifel. 2012. "Small Area Estimation-Based Prediction Methods to Track Poverty: Validation and Applications." *Journal of Economic Inequality* 10 (2): 267–97.

IHS (Integrated Household Survey). 2013. GeoStat, Tbilisi. http://www.geostat.ge /?action=meurneoba&mpid=1&lang=eng.

Ravallion, Martin. 2011. "On Multidimensional Indices of Poverty." *Journal of Economic Inequality* 9 (2): 235–48.

Rawlings, Laura, Sheila Murthy, and Natalia Winder. 2013. "Common Ground: UNICEF and World Bank Approaches to Building Social Protection Systems." Social Protection and Labor Policy Note 15, World Bank, Washington, DC.

UNICEF and USAID. 2011. "Survey of Barriers to Access to Social Services: Georgia 2010." http://unicef.ge/uploads/Survey_of_Barriers_to_Access_to_Social_Services._Georgia _2010_eng.pdf.

World Bank. Various years. SPEED (Social Protection Expenditure and Evaluation Database) for Europe and Central Asia. World Bank, Washington, DC.

———. 2015a. *The Impact of Targeted Social Assistance on Labor Market in Georgia: A Regression Discontinuity Approach.* Washington, DC: World Bank. https:// openknowledge.worldbank.org/handle/10986/22502.

———. 2015b. *Promoting Labor Market Participation and Social Inclusion in Europe and Central Asia's Poorest Countries.* Washington, DC: World Bank. https://openknowledge .worldbank.org/handle/10986/22501.

Abbreviations

CBP	Child Benefit Program
GDP	gross domestic product
GEL	Georgian lari
GeoStat	National Statistics Office of Georgia
GoG	government of Georgia
IDP	internally displaced person
IHS	Integrated Household Survey
MoLHSA	Ministry of Labor, Health, and Social Affairs
OLS	ordinary least squares (regression)
PAE	per adult equivalent
PMT	proxy means test
PPP	purchasing power parity
SFC	special functioning contingent
SPEED	Social Protection Expenditure and Evaluation Database (World Bank)
SRIS	Social Registration Information System
SSA	Social Services Agency
TSA	Targeted Social Assistance
UNICEF	United Nations Children's Fund
WBG	World Bank Group
WMS	Welfare Monitoring Survey

CHAPTER 1

Introduction

Objective

At the end of 2013, the government of Georgia (GoG) began a technical review of its main social assistance program: Targeted Social Assistance (TSA). When the current administration took office in 2012, it made a promise to pay more attention to social issues in the country. The government needed to be convinced of the efficiency and transparency of the TSA as a last-resort social assistance program and to present it to its constituency. There was concern that too many poor people were not covered by the TSA and, conversely, that too many nonpoor were benefiting from it, therefore draining resources. The GoG was also worried that the subjective elements of determining eligibility and the reliance on assets that could be concealed in the eligibility formula were leaving room for abuses of the system. Since then, Georgia took several steps to address these concerns: (1) the technical features of the TSA were reviewed, (2) the administrative and business processes of the program's implementation were improved, and (3) new legislation was passed. The latter modified the targeting formula and the scheme of benefits of the TSA, and created a new targeted program: the Child Benefit Program (CBP). Implementation of the TSA and the CBP started in June 2015, and compensation measures were introduced in August 2015.

This report describes and assesses the TSA's revision process and the technical work behind it. It also provides an initial and basic set of recommendations for the GoG in order to move toward building a comprehensive and efficient social protection and labor system. This report documents and assesses the technical work that led to the just mentioned policy actions. Such documentation is of particular importance given the high turnover of officials (technical staff and decision makers) working with the TSA during the reform period, resulting in scant institutional memory. In addition, the report provides guidance about next steps in light of the findings from the deep analytical work and the political actions taken by the government.

The technical work was carried on by UNICEF and the World Bank Group (WBG) in collaboration with the Ministry of Labor, Health, and Social Affairs (MoLHSA) and the Social Services Agency (SSA) of the GoG. UNICEF initiated the collaboration with the GoG, and thus took the lead in the technical work behind the revision of the proxy means test (PMT) used for targeting recipients and the needs index (see chapters 3 and 4). The WBG came on board later and took the lead on the analysis of distributional impact of the policy actions before and after the introduction of compensation measures (see chapters 6, 7, and 9). The pretesting of the TSA was led by UNICEF with input from the WBG (chapter 8). This report is a joint effort of UNICEF and the WBG, and it reflects the technical opinions only of the teams in both institutions.

The TSA program is the main instrument of the GoG to support consumption in extremely poor households. The TSA budget is the third largest expenditure item among total social spending in Georgia, after social pensions and education; 14 percent of total social spending goes to this program.[1] This is the main vehicle through which to alleviate poverty in a country that spends relatively low amounts by international standards on social protection and labor, although it is not much less than the average spending in social protection of the countries in the region. Georgia spends 1.2 percent of the gross domestic product (GDP) in social assistance excluding social pensions, while the average for Eastern Europe and Central Asia is 1.8 percent.[2] In 2013, the TSA program lifted 6 percent of the population out of extreme poverty, lowering the extreme poverty rate from 9.7 to 3.9 percent.

The TSA program targets the poor using a PMT formula. Introduced in 2006, the TSA and the PMT were a means of increasing efficiency of social assistance spending. The PMT mechanism was chosen as suitable for Georgia because income from formal sources is a less accurate indicator of household welfare given the high levels of informality in the country. Since 2006, many categorical benefits have been phased out and gradually replaced by the TSA. For example, households cannot receive the family allowance or the benefits for internally displaced persons (IDPs) while they are receiving TSA support.

Compared to other social assistance programs in the region, Georgia's TSA is a reasonable performer in terms of targeting and a solid performer in terms of coverage of the bottom quintile of the population sorted by levels of well-being. However, the TSA is one of the strongest programs in the region if targeting and coverage, or poverty and coverage, are assessed jointly. In 2013, the TSA covered 12 percent of households. In the same year, coverage of the bottom quintile of the population was 48 percent (and of the bottom decile 71 percent); the benefit incidence was 53 percent. In general, it is easier to achieve good targeting in relatively small programs and easier to achieve higher coverage by tolerating weaker targeting accuracy. Figure 1.1 shows that for the level of poverty, coverage, and targeting accuracy, the TSA performs relatively better than programs of other countries in the region.

In spite of the several measures taken since the conception of the TSA to continuously improve it, in 2013 it was time to proceed with a technical evaluation of the formula. Various complementary and practical measures have been taken over time to maintain the TSA's efficiency. These include updating the software, network, and hardware for business processes; rehabilitating offices; simplifying procedures; and adjusting the level of benefits. On the technical side,

Figure 1.1 Poverty Incidence and Benefit Incidence, Coverage in the Bottom Quintile, Georgia and Regional Comparators

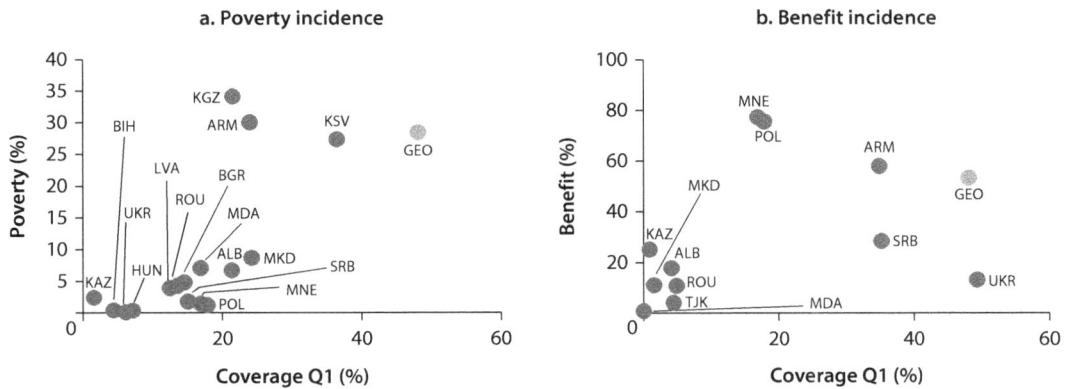

Source: Europe and Central Asia Social Protection Expenditure and Evaluation Database (SPEED), latest year available.
Note: Q1 = bottom quintile; the country-years in the graphs are ALB/Albania (2012); ARM/Armenia (2012); BGR/Bulgaria (2008); BIH/Bosnia and Herzegovina (2007); GEO/Georgia (2013); HUN/Hungary (2007); KAZ/Kazakhstan (2010); KGZ/Kyrgyz Republic (2007); KSV/Kosovo (2011); LVA/Latvia (2010); MDA/Moldova (2011); MKD/Macedonia, FYR (2010); MNE/Montenegro (2011); POL/Poland (2011); ROU/Romania (2011); SRB/Serbia (2010); TJK/Tajikistan (2009); UKR/Ukraine (2010).

it is good practice to revisit the validity of PMT formulas every five years or so, as patterns of consumption change and readjustments are needed. Given that the PMT was updated only once, in 2010 (and not using all the relevant data), and that the needs index was never reassessed, it was time to pay attention to these technical aspects of the program.

Besides the need to improve the efficiency of the program, there were concerns about weaknesses in the design that could allow households to "fool" the system. It was believed that there were leakages and work disincentives in the program that needed to be either disproved or addressed. As noted, there also were concerns about households concealing goods in order to gain eligibility to the TSA and that the subjective evaluations in the eligibility formula could be manipulated. The evidence came from reports by social agents and by observations that the TSA spiked in the months prior to elections (as will be seen later in figure 1.6). To better understand the issue of work disincentives, the WBG with donor funding recently analyzed the issue as part of a regional report on jobs.[3] The study showed that work disincentives were present in Georgia for women with underage children living in rural areas, thus indicating that work disincentives were not embedded in the TSA design. This enabled the GoG to focus on other sets of issues.

Generally, the reform of the TSA could be also perceived as a first step in the development of a social protection and labor *system*. This system can be defined as the comprehensive and articulated set of social policies and programs that support persons and families at different moments in their life in order to help them cope with permanent and transitory risks and to escape poverty (World Bank 2015a). In Georgia there are smaller (mostly categorical) social programs, policies, and services directed toward vulnerable households, the whole population, or parts of the country. For example, there is a birth subsidy that is offered to families giving birth to a third or subsequent children living in regions with negative population growth, and there are additional benefits for the pensioners in high mountainous regions.[4] Many of these programs and services have positive impacts on the well-being of the population. However, less is known about them than is known about the TSA in terms of their effectiveness, the populations they serve, the overlap of the groups of populations they target, and even the government agency that is in charge of designing and implementing them.

In some instances, subnational governments provide additional social assistance and deliver local services using the vulnerability score of the TSA. These programs are diverse in scope, objective, and target population. For example, the municipality of Tbilisi has a program that offers a basket of benefits such as the "communal subsidy" for electric energy, cleaning, and water payments and provides additional pecuniary transfers for families with a TSA vulnerability score below 70,000. A different program offers free public transport to certain groups of residents (doctors employed in municipal polyclinics, school teachers, and so forth).

A social protection and labor system exploits synergies and provides efficiency gains. The coordination of programs avoids duplications, saves administrative resources (by bundling services that go to a same group of beneficiaries), and creates filters or layers of services that provide specific resources for distinct groups. Also, the system serves to solve information asymmetries and to give everybody knowledge of his or her rights and opportunities. Another by-product of having a system is that the Ministry of Finance can have more tools for better budgeting of social expenses, as the system can more accurately provide a ceiling value of social spending.

Linking social assistance to labor markets should wait until job creation picks up and public employment services are fully developed. It has already been pointed out that the next natural step for Georgia is to link the TSA to the labor market (World Bank 2012). However, unlike many other countries, Georgia did not have any labor market policy until very recently. Georgia does not have unemployment insurance or a binding minimum wage, and the public employment services were fostered in just the recent past. For instance, the current web portal for registration of job seekers—*Worknet*—was introduced only in 2013, and it has only one functionality: registration of job seekers and vacancies by employers. It is still used minimally, especially among employers, relative to the magnitude of the unemployment rate. Moreover, linking social assistance to labor outcomes requires the adoption of a formal definition of unemployment from the government, something that still needs to happen in Georgia. Last but not least, it is critical to have a dynamic labor market with solid job creation in order to tie benefits to job seeking, and this still needs to materialize in Georgia. The timid pickup in job creation during 2014 is not enough for the country to embark on costly reforms of uncertain payoff. Moreover, additional analysis of the employment and employability characteristics of TSA beneficiaries needs to be conducted.

The objective of this publication is to assess the reform process and the technical work behind it, and to provide an initial set of recommendations for the government in order to move toward building a comprehensive and efficient social protection and labor system. The remainder of this chapter provides some context on the TSA and briefly describes what the reform consists of. The rest of the report is organized following the sequence of events and policy actions taken by the GoG. The second chapter presents the data used and discusses some of the definitions, as the three parties involved in this process work with different definitions, in particular when it comes to poverty measurement. In the third chapter, the revision for the consumption index (PMT estimate) is discussed, and the fourth chapter discusses the needs index. Chapter 5 presents the new structure of benefits and other aspects of the reform. Chapters 6 and 7 delve deeper and describe the "winners" and "losers" of the TSA and the CBP, using a distributional analysis. Winners and losers will be narrowly defined as newly eligible or newly ineligible persons to the TSA program or those who gain and lose in terms of the transfers of the TSA and the CBP. This discussion, though informative, is not complete; it is preferable in these cases to take into account the total transfers from all programs and services, not only the program in question. Chapter 8 describes the pretesting of the PMT formula. Chapter 9 evaluates the compensation measures introduced in August 2015 to diminish the number of losers. Finally, the last chapter discusses future policy options related to the TSA and options for moving toward strengthening the system of social protection and labor. Each chapter concludes with a summary of the main messages discussed.

The Targeted Social Assistance Program circa 2013

Georgia has a wide range of social protection programs. These encompass the TSA, pensions, disability, and child and foster care programs among others. In 2013, government expenditure earmarked for social protection was slightly above 6 percent of Georgia's GDP, or close to 20 percent of overall government expenditure. The majority of this budget went to noncontributory pensions (4.8 percent of GDP, which is four times larger than the spending earmarked for other social assistance programs). In total, the TSA program encompassed about 13 percent of Georgia's social protection budget in 2013. Figure 1.2 presents an overview of budget allocations toward social protection in Georgia and other countries in the region. Figure 1.3 breaks down Georgia's 2013 social protection budget into the various programs.

The current administration has committed itself to improving social sector outcomes, including in health and education. These sectors were severely underfunded in 2013, especially when compared to other countries. Health has experienced major reforms with the introduction of universal health care. The budget of universal health care increased from GEL (Georgian lari) 70 million in 2013 to GEL 338 million in 2014, with a planned budget of GEL 470 million in 2015. The expenditure on universal health is one-third of the expenditure on noncontributory Old Age Pension (which was about 7 percent in 2013). Similarly, the state expenditure on education rose, even when the spending on free universal preschool is not taken into account.[5]

Figure 1.2 Social Protection Spending in Select Eastern European and Central Asian Countries

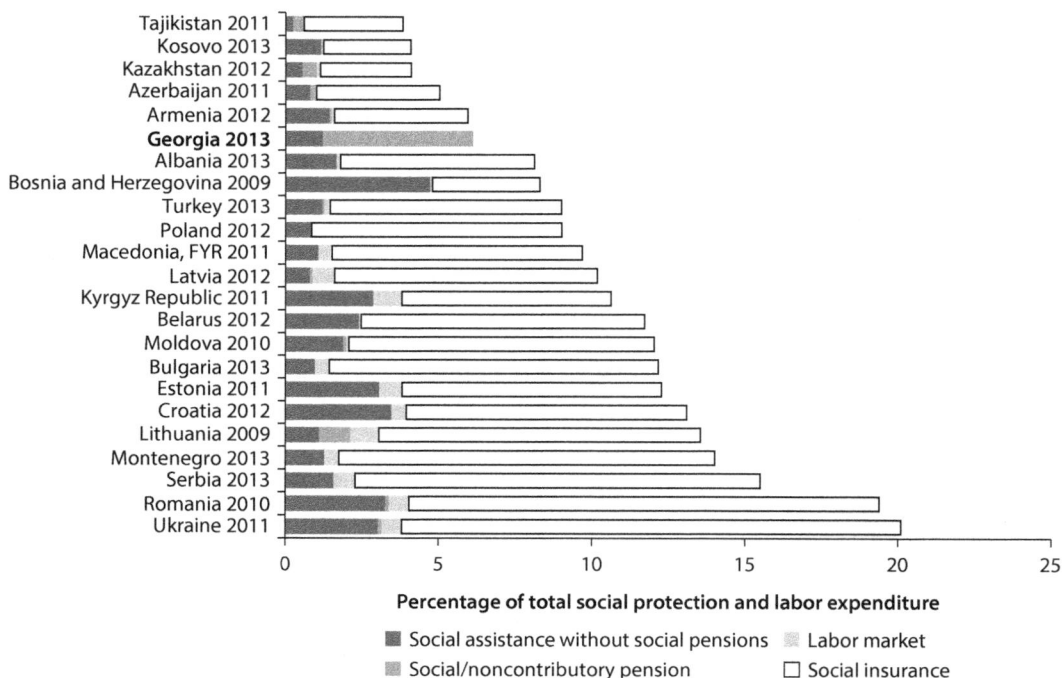

Tajikistan 2011
Kosovo 2013
Kazakhstan 2012
Azerbaijan 2011
Armenia 2012
Georgia 2013
Albania 2013
Bosnia and Herzegovina 2009
Turkey 2013
Poland 2012
Macedonia, FYR 2011
Latvia 2012
Kyrgyz Republic 2011
Belarus 2012
Moldova 2010
Bulgaria 2013
Estonia 2011
Croatia 2012
Lithuania 2009
Montenegro 2013
Serbia 2013
Romania 2010
Ukraine 2011

Percentage of total social protection and labor expenditure

■ Social assistance without social pensions   ▨ Labor market
▨ Social/noncontributory pension   □ Social insurance

Source: Social Protection Expenditure and Evaluation Database (SPEED; World Bank).

The TSA has been constantly revised since 2006 and has had its benefit amounts updated. Households apply to the unified database for socially vulnerable families under the SSA, and social agents visit the households to assess and verify their vulnerability status. As of June 2015, more than half of the families of the country had applied to the TSA and were registered in the database (about 43 percent of the total population). However, only 10 percent of the population and 12 percent of families qualified for the cash benefit.[6] Until January 2009, the first family member in qualifying households received GEL 30 and each subsequent member received GEL 12. In 2009, while the first family member benefit remained unchanged, the benefit for each subsequent family member was doubled to GEL 24 (SSA 2011). In July 2013, the cash benefit amount was raised again—doubled for every family member. The first family member started receiving GEL 60 and each subsequent member GEL 48.[7] See figure 1.4 for the evolution of these TSA indicators.

In 2013, there was also an increase of the proportion of recipients in the bottom quintile and a reduction of recipients in the upper half of consumption distribution. UNICEF's Welfare Monitoring Survey of 2013 showed that the TSA increased the proportion of its recipients in the bottom quintile among all recipients from 54 percent to 72 percent. This improvement was probably due to improvements in the administration of the program. For instance, the SSA has

Figure 1.3 Primary Government Social Spending as a Percentage of GDP, 2013

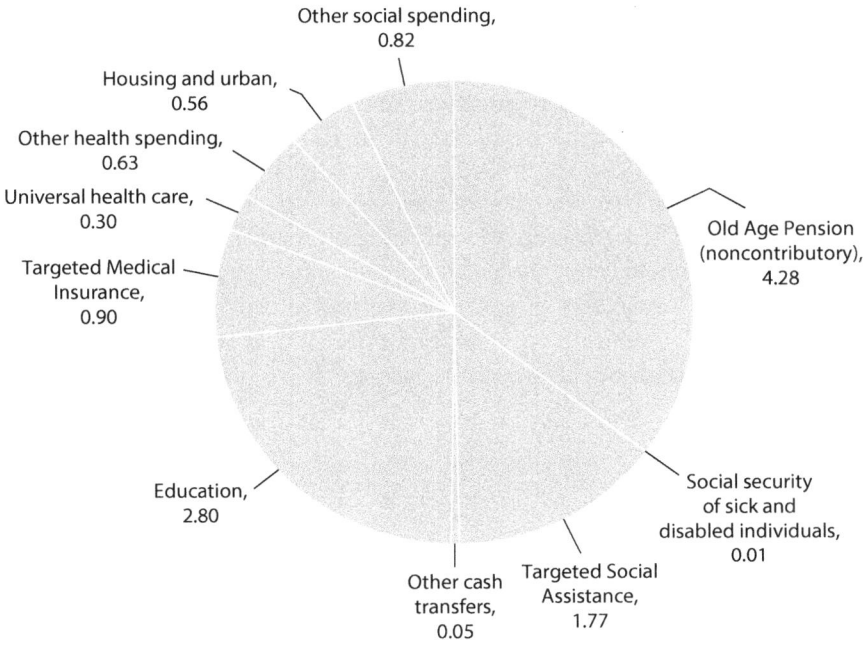

- Other social spending, 0.82
- Housing and urban, 0.56
- Other health spending, 0.63
- Universal health care, 0.30
- Targeted Medical Insurance, 0.90
- Old Age Pension (noncontributory), 4.28
- Education, 2.80
- Social security of sick and disabled individuals, 0.01
- Other cash transfers, 0.05
- Targeted Social Assistance, 1.77

Source: World Bank 2015c, table 2.2.

Figure 1.4 TSA Indicators, 2008–14

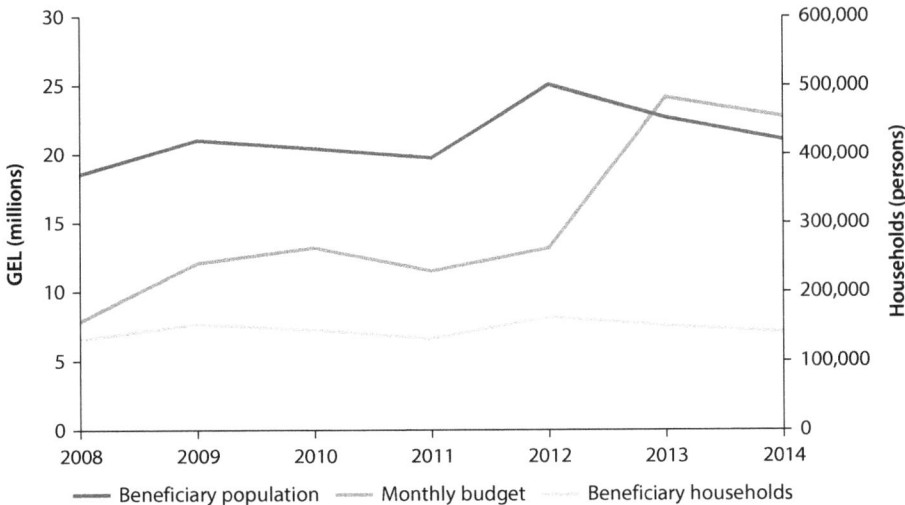

Legend: Beneficiary population — Monthly budget — Beneficiary households

Source: Social Services Agency.
Note: The data are for December of each year. Population estimated based on number of household members of TSA-eligible households. GEL = Georgian lari; TSA = Targeted Social Assistance.

taken seriously the reassessment of families to ensure there are no inclusion errors. In addition, it has reduced the proportion of households in the upper half of the consumption distribution to 12 percent (see figure 1.5).

The TSA program seems to adjust quickly to a changing environment, registering beneficiaries in and out of the program. This gives dynamism to the static PMT but raises concerns about its manipulation. In February and March 2013, the coverage of the program decreased substantially by 113,708 beneficiaries. From April to June of that year, the program was enlarged by 39,468 beneficiaries (see figure 1.6).[8] These flows in and out of the program could mirror poverty dynamics, as households are very likely to move around the poverty line (World Bank 2014), but more research would be needed to corroborate this hypothesis.

Figure 1.5 TSA Coverage of Households, 2009–13

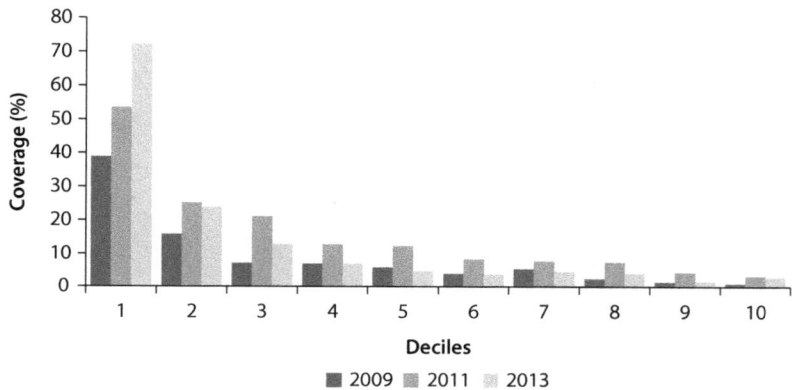

Source: Welfare Monitoring Survey rounds 2009, 2011, and 2013.
Note: Pre-TSA consumption deciles. Consumption aggregate measured according to UNICEF definition. For details on the definitions, see chapter 2 and "Glossary." TSA = Targeted Social Assistance.

Figure 1.6 TSA Beneficiaries by Month, 2010–15

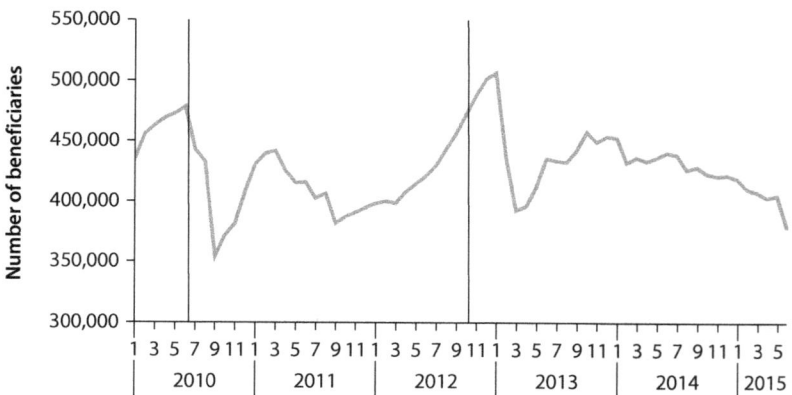

Source: Social Services Agency.
Note: Real number of population covered. The vertical lines indicate dates of elections. TSA = Targeted Social Assistance.

Notice there are spikes in the number of beneficiaries in the months before elections (marked by the vertical lines). This fact has fed the doubts about the manipulation of the program, in particular by the subjective assessments. Moreover, TSA coverage varies substantially across regions, as expected from a country with poverty unevenly distributed across its landscape. Map 1.1 shows the coverage of the TSA across regions in Georgia, and chapter 2 includes a description of regional poverty incidence, jointly with the discussion on measurement.

The improvement of the TSA targeting, coupled with the increase in the benefit size, made the TSA scheme more effective in lifting populations out of extreme poverty. As a result of the increase of the TSA benefits in 2013, the program has become approximately 60 percent more effective in lifting the population out of extreme poverty, as compared to 2011. Table 1.1 shows the percentage point difference between the poverty incidence with and without TSA and indicates an important jump in 2013 toward greater efficiency.

Map 1.1 TSA Coverage by Region

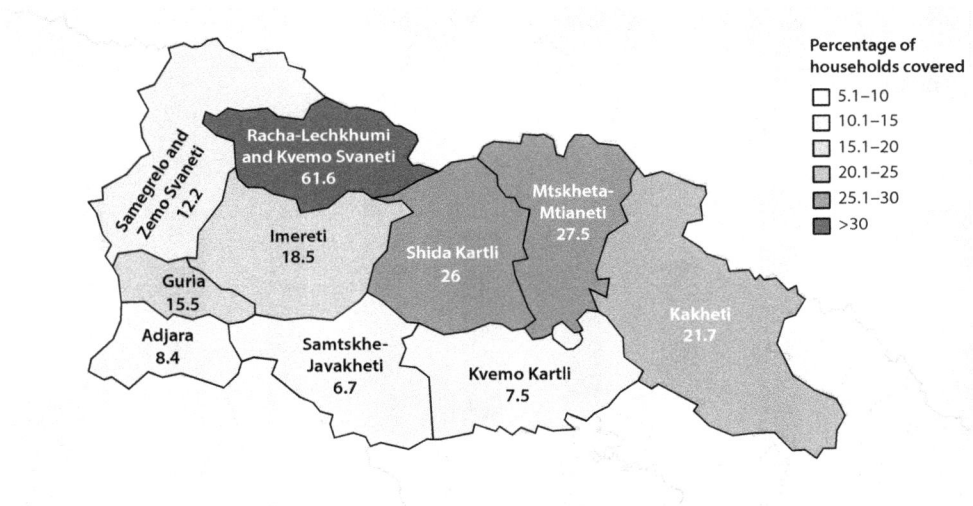

Note: Administrative data percentages are calculated using official National Statistics Office of Georgia (GeoStat) population data for 2013–14, which assumes 4.5 million people and 1.167 million households in Georgia. Estimations for this map are based on the sampling weights that GeoStat uses and assumes 3.63 million people and 1.022 million households. TSA = Targeted Social Assistance.

Table 1.1 Extreme Poverty Incidence with and without TSA, 2009–13

	2009	2011	2013
With TSA	9.9	9.1	3.9
Excluding TSA	13.6	12.7	9.7
Percentage point effect	3.7	3.6	5.8

Source: Welfare Monitoring Survey.
Note: Weighted data at population level. Poverty incidence is measured using the US$1.25 per adult equivalent (PAE) a day poverty line and the welfare aggregated as measured by UNICEF. TSA = Targeted Social Assistance.

Despite these important efficiency gains, the TSA program continues to seek improvements, as poor families with children are less likely than poor families without children to be eligible for the TSA. Children and families with children are overrepresented in the lowest consumption deciles. Despite the overall improvements in terms of economic growth and the expansion of cash transfer programs, these groups are less likely to qualify for TSA benefits than equivalent childless households. Coverage of childless households is always higher than coverage of households with children (figure 1.7). Around 8 percent of childless households fall into the first decile and 74 percent of those are covered by the TSA. At the same time, around 13 percent of households with children fall in the first decile and only 71 percent of those are covered by the TSA. For those in deciles 2 through 4, coverage of households with children is half of that of households without. Evidently, households with children have a more difficult time in qualifying for the TSA scheme. At the same time, the major driver of the inclusion error are households without children. Even though about 30 percent of

Figure 1.7 Distribution of Households with and without Children and TSA Coverage by Decile, 2013

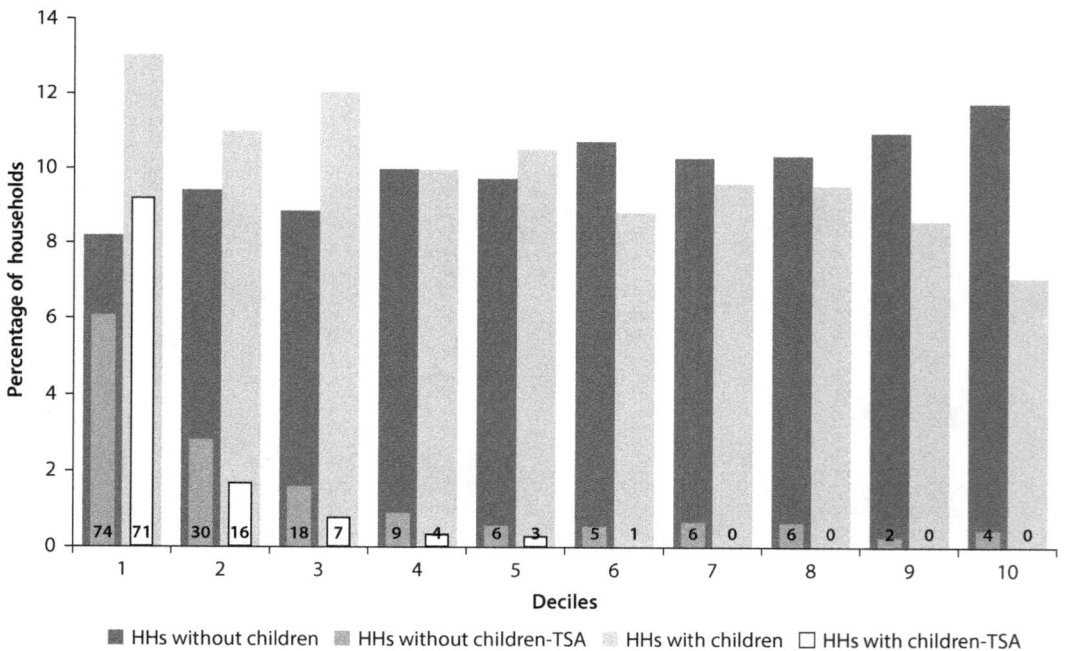

Source: Welfare Monitoring Survey 2013 (http://data.unicef.ge/en/datasets/2013-welfare-monitoring-survey).
Note: Pre-TSA PAE consumption deciles are shown. Consumption aggregate is measured according to the UNICEF definition. See chapter 2 and "Glossary." The numbers at the bottom of each bar indicate the percentage of total households in that decile that have children. For example, in the first decile 74 percent is the percentage of households without children that receive TSA and 71 percent is the percentage of households with children that receive TSA. The sum of the height of the blue bars across deciles gives you the total population without children (100%), and the sum of the orange bars across deciles gives you the total percentage of covered families without children (15%). Similarly, the sum of the height of the green bars across deciles gives you the total population with children. The sum of the white bars across deciles gives you the percentage of families with children covered by TSA (13%). HH = households; PAE = per adult equivalent; TSA = Targeted Social Assistance.

poor households with and without children are covered by TSA (8.8 percentage points out of 27.6 percent and 5.4 percentage points out of 18.4 percent, respectively), the coverage of nonpoor households (inclusion error or leakage) is more than twice as high in households without children (9.1 percentage points out of 81.7 percent versus 3.8 percentage points out of 72.4 percent, respectively, and this difference is statistically significant).

Some improvements to the coverage and targeting of the program could be achieved by improving outreach and decreasing the inclusion errors in the higher deciles. Almost 20 percent of households in the first decile of the consumption per adult equivalent (PAE) distribution received PMT scores that were too high to qualify for TSA (that is, scores greater than 57,000),[9] and only 8 percent were not registered (see figure 1.8). The coverage of the second decile is 24 percent, which could have been a good indicator if all 100 percent of the first decile was covered and considering overall coverage of the program was 12 percent. For households in the second and third deciles of the consumption PAE distribution, more than 50 percent had too high of PMT scores.[10] At the same time, over 20 percent of households in the second and more than 35 percent of households in the third decile were not registered in the database. Again, this shows that there is still room for improving the outreach of the program.

Incomes of households in the bottom 40 percent do not vary between those who qualify for TSA and those who are above the threshold but still vulnerable. Figure 1.9 shows household income by consumption decile for two groups of households: (1) households with a reported vulnerability score below 57,000 who were eligible to receive the TSA and (2) households with a reported score

Figure 1.8 Percentage of Families per Group of TSA Score and Consumption Decile, 2013

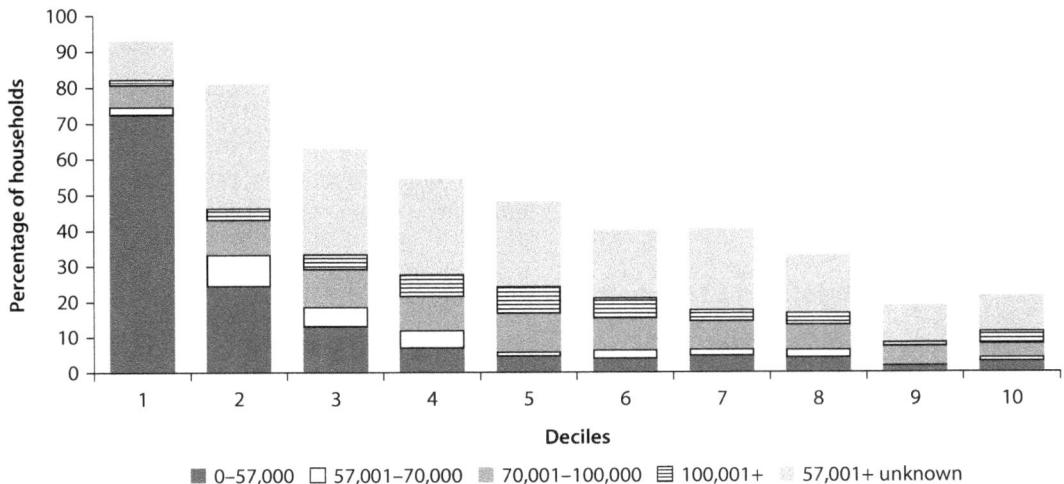

■ 0–57,000   □ 57,001–70,000   ▨ 70,001–100,000   ▤ 100,001+   ░ 57,001+ unknown

Source: Welfare Monitoring Survey 2013.
Note: Pre-TSA PAE consumption deciles are shown. Consumption aggregate is measured according to the UNICEF definition. See chapter 2 and "Glossary." The distance (percentage) that is missing until 100 represents the households that are not registered in the TSA program. PAE = per adult equivalent; TSA = Targeted Social Assistance.

Figure 1.9 Income per Adult Equivalent for TSA-Eligible and TSA-Vulnerable Households, 2013

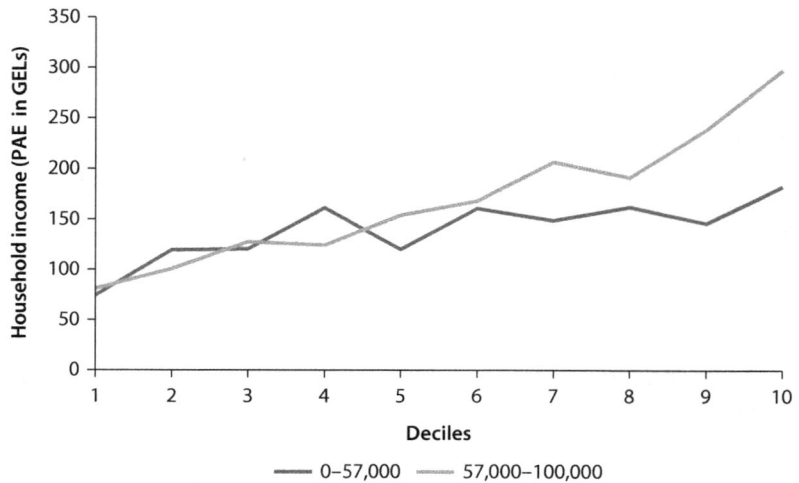

Source: Welfare Monitoring Survey.
Note: Pre-TSA PAE consumption deciles are shown. Consumption aggregate is measured according to the UNICEF definition. See chapter 2 and "Glossary." GEL = Georgian lari; PAE = per adult equivalent; TSA = Targeted Social Assistance.

between 57,000 and 100,000, who were not eligible to receive the transfer but nevertheless are vulnerable. If the PMT had more accurately estimated household income, the income of TSA-vulnerable households would be well above income of TSA recipient households. This is more or less true in the four top consumption deciles. Nonetheless, households in the bottom forty of the welfare distribution who apply for TSA and are rejected might not be much different from those who are accepted. This suggests a high concentration of population around the qualification cutoff. When the consumption decile is held constant, a household qualifying for the TSA scheme might be in similar need of support as a household who is rejected. Even at the upper edge of the consumption distribution (upper 40 percent of distribution), the average household scoring below 57,000 barely manages to avoid having income PAE below the monthly subsistence minimum.

The Reform in a Nutshell

Early in 2014, the GoG started to work closely, first, with UNICEF and, later, with the WBG on the technical assessment of the TSA and its translation into policy actions. Since then, UNICEF and the WBG have been providing technical and financial assistance to the MoLHSA and the SSA.[11] Most of the technical assistance consisted of analyses that enabled the technical teams and high-level government officials to make decisions about the design of the TSA and the introduction of the CBP. Figure ES.2 (in the "Executive Summary") summarizes the milestones of the policy dialog among the institutions and how the GoG used the technical outputs to design and implement the five elements of the reform already mentioned. By the end of 2015, the GoG had completed the technical revision, initiated implementation, and introduced compensation measures. The plan of the SSA is to reassess about a twelfth part of the registry each month to complete the process in a year's time or by the end of 2016. The following paragraphs describe the salient messages coming from each piece of the technical work and how the technical work fed the policy actions.

The objective of the government was to validate and improve the effectiveness of the TSA. In particular, the GoG wanted to (1) minimize inclusion and exclusion errors associated with the program, given the changing economy; (2) remove from the PMT formula easily concealable durable goods, as there was a belief that households were indeed concealing them in an effort to be eligible for assistance; (3) include new easily verifiable and potential income-generating items; (4) reduce the total number of variables used in the PMT formula; and (5) remove from the PMT formula the subjective assessment by the social agents.

This technical assessment led to a reform of the TSA program and the introduction of the CBP. Thus, this reform comprised five elements: (1) update of the PMT formula that gives place to the consumption index; (2) update and simplification of the needs index; (3) establishment of a new benefit structure that varies with the vulnerability score; (4) revision of the calculation of total household transfer depending on household demographic composition; and (5) introduction of an associated program: the CBP. In the rest of this report, elements 1–4 will be referred to as the *TSA reform* and elements 1–5 as the *reform package*, or TSA+CBP. In addition, compensation measures to reduce the unavoidable harming effects of the reform were introduced in August 2015.

The reform package, TSA+CBP, is expected to further contribute to reducing extreme poverty, and in particular child poverty. Specifically, through this package the SSA seeks to better target TSA benefits to the poor, increase investment in the human capital of children, and redirect some funds to better protect vulnerable groups who may be relatively better off but still experience significant risk of slipping below the poverty line and who are considered poor according to absolute poverty lines set for the region. Although it is difficult to have large efficiency gains with a program like the TSA that is already well targeted, there is always scope for improvement. At a minimum, the revision of the PMT of the TSA is expected to help maintain the targeting performance of the TSA. Marginal gains are also expected, especially in the second decile—partially covered by the TSA— contributing to a reduction in poverty incidence. In addition, given that poor families without children were more likely to be in the TSA than families with children, this revision of the PMT was an opportunity to address this bias and reduce child poverty. For example, using the US$2.50 per day per capita poverty line, 36 percent of the population was poor in 2013 (World Bank 2015b). In addition, the national average disguises the important variations across the country, with rural poverty almost doubling urban poverty

(46.1 and 25.6 percent, respectively, for 2013), which calls attention to the need for updates in the eligibility formula.[12]

Periodic updates to the PMT formula help maintain the targeting efficiency of PMT-based poverty-targeted schemes. Over the years, consumption patterns change in response not only to income growth in the country (some goods become accessible to the whole population) but also to technological or norms changes. For example, mobile devices are no longer considered luxury items.

As a by-product, this revision of the PMT formula seeks to enable smaller gains that facilitate the administration of the program, its transparency, and its evaluation. For example, simplifying some of the variables that enter in the PMT formula could help to add transparency to the implementation and eliminate some of the concerns about its level of effectiveness. Also, the formula tradition-ally included the subjective evaluation by social agents. While this was well intentioned when introduced, it was not clear how effective it was in improving the targeting efficiency, and so it has been removed.

Revisions to the benefit structure aimed to promote a more pro-poor distribu-tion of benefits by extending higher per capita benefit amounts to the poorest households. This staggered benefit structure also is expected to contribute to reducing work disincentives as the marginal tax rate of taking a job at the cost of losing program eligibility becomes lower.[13] One caveat and usual criticism to this type of structure is that the PMT is never accurate enough to generate signifi-cantly different brackets to differentiate groups of the population. One alterna-tive to this method of differentiating the size of the transfer is to introduce layers of benefits, as further discussed in chapter 10. In addition, the equalization of the benefits for each member of the household reduces the incentive for artificial division of the households.

The newly introduced benefit structure responded to clear parameters established by the government. The new cutoffs for the revised benefit structure are in accordance with the following requests set by the GoG: (1) households scoring below 57,000 should continue to receive the same amount, (2) total population coverage should not be decreased, (3) total monthly budget of the TSA should not be increased substantially, and (4) all household members should receive equal amounts. One key concern of the SSA is to maintain a healthy system without work disincentives. A sound study using a reliable econometric methodology revealed that the TSA generated only small work disincentives for women with young children living in rural areas.[14] The work disincentives of this group are more likely to be minimized with support for childcare and flexible, family-friendly work schedules rather than by changing the design of the TSA.

Furthermore, the revised benefit structure took into account the introduction of another program: the CBP, which consists of an additional transfer of GEL 10 per child under 16. The CBP has a higher eligibility threshold than the TSA, resulting in increased coverage of the vulnerable. This benefit is intended as an additional protection for households that move in and out of poverty or that would be considered poor using absolute poverty lines determined by the World Bank. (Figure 2.5 in chapter 2 shows significant mobility prevailing in Georgia.)

Table 1.2 Distribution of New TSA and CBP Beneficiaries

Vulnerability score	TSA only		CBP only		TSA+CBP	
	Percent	Cumulative (%)	Percent	Cumulative (%)	Percent	Cumulative (%)
0–30,000	20.60	20.60	13.85	13.85	12.29	12.29
30,001–57,000	54.80	75.40	24.27	38.12	32.70	44.99
57,001–60,000	9.18	84.58	4.32	42.44	5.48	50.47
60,001–65,000	15.42	100.00	5.23	47.67	9.20	59.67
65,001–100,000	0	100.00	52.31	100.00	40.32	100.00
Over 100,000	0	100.00	0	100.00	0	100.00

Source: Government of Georgia, Resolution No. 758, December 31, 2014.
Note: Households are sorted by TSA score before the introduction of compensation measures. Table A.2 (appendix A) shows the distribution as a percentage of the total population. CBP = Child Benefit Program; TSA = Targeted Social Assistance.

In this way, the package serves to avert perpetuating poverty effects in future generations. Table 1.2 shows the distribution of households by vulnerability score and program eligibility.

Finally, to minimize the number of newly ineligible TSA beneficiaries the government introduced compensation measures. The distributional analysis identified single nonworking pensioners as one of the groups that would lose eligibility in the TSA. It is worth mentioning that the number of nonworking pensioners would have gone down due to revisions in the pension amount accounted in the formula, and not by changes in the formula per se. To minimize the impact of the reform on these pensioners, the government increased the coefficient of the needs index for this sociodemographic group. The increment undoes the reduction that was estimated based on the changes in the prices of goods consumed by single pensioners (mostly due to the adoption of universal health care covering medicines) and further increases it. Clearly, the compensation measure achieved its objective. Nevertheless, and as is further discussed in chapter 9, compensation measures should be reexamined based on additional analyses of their fiscal sustainability and alignment with the objectives of the reform and the other transfers received by this group.

Summary

Established in 2006, the TSA program has been constantly revised and has had its benefit amounts updated. In 2013, the improvement of the TSA targeting, coupled with the increase in the benefit size, made it more effective in lifting populations out of extreme poverty. Yet the program continues to seek improvements in order to keep the PMT up to date in terms of correlates with changing consumption patterns and as poor families with children are less likely than poor families without children to be eligible for the TSA. The program also witnessed constant changes of beneficiaries over time that can be explained by high movement of families across the consumption quintiles; the program was able to capture the well-being of a family only at a particular moment in time. It is worth mentioning that the households that did not qualify for TSA in 2013 were not necessarily well off or much different from the households that did qualify. The incomes of households in the bottom 40 percent of the welfare distribution did not vary between those who qualify for TSA and those who are above the threshold but still vulnerable. All these suggest the need to (1) refine the TSA program further and (2) develop additional safety nets to support vulnerable families, and in particular children.

Periodic updates to the PMT formula are part and parcel of running a PMT-based poverty-targeted scheme. In addition, the GoG was interested in validating the efficacy and transparency of the program. The major priorities of MoLHSA and SSA for refining the PMT were to (1) improve leakage and undercoverage results, (2) remove the easily concealable durable goods from applications, (3) include easily verifiable and potential income-generating items, (4) reduce the total number of variables used, and (5) remove the subjective assessment of social workers.

The package of TSA reforms comprised five elements: (1) update of the PMT formula that produces the consumption index, (2) update of the needs index, (3) establishment of a new benefit structure that varies with the vulnerability score, (4) revision of the calculation of total household transfer depending on household demographic composition, and (5) introduction of an associated program: the CBP. Revisions to the benefit structure aim to promote a more pro-poor distribution of benefits by extending higher per capita benefit amounts for the poorest households. These changes were followed by compensation measures to minimize the undesirable consequences of the package, at least in the short run. The introduction of the CBP, which consists of an additional transfer of GEL 10 per child under age 16, is an additional protection for households who move in and out of poverty or who would be considered poor using the absolute poverty line as a way to avert perpetuating poverty effects in future generations.

The introduction of the CBP can also be perceived as a first step toward a comprehensive and efficient social protection and labor system. Little is known about how different programs and services in Georgia complement and substitute for each other. Although the total spending in social assistance and labor is not large relative to other countries in the region, there seems to be no or little coordination among programs. However, at the same time, and based in the fact that about half of the population of the country registers with the TSA when only 12 percent benefit from this program, it can be presumed that some of these other programs—even at different government levels—use the TSA vulnerability score to target beneficiaries.

This report recommends that the GoG move toward building a comprehensive and efficient system of social protection and labor. The final chapter of this report briefly delineates the main principles that underlie the building of systems, based on the common understanding of systems by UNICEF and the WBG (Rawlings, Murthy, and Winter 2013). Further analysis is needed to thoroughly describe the demand of programs and services by the population of Georgia. At the same time, the analysis should take stock of the programs and services currently offered by the GoG.

Notes

1. Based on the estimates for the years 2009 to 2015.

2. Based on the Social Protection Expenditure and Evaluation Database (SPEED) for Europe and Central Asia. The average is calculated over 23 countries of Eastern Europe and Central Asia. The countries are selected based on their data availability.

3. Using a regression discontinuity econometric model, the authors compared the labor market engagement of a household's members around the eligibility threshold of the TSA. The results showed the presence of work disincentives for women. Women just below the eligibility threshold were 7 to 11 percentage points less likely to work than women just above it, in 2011. The reader interested in comparing performances across countries can consult the multicountry report (World Bank 2015e). The details of the analysis for Georgia are discussed in a background paper (World Bank 2015d).

4. The government gives additional GEL 30 to old age pensioners in Svaneti, for example.

5. The provision of preschool service is decentralized and it is hard to estimate the total budget.

6. The population size is updated to the most recent census data's preliminary findings. The total population of the country has changed from 4.5 million to 3.7 million. Retrieved from the SSA and National Statistics Office of Georgia (GeoStat) web pages.

7. UNICEF 2014.

8. SSA administrative data, actual transfers to beneficiary households.

9. The "unknown" category in figure 1.8 refers to the families who are registered in the database and do not know their exact score but whose scores are too high to be eligible for the benefit.

10. According to the Survey of Barriers to Access to Social Services (UNICEF and USAID 2011), among the reasons for not applying for TSA benefits, the major disincentives are suspicion about the accuracy of the evaluation (33 percent) and lack of awareness about where to submit the application (24 percent).

11. The portion of the reform of the TSA that reviews the PMT formula was included as a prior action in the WBG Inclusive Growth Development Policy Operation.

12. Also using the US$2.50 a day absolute poverty line. As explained in chapter 3, the PMT formula is estimated for four regions, thus the reestimation of the status quo model as well as this revision take care of changes in consumption patterns in rural and urban areas.

13. Work disincentives in Georgia are present only among certain groups of the population: mostly women with young children living in rural areas (Santos et al. 2015 using a regression discontinuity approach). More information about how to measure work disincentives as a tax wedge can be found at OECD (2005).

14. Santos et al. (2015) analyze the impact of the TSA program on individual's labor market decisions. Using a tailored survey of approximately 2,000 households chosen based on administrative data and around the eligibility threshold and a regression discontinuity identification strategy, the results suggest that the TSA program indeed generates work disincentives around the threshold, although these disincentives are concentrated among women. On average, women who receive TSA are 9 to 11 percentage points less likely to be economically active than women who live in households that do not receive the transfer. The disincentives' effects are larger for women who are not married and have children that are school-aged.

References

OECD (Organisation for Economic Co-operation and Development). 2005. "Increasing Financial Incentives to Work: The Role of In-Work Benefits." In *OECD Employment Outlook*, chap 3. Paris: OECD. https://www.oecd.org/els/emp/36780865.pdf.

Rawlings, Laura, Sheila Murthy, and Natalia Winder. 2013. "Common Ground: UNICEF and World Bank Approaches to Building Social Protection Systems." Social Protection and Labor Policy Note 15, World Bank, Washington, DC.

Santos, I., B. Kits, A. Isik-Dikmelik, and O. Smith. 2015. *The Impact of Targeted Social Assistance on Labor Market in Georgia*. World Bank Report 98707. Washington, DC: World Bank.

SSA (Social Services Agency of Georgia). 2011. *Annual Report 2011*. Tbilisi.

UNICEF. 2012. *Georgia: Reducing Child Poverty: A Discussion Paper*. Tbilisi, UNICEF. http://unicef.ge/uploads/UNICEF_Child_PovertyENG_web_with_names1.pdf.

———. 2014. *The Well-Being of Children and Their Families in Georgia: Georgian Welfare Monitoring Survey, Third Stage 2013*. Tbilisi, UNICEF. http://unicef.ge/uploads/WMS_2013_eng.pdf.

———. 2015. *Reducing Child Poverty in Georgia: A Way Forward*. Tbilisi, UNICEF. http://unicef.ge/uploads/UNICEF_Poverty_Paper_2015_ENG_FINAL_.pdf.

UNICEF and University of York. 2010. *How Do Georgian Children and Their Families Cope with the Impact of the Financial Crises? Report on the Georgia Welfare Monitoring Survey, 2009*. Tbilisi, UNICEF. http://unicef.ge/uploads/en_How_do_Georgian_children_and_their_families_cope_with_the_impact_of_the_financial_crises_-_Report_on_the_Georgia_Welfare_Monitoring_Survey_2009_-_english_version.pdf.

UNICEF and USAID. 2011. "Survey of Barriers to Access to Social Services: Georgia 2010." Tbilisi, UNICEF. http://unicef.ge/uploads/Survey_of_Barriers_to_Access_to_Social_Services._Georgia_2010_eng.pdf.

UNICEF, USAID, and University of York. 2012. *The Well-Being of Children and Their Families in Georgia: Welfare Monitoring Survey, Second Stage, 2011*. Tbilisi, UNICEF. http://unicef.ge/uploads/WMSFinal_final_Copy_for_web_1_USAID.pdf.

Welfare Monitoring Survey. 2013. UNICEF. http://data.unicef.ge/en/datasets/2013-welfare-monitoring-survey.

World Bank. Various years. SPEED (Social Protection Expenditure and Evaluation Database) for Europe and Central Asia. World Bank, Washington, DC.

———. 2012. *Georgia—Public Expenditure Review: Managing Expenditure Pressures for Sustainability and Growth*. Washington, DC: World Bank. https://openknowledge.worldbank.org/handle/10986/12315.

———. 2014. *Georgia Public Expenditure Review: Diagnostics of Public Investment Management System*. Washington, DC: World Bank. https://openknowledge.worldbank.org/handle/10986/19302.

———. 2015a. "Avanzando hacia sistemas de protección social y trabajo en América Latina y el Caribe." Social Protection and Labor Global Practice, Latin America and Caribbean Region, World Bank, Washington, DC.

———. 2015b. "Georgia Poverty Assessment: Poverty Reduction and Shared Prosperity since the Crisis." Note prepared under the FY15 South Caucasus Programmatic Poverty Assessment (P151474), World Bank, Washington, DC.

———. 2015c. *Georgia Public Expenditure Review: Selected Fiscal Issues.* Washington, DC: World Bank. https://openknowledge.worldbank.org/handle/10986/22259.

———. 2015d. *The Impact of Targeted Social Assistance on Labor Market in Georgia: A Regression Discontinuity Approach.* Washington, DC: World Bank. https://openknowledge.worldbank.org/handle/10986/22502.

———. 2015e. *Promoting Labor Market Participation and Social Inclusion in Europe and Central Asia's Poorest Countries.* Washington, DC: World Bank. https://openknowledge.worldbank.org/handle/10986/22501.

CHAPTER 2

Data and Definitions

Introduction

Important challenges in the effort to revise the Targeted Social Assistance (TSA) program were filling in data gaps, reconciling differences arising from various data sources, and addressing the discrepancies in the definitions of key variables and measures among all institutions involved. This chapter explains how the team addressed these issues and makes explicit the data sources and definitions used in the rest of the report, being candid about the costs and benefits of the compromises made.

Data

The first problem to tackle was data availability, because none of the existent sources included information on both consumption and the household declaration variables retrieved in the TSA registry. The helpful but limited data sources comprised administrative social assistance records, the Welfare Monitoring Survey (WMS) conducted by UNICEF, and the Integrated Household Survey (IHS) collected by the National Statistics Office of Georgia (GeoStat). As is the case in many countries, the government of Georgia did not allow cross-checking the information from the administrative records with that of household surveys.

To address this data gap, UNICEF worked with the Social Services Agency (SSA) and GeoStat to implement the collection of an additional module in the IHS that included the household declaration variables of the TSA registry. The sampling frame for the additional module was designed using the third quarter (Q3) of the 2013 IHS (called *estimation sample* hereafter), and enumerators in the field retrieved the additional variables between February and March 2014. This sample comprises 2,601 households and is used to conduct all the analyses that follow in this report: the construction of the proxy means test (PMT; for more see chapter 3) and the analysis of winners and losers (chapters 6, 7, and 9).[1]

Readers interested in replicating the work should notice a few caveats. First, because in spring 2014 not all the households were found, a total of 166 household observations from Q3 2013 were deleted from the estimation sample.[2] Second, there could be and actually are some changes for a few variables between Q3 2013 and spring 2014 when the additional data were retrieved. Some of these variables such as household size are corrected, while others such as consumption come from the core IHS in Q3 2013 (the core survey). Additional data were collected for those households that were interviewed for the first time in Q4 2013 to have a *validation sample*. Table A.1 (in appendix A) shows the differences between the estimated sampling frame and the actual number of households interviewed. The rest of this section describes the main features of the data to be transparent about their strengths and weaknesses.

The IHS is a nationally representative survey. It is conducted by GeoStat on a continuous basis. The sample is a rotating panel of approximately 2,500 households in which each household is interviewed in four consecutive quarters and a fourth of the sample is renewed every quarter. During 2013, 11,101 interviews were performed. The survey includes modules on food consumption, durables, assets, agricultural production, health and educational expenses, and employment. The IHS is also nationally representative by quarters and by regions, although, the least populated regions need to be consolidated for meaningful significance. GeoStat is transparent in the management of the information, and the datasets for the past several years are available online.[3]

The WMS is a nationally representative survey as well. However, working with this survey would have delayed the reform as its next round was scheduled for July–October 2015. It is conducted by UNICEF Georgia biennially on a longitudinal sample. The first survey was conducted in 2009 with 4,646 fully completed interviews, with attrition rates of 14 and 10 percent in 2011 and 2013, respectively. The survey includes modules on consumption, income, durables, assets, health and education, economic and social factors, and child development. Even though the methodology for computing consumption aggregates is somewhat different for the WMS and IHS, the trends are similar when comparing the respective years.

In the past, the WMS was the only instrument that allowed a reliable evaluation of the performance of the TSA because it retrieved information about the consumption variables and the TSA vulnerability score of the household. Even if today the IHS records the TSA transfers separately from other transfers, it cannot be used for performance monitoring, let alone for a full evaluation, as is the objective of the current report. A recommendation coming from this report is for GeoStat to modify the IHS to routinely collect the TSA household declaration variables, as well as to be alert to include any other variables that could help to improve the eligibility formula of the TSA.

Finally, a pretesting was carried out with the help of social agents and the revised registry to validate the results before implementation. The pretesting was conducted between March and April 2015 and covered 5,565 households. Full interviews were conducted using the revised household declaration. More details on this are presented in chapter 8.

Definitions

Welfare Aggregate

The welfare aggregate is total monthly household consumption, using GeoStat's definition. However, results should be consistent if using the World Bank's or UNICEF's measures of welfare aggregate. The measure used in this report comes from GeoStat.[4] This measure of consumption aggregate differs slightly from the one used by the World Bank Group (WBG) and by UNICEF to track poverty in the country, but it does not lead to a wildly different reranking of households. Figure 2.1 shows that the two measures of the consumption aggregate are highly correlated; the correlation coefficient between measures is estimated at 0.83 (GeoStat and World Bank) and at 0.75 (GeoStat and UNICEF) and statistically significant at 1 percent in all cases. The consumption aggregate reported by GeoStat captures all expenditure consumption and is reported in nominal terms. In contrast, the consumption aggregate developed by the WBG excludes certain categories that are infrequent expenses (for example, weddings) and adjusts by time and spatial price differences. The main objective of the WBG measure is not only to track poverty in the country but also to produce a measure that is suitable for international comparisons. The UNICEF consumption aggregate is closer to GeoStat's measure.

Seasonality

Seasonality affects consumption throughout the year in Georgia. One of the main concerns was that working with only Q3 data could bias the results due to seasonality, as World Bank (2015) found differences in poverty throughout the year. Figure 2.2 reports average household consumption for the year 2013. Panel a shows that consumption was the highest in the last quarter of the year and the lowest in the second quarter. This pattern is clearly observed in urban areas as well. In rural areas, the second quarter was also the lowest, but

Figure 2.1 Household-Level Consumption Aggregates: GeoStat, UNICEF, and World Bank

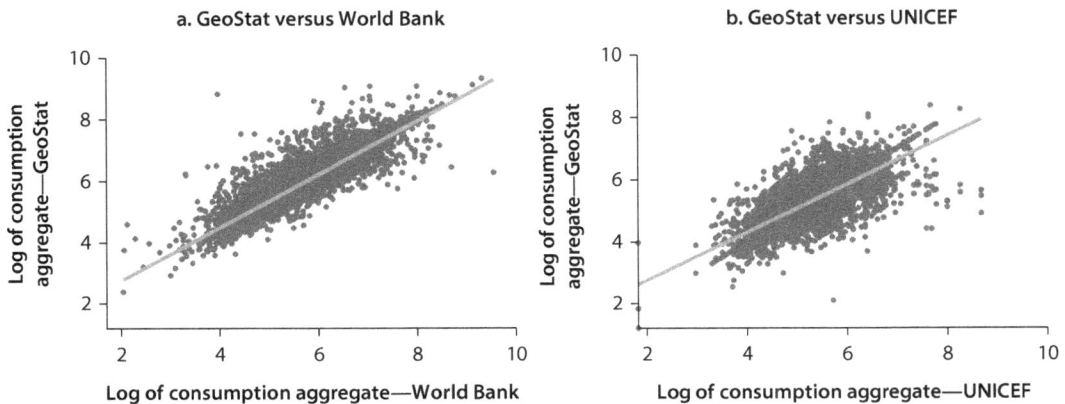

Source: Elaboration based on GeoStat and Europe and Central Asia Poverty (ECAPOV) estimates from IHS 2013. Natural logarithm of the monthly household consumption in local currency units. GeoStat = National Statistics Office of Georgia.

Figure 2.2 Household Consumption by Domain and Quarter (per Adult Equivalent), 2013

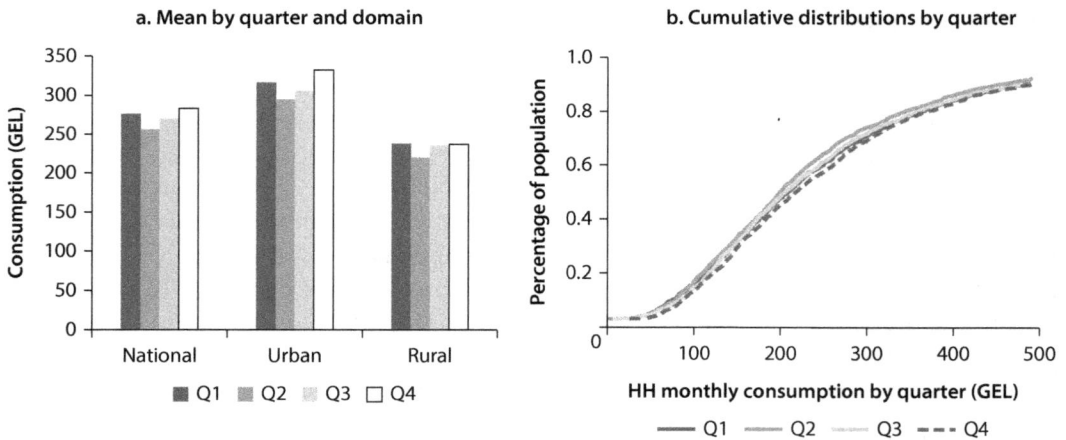

a. Mean by quarter and domain

b. Cumulative distributions by quarter

Source: Calculation based on IHS 2013.
Note: Monthly per adult equivalent household consumption, GeoStat consumption aggregate. Values reported in 2013 GEL, deflated by GeoStat monthly per national consumer price index (2013 = 100). GEL = Georgian lari; GeoStat = National Statistics Office of Georgia; HH = household; Q = quarter.

the differences between first, third, and fourth quarters are negligible. Panel b complements this information by showing that the distributions of the consumption aggregate by quarter shifted slightly from one quarter to another, suggesting that the differences in mean values are not driven by outliers. The orange line above all the others corresponds to the lowest values in the second quarter, and the dashed line below all the others corresponds to the fourth quarter. Although more analysis is required, a potential explanation is that the consumption shift results from the increase in heating expenses during the cold months of the year.

Seasonality affects other variables, such as unemployment, that are highly correlated with consumption and well-being. Employment (and unemployment) vary across the quarters of the year, with the lowest employment (highest unemployment) rate in the first quarter of the year, probably affected by the reduction of activities for industries that operate in open air (for example, construction and agriculture). Figure 2.3 shows these statistics by quarter.

However, the changes in consumption due to seasonality do not lead to changes in the targeting of the TSA and should not affect the results of the analysis of the following chapters. Taking advantage of the structure of the survey, one is able to follow TSA beneficiary households during the four quarters in order to identify their ranking in the distribution during the year. Households followed during the four quarters are a fourth of the whole sample and are slightly poorer than the rest of the distribution, but the distributions are considerably similar. The analysis indicates that there are no changes in the targeting of the program in spite of the seasonal changes in consumption. Figure 2.4 shows the coverage and the distribution of TSA beneficiaries across quarters of the year, by decile. The figure suggests that, although there are some variations in coverage and distribution of beneficiaries, there are no considerable changes, especially in the bottom decile.

Figure 2.3 Employment and Unemployment Rates for Household Head

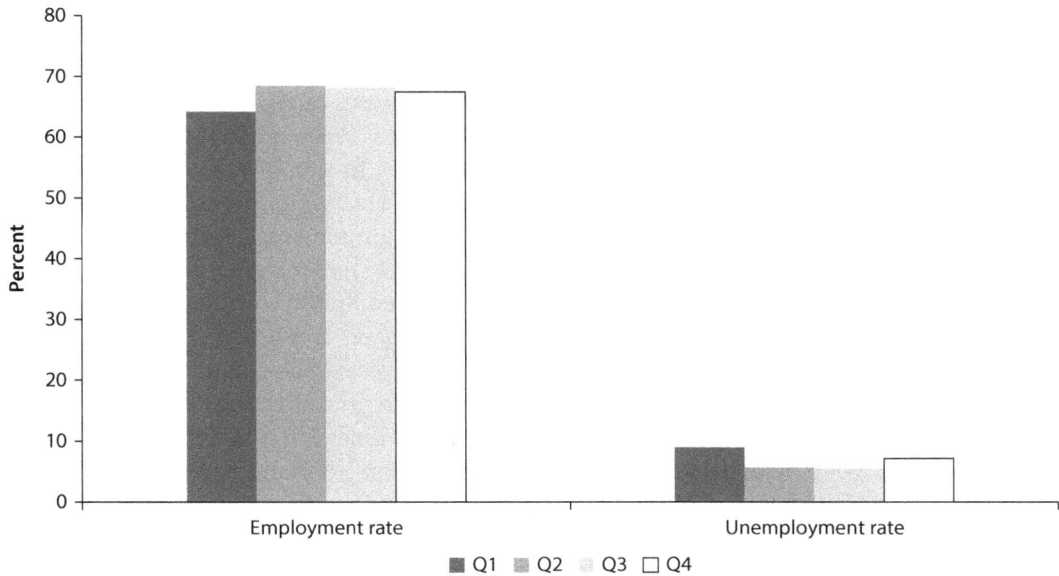

Q1 Q2 Q3 Q4

Source: Calculations based on IHS 2013.
Note: Q = quarter.

Figure 2.4 TSA Coverage and Distribution of Beneficiaries

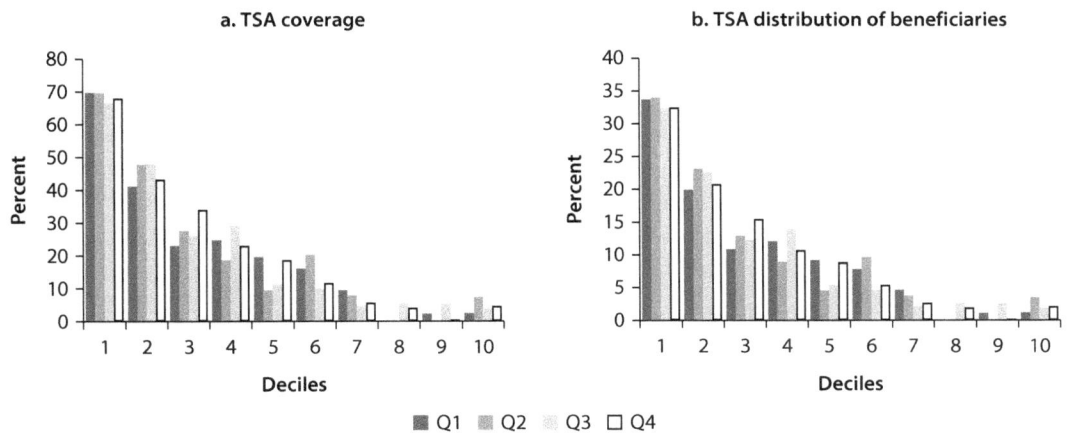

a. TSA coverage
b. TSA distribution of beneficiaries

Q1 Q2 Q3 Q4

Source: Calculation based on IHS 2013.
Note: Deciles estimated using household per adult equivalent consumption. Q = quarter; TSA = Targeted Social Assistance.

In sum, although rudimentary, the analysis conducted on the comparison of the measures of welfare aggregate of the various institutions and seasonality suggests that the results presented in what follows would not have been affected—at least qualitatively—by working with another definition of consumption aggregate or with yearly data.

Poverty

Nevertheless, when it comes to poverty measurement, there are irreconcilable differences among all the parties involved. All three institutions—the government of Georgia, UNICEF, and the WBG—work with different measures of poverty (see table 2.1). While the government uses relative measures of poverty, the WBG and UNICEF have absolute measures. The rest of this section briefly describes and contrasts the poverty definitions. To simplify the analysis, the rest of the report abstains from entering into an evaluation of the reform in terms of poverty. Instead, it works with the entire distribution of the consumption aggregate, which relies on rankings of well-being that were proved to be of little variation across measures and which are not affected by the choice of poverty line.

A myriad of poverty lines are being used by different institutions to measure poverty in Georgia, resulting in diverging estimates. The comparison of all these results is examined in World Bank (2015). The official poverty rate is estimated by GeoStat using a relative measure: a line established at 60 percent of the median per-adult-equivalent (PAE) consumption.[5] This method is appropriate in identifying households lagging in the consumption distribution, but it is not designed to capture changes over time to satisfy a minimum standard of well-being. These poverty estimates have remained quite stable in the past few years, estimated at 21.4 percent in 2013.

The World Bank, in contrast, follows an absolute poverty approach. In its methodology, the World Bank estimated poverty at 36 percent in 2013, using a line equivalent to $2.50 per day in 2005 purchasing power parity (PPP) terms. For this estimate, the consumption was estimated in per capita terms. Other World Bank reports use poverty lines set at $5.00 per day, resulting in poverty rates of 73.3 percent in 2013, and at $1.25 per day, resulting in poverty rates of 10.3 percent in 2013. This second rate is typically not reported for the region because of the extremely low incidence rates obtained in most countries. Independently of the choice of measure, the poverty incidence trend since 2010 is clearly decreasing, falling by more than 10 percentage points between 2010 and 2013 (46.7 to 36.0 percent using the $2.50 per day poverty line). Regional disparities in poverty

Table 2.1 Poverty Rates by GeoStat, UNICEF, and World Bank Group, 2009–13
percent

Definition	2009	2011	2013
GeoStat	21.0	23.0	21.4
UNICEF US$2.50 per day PAE	44.8	37.9	24.6
UNICEF child poverty US$2.50 per day	49.0	40.8	28.4
WBG US$2.50 PPP per day per capita	45.1	44.8	36.0
WBG US$5.00 PPP per day per capita	78.9	80.0	73.3

Source: Estimates retrieved from GeoStat web portal on August 13, 2015, http://geostat.ge/index.php ?action=page&p_id=188&lang=eng. WBG estimates from World Bank 2015. UNICEF estimates obtained from WMS 2013.
Note: UNICEF poverty rate estimates headcount rate PAE. GeoStat = National Statistics Office of Georgia; PAE = per adult equivalent; PPP = purchasing power parity; WBG = World Bank Group; WMS = Welfare Monitoring Survey.

incidence are evident when dividing the country into urban and rural areas. While urban areas reported a poverty rate close to 25 percent, rural areas almost doubled it, with 46.1 percent in 2013.

UNICEF calculates poverty using one relative and two absolute poverty lines. The relative poverty line is calculated using the same definition as GeoStat's. In each survey, the line corresponds to 60 percent of the weighted median consumption of households. The absolute poverty lines, extreme and general, correspond to the US$1.25 and US$2.50 daily consumption PAE. GEL values of absolute poverty lines are calculated with a 2009 base using May–July real exchange rates. In subsequent rounds of the survey, absolute poverty lines are updated for consumer price index changes in the survey months. In spite of UNICEF's and WBG's poverty lines being defined at $2.50 per day, the poverty incidence rates are not the same, as the definition of consumption varies; for example UNICEF measures it per adult equivalent and the WBG does it per capita.

Child poverty measures are also calculated by UNICEF, which also calculates the household poverty rates and performs a head count. The poverty lines are not adjusted when measuring the poverty rates of different subpopulations, since the PAE consumption already takes into account the demographic composition of the household. Instead, the household statistical weights are multiplied by the number of children in the household to estimate the percentage of children under the poverty line.

When a poverty line is needed, this report uses a relative line set at the 15th percentile of total monthly consumption. With this line, the poverty incidence varies significantly across space. Most of the analysis is thus conducted using the whole distribution of consumption. This choice of relative poverty line responds to the needs of the analysis. The line of the PMT is set at the 15th percentile in order to maintain coverage of the TSA constant, and at the 30th percentile to facilitate comparisons with similar studies of other countries. Based on these measures, important variations in welfare across regions in Georgia are observed. Maps 2.1 and 2.2 show poverty incidence by region.[6] If using the lowest poverty cutoff (15th percentile), the poorest region is Shida Kartli and the least poor regions are Adjara and Samtskhe-Javakheti.

Another feature of poverty in Georgia is the high mobility of households along the welfare distribution. Figure 2.5 shows the movement across quintiles of households between 2011 and 2013 using the longitudinal data of the WMS. Each bar represents a quintile in the 2011 welfare distribution and each color (across bars) represents a quintile in the 2013 welfare distribution. Twenty-four percent of the population in the bottom quintile of the population in 2011 continued in the bottom quintile in 2013 (blue) while 7.2 percent of the population in the bottom quintile in 2011 moved to the top quintile in 2013 (stripes). Thus, the figure shows there has been significant mobility along the welfare distribution in those two years. If the neighboring quintiles are excluded, for each quintile of 2011, about 40 percent of the population "relatively" moved 20 percentage points or more in the welfare distribution.[7]

Map 2.1 Percentage of Households below the 15th Percentile (GEL 121.57 PAE), by Region

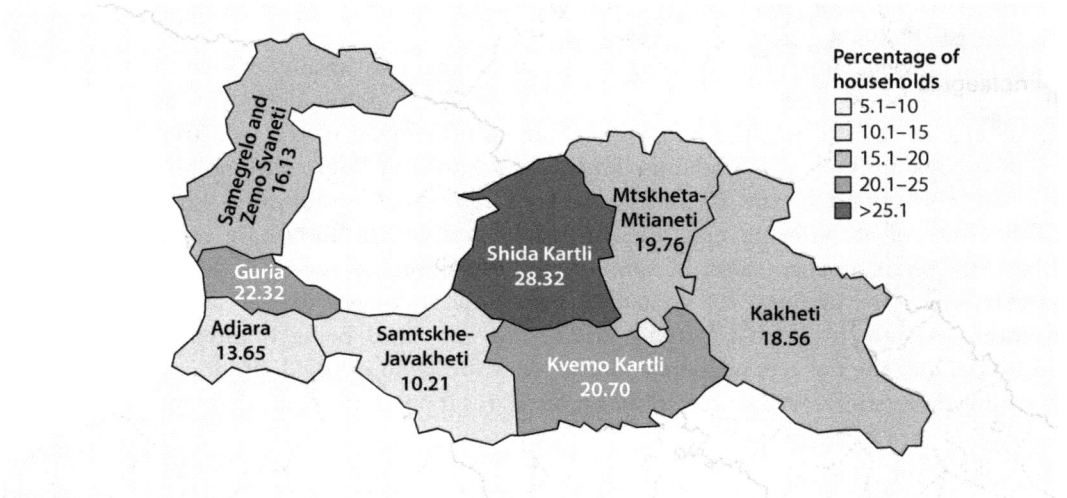

Percentage of households
☐ 5.1–10
☐ 10.1–15
▨ 15.1–20
▨ 20.1–25
■ >25.1

Samegrelo and Zemo Svaneti 16.13
Guria 22.32
Adjara 13.65
Samtskhe-Javakheti 10.21
Shida Kartli 28.32
Kvemo Kartli 20.70
Mtskheta-Mtianeti 19.76
Kakheti 18.56

Note: Additional module data. Information on Racha-Lechkhumi-Kvemo Svaneti is merged with Imereti in the study's dataset, which is why information on those regions is not displayed. GEL = Georgian lari; PAE = per adult equivalent.

Map 2.2 Percentage of Households below the 30th Percentile (GEL 121.57 PAE), by Region

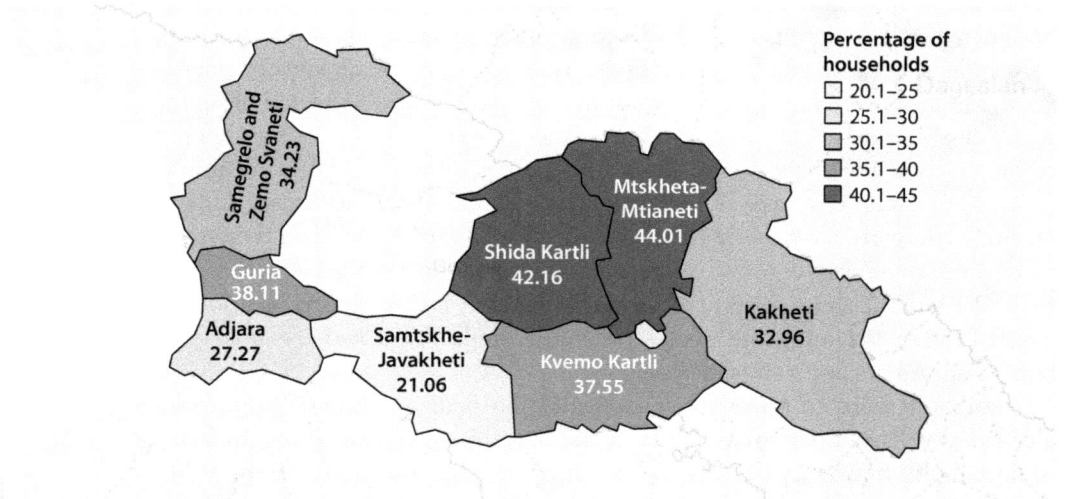

Percentage of households
☐ 20.1–25
☐ 25.1–30
▨ 30.1–35
▨ 35.1–40
■ 40.1–45

Samegrelo and Zemo Svaneti 34.23
Guria 38.11
Adjara 27.27
Samtskhe-Javakheti 21.06
Shida Kartli 42.16
Kvemo Kartli 37.55
Mtskheta-Mtianeti 44.01
Kakheti 32.96

Note: Additional module data. Information on Racha-Lechkhumi-Kvemo Svaneti is merged with Imereti in the study's dataset, which is why information on those regions is not displayed. GEL = Georgian lari; PAE = per adult equivalent.

Multidimensional poverty measures show improvements in all the dimensions, although progress in some areas is stickier. Together with the monetary poverty measures, UNICEF calculates the multidimensional poverty indices for population and children biennially. The indexes show continual improvement in all aspects of multidimensional poverty from 2009 to 2013 (table 2.2).

Figure 2.5 Movement of Households through Different Consumption Quintiles

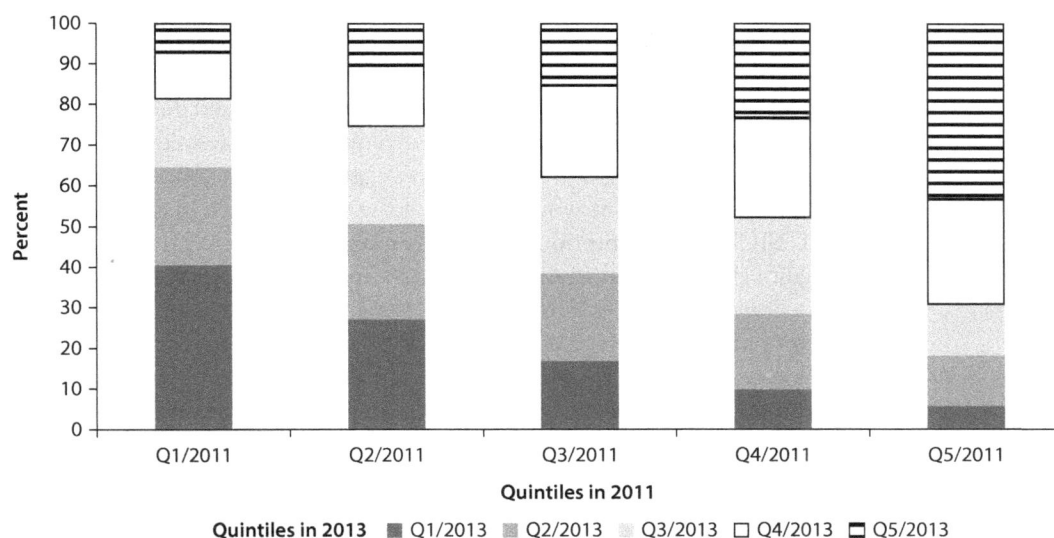

Source: Welfare Monitoring Survey rounds in 2011 and 2013.

Table 2.2 Multidimensional Poverty Rates of Population and Children, 2009–13

Dimension	Population in poor and deprived households (%)			Children in poor and deprived households (%)		
	2009	2011	2013	2009	2011	2013
Extreme poverty	9.9	9.1	3.9	11.5	9.4	6.0
General poverty	44.8	37.9	24.6	49.0	40.8	28.4
Material deprivation	12.7	7.6	3.6	13.1	5.7	2.9
Subjective poverty	37.1	35.2	24.3	36.4	31.1	22.9
Social exclusion	8.1	5.6	4.1	8.6	6.7	5.6
Lack of utilities	61.5	62.4	55.6	60.3	59.8	53.7

Source: Welfare Monitoring Survey rounds in 2009, 2011, and 2013.

However, progress has not been even across all dimensions. While material deprivation has rapidly decreased in terms of monetary poverty measures, subjective poverty, social exclusion, and utilities have not responded at the same pace. Particularly worrisome is the social exclusion dimension that includes achievements in education and economic opportunities.

Summary

To address the lack of suitable data that combined variables in the household declaration of the TSA registry and consumption data, UNICEF worked with the SSA and with GeoStat to implement the collection of an additional module in the IHS with such variables. The sampling frame for the additional module was designed using Q3 of the 2013 IHS.

The consumption aggregate used for the analysis of the reform is the consumption expenditures reported by GeoStat. The analysis is performed focusing on the entire distribution, rather than on poverty categories, given that different noncomparable definitions of poverty exist for the country (GeoStat, WBG, and UNICEF) leading to different estimates. Statistical estimates and graphical analysis show that there is a high correlation in the ranking of households when using any of the different measures of consumption aggregate. This simple correlation suggests that the conclusions would remain if the analysis were performed using WBG or UNICEF's consumption aggregate variables.

Seasonality affects the consumption estimate used for this study, but this does not lead to dramatic changes in the location along the income distribution of the beneficiaries or in the coverage of the program. A simple graphical analysis shows that the location of beneficiaries in the welfare distribution curve does not change from quarter to quarter. Most beneficiaries stay in their same decile across the year and are largely concentrated in the lowest deciles. Other variables that enter into the PMT formula such as employment do not change wildly across quarters, suggesting that the definition of beneficiaries should not be affected by the quarter in which the household reports its data.

The main recommendation for the government going forward is to routinely gather the necessary information in the IHS of GeoStat to be able to regularly monitor and evaluate the performance of the TSA. There are different layers of additional information needed. First, GeoStat needs to continue tracking the transfers received from all programs separately and avoid pooling the information into a single source of additional income. Second, GeoStat could integrate the ad hoc module collected for this revision to the core questionnaire. In this way, the additional information to monitor the performance of the PMT and the TSA could be evaluated yearly or every other year. This will also serve to erase doubts about seasonality biases. Third, in order to continuously improve the PMT formula, GeoStat should collect potential variables that respond to changes in consumption driven by changes in technology or norms. For example, it might be important to collect further details not only on access to the Internet but also on the type of Internet service (Wi-Fi versus DSL) accessed. Another potentially important data enhancement is having data representative at even lower geographic levels. More of this discussion follows in chapters 3 and 10.

Notes

1. The revision of the needs index used the IHS and did not need to use the additional module.
2. See table A.2 in appendix A for a distribution over the welfare aggregate curve of these 166 observations.
3. They can be found under "Integrated Household Survey Databases 2009, 2010, 2011, 2012, 2013 and 2014 Years," http://geostat.ge/index.php?action=meurneoba&mpid =1&lang=eng.

4. The details of the procedure used by GeoStat to compute consumption can be found in "Description of Integrated Household Survey Database Variables," http://geostat.ge/cms/site_images/_files/databases/Description%20of%20IHS%20 database%20variables%20-%20Eng.doc.

5. The number of equalized adults per household is obtained assigning different coefficients to each member, as follows: (1) child (ages 0–7) coefficient 0.64; (2) children (ages 8–15) coefficient 1; (3) working-age male (ages 16–64) coefficient 1; (4) working-age female (ages 16–59) coefficient 0.84; (5) pension-age male (ages 65 and older) coefficient 0.88; and (6) pension-age female (ages 60 and older) coefficient 0.76. Corresponding coefficients are assigned to every household member and then summed for each household. The resulting number is raised to the power of 0.8, to account for cohabitation effects.

6. Later we use monthly consumption and correct by the needs index in a second stage.

7. This does not mean that every household moving up is better in absolute terms, as part of the "relative" moves can be originated by people that were better off and now have gone down in absolute terms.

References

IHS (Integrated Household Survey). 2013. GeoStat, Tbilisi. http://www.geostat.ge/?action =meurneoba&mpid=1&lang=eng.

UNICEF. 2012. *Georgia: Reducing Child Poverty: A Discussion Paper.* Tbilisi, UNICEF. http://unicef.ge/uploads/UNICEF_Child_PovertyENG_web_with_names1.pdf.

———. 2015. *Reducing Child Poverty in Georgia: A Way Forward.* Tbilisi, UNICEF. http://unicef.ge/uploads/UNICEF_Poverty_Paper_2015_ENG_FINAL_.pdf.

World Bank. 2015. "Georgia Poverty Assessment: Poverty Reduction and Shared Prosperity since the Crisis." Note prepared under the FY15 South Caucasus Programmatic Poverty Assessment (P151474), Washington, DC, World Bank.

CHAPTER 3

Revision of the PMT Formula

Introduction

The revised proxy means test (PMT) formula builds on the existing methodology, but it updates the list of proxies of consumption and their weights. The new PMT formula calculation is based on the nationally representative 2013 Integrated Household Survey (IHS) of Georgia, as discussed in chapter 2. The key features of the original PMT formula are retained because the methodology has for the most part performed well thus far,[1] but the coefficients on the existing predictors of welfare (that determine the contribution of each proxy to the total TSA vulnerability score) were updated, and some variables were removed if they proved difficult to collect or difficult to justify to the public as an indicator of better-off households (for example, ownership of refrigerators).

The Targeted Social Assistance (TSA) vulnerability score consists of a household consumption index, calculated using a PMT and a household needs index. Box 3.1 presents the main features of the vulnerability score formula of the TSA. The household consumption index uses regression methods to proxy total monthly household consumption. The needs index adjusts for the potential needs of the different household members. It is a unique component of the PMT formula in Georgia as it does not appear in PMT methodologies of other countries. This index has also been revised (see chapter 4).

Under the new formula, the TSA benefit eligibility threshold increases from a 57,000 to a 65,000 TSA vulnerability score to maintain coverage constant. In the prereform PMT formula, the eligibility cutoff was set at 57,000. At the earlier threshold, the TSA was able to reach 12.6 percent of Georgia's population. Under the revised PMT formula, a slightly higher nationwide coverage of 13.4 percent is attained at the 65,000 threshold.[2]

Thus, the increase in the eligibility threshold is not intended to raise coverage, but to maintain it. The change in the eligibility threshold only responds to the change in the PMT formula and scale of the new vulnerability score; it is done to maintain equivalence in the coverage pre- and postreform. It would be incorrect to conclude that the increment of the cutoff score from 57,000 to 65,000

Box 3.1 PMT Formula for the TSA

Compared to the models employed in other countries, the proxy means test (PMT) formula of the Targeted Social Assistance (TSA) program is more complex. In addition to a long list of predictor variables whose coefficients vary over four geographic areas in the country, it implies calculation of the household welfare index in the following way:

$$I = \frac{C}{N},$$ (B3.1.1)

where I = household welfare index, C = household consumption index, and N = household needs index.

The **consumption index**, C, has the following features:

- It is estimated in a conventional way for PMT formulas, using an ordinary least squares (OLS) regression.
- Monthly household consumption—rather than per capita or per adult equivalent consumption—is used as the dependent variable (proxy of welfare) to allow the inclusion of demographic variables as explanatory variables. The needs index serves to account for household economies of scale.
- Traditional predictors are used, such as sociodemographic and location variables, and ownership of durable goods and of productive assets.
- Self-reported income is used as one of the predictors, except for pensioners.
- The household consumption is predicted separately for four areas: Tbilisi, big cities, small towns, and villages.
- The weighted sum of targeted social assistance—or any other TSA benefit—received by the household is deducted from the amount of predicted household consumption.

The **needs index**, N, is calculated as

$$E = \sum_{i=1}^{n} e_i,$$ (B3.1.2)

where E is the number of equivalent members in the household. e_i is the coefficient of each household member based on gender, age, physical condition, and social condition explaining the need of member i of the household in relation to the needs of an equivalent adult,

$$N = \frac{E}{n^\beta} * B,$$ (B3.1.3)

where N is the needs index, E is the number of equivalent members in the household, n is the number of household members, $\beta = 0.2$ are the economies of scale, and B is the value of the subsistence minimum basket at the time of developing the formula (GEL 149.6).

The needs index has the following features:

- It takes into consideration specific needs of such groups as persons with disabilities and severe chronic diseases, pregnant and breastfeeding mothers, pensioners, orphans, and single mothers.

box continues next page

Box 3.1 PMT Formula for the TSA *(continued)*

- It differentiates by age and gender groups.
- It calculates the subsistence minimum of different categories in relation to the subsistence minimum of a healthy 30- to 39-year-old male.
- It is estimated on the basis of evaluation of expert opinions and specific calculations.
- The needs are divided into two main categories: caloric and noncaloric. Caloric needs consist of food and caregiver needs. Noncaloric needs include transportation, medical services, special means,[a] and other needs, with medical services and special means having subgroups. The needs are translated into coefficients and summed for the final coefficient. The ratio of the food to nonfood consumption is 70:30.
- It was also revised during this process.

Final adjustments are applied to the household welfare index. This index—referred to throughout the report as the TSA *vulnerability score*—is rounded and rescaled according to the following formula:

$$Q = max \left(10 * int (10{,}000 * I), 1{,}000 \right), \tag{B3.1.4}$$

where Q = household rating score and I = household welfare index.

The fact that the household rating score is a ratio of observed consumption to the expected needs level for a household of a given composition—albeit a rescaled one—allows us to interpret it as a fraction of the needs met by predicted household consumption. For instance, a household with Q = 65,000 can be interpreted to have an estimated consumption (I) level equivalent to 65 percent of its needs (N).

Source: Resolution No. 758, December 31, 2014, of the government of Georgia.
a. *Special means* refers to all the additional expenses needed by different groups of the population, from books for children of school age to special equipment for persons with disabilities.

---

constitutes an expansion of coverage to groups that were not previously targeted. However, the higher score, which maintains the coverage, indicates the overall improvement in the households' welfare situation in relation to the state-established subsistence minimum.

Estimation of the New PMT Formula

The revision of the PMT formula is carried out following best practices around the world. These practices are discussed in the rest of the chapter and imply working with two samples: one for estimation and another one for validation; using various econometric models to ensure goodness of fit; and balancing parsimonious models for implementation simplicity and rich models with (new) variables to reduce the measurement errors.

Additional data were collected to design the reform. The analysis uses one sample for the estimation and another sample for the validation of results.[3] The *estimation sample* comes from the third quarter (Q3) of the 2013 IHS with 2,601 households, and the *validation sample* comes from Q4 of the same year survey, with 661 newly included households. Georgia's National Statistics Office (GeoStat) collected the data specifically for the analysis of the reform of the TSA in 2014. It added a module to the IHS that incorporated the variables used in the household declaration registry, as well as new salient variables that previous research based on the Welfare Monitoring Survey of 2013 showed could have high predictive power. Variables such as number of employed salaried adults, quality of roofing material, mountain region, number or/and square meters of rooms of the dwelling, ownership of summer house, and others were tested.

Among the several regression models investigated, ordinary least squares (OLS) results performed well and were chosen for their simplicity. Applications in other countries used different regression models, each of them having advantages and disadvantages. OLS and probability models (such as probit or logit) aim to minimize the sum of the squared error around the mean for linear and nonlinear fitted values. Instead, quantile regressions are used to minimize the fitted error at the bottom of the distribution, where the targeting is more relevant. OLS and probit regressions tend to overestimate household consumption, and although the quantile (50th percentile) regression performed best in estimating the consumption, it showed worse leakage results. Table 3.1 presents the estimates of the main indicators for different models (Berulava 2014). As the status quo model was estimated using an OLS regression and the other regression models showed similar qualitative results, the OLS was preferred.

Various features of the PMT are maintained in this revision. In what follows, the results discussed in this chapter correspond to OLS regressions. Generally, PMT models use OLS, because the regressions performed better (both in terms of R-squared and prediction accuracy). The same approach was implemented at the beginning of the program. The explained variable is the log of monthly household consumption, instead of consumption per adult equivalent. This feature was also introduced in the original design of the TSA.

The estimation of the PMT involved several steps that complemented each other. These steps consist of: (1) correlation analysis to find a set of variables that

Table 3.1 Undercoverage and Leakage for Select Econometric Models at the 15th and 30th Percentiles

Models	Undercoverage 15%	30%	Leakage 15%	30%	Coverage 15%	30%	R-squared Tbilisi	Cities	Towns	Villages
OLS	61.23	53.46	41.90	29.90	10.00	19.91	0.490	0.485	0.514	0.502
Probit	66.89	48.98	32.84	32.30	7.39	22.60	0.207	0.312	0.318	0.287
Quantiles										
P45th	43.27	33.93	49.28	39.68	16.76	32.82	0.309	0.321	0.333	0.323
P50th	48.93	40.47	46.81	36.74	14.38	28.22	0.301	0.300	0.342	0.317
P55th	53.02	54.94	45.32	33.58	12.75	24.69	0.296	0.292	0.310	0.313

Source: IHS 2013 (additional module data).
Note: OLS = ordinary least squares; P = percentile. Models are not corrected for the needs index. The cutoffs correspond to the values of the actual household consumption. Pseudo R-squared reported for probit and quantile regressions.

closely predict the household consumption variable; (2) collinearity diagnostics to drop collinear indicators from the model; and (3) stepwise option of the OLS regression to leave only statistically significant variables.

Regression analysis is used to predict household welfare based on a set of observable and verifiable household and individual variables. Building on the existent formula, the dependent variable used to proxy welfare is monthly total household consumption. The predictors selected are highly correlated with the welfare proxy and need to be verifiable. The following group of variables were tested in the estimation:

- *Location*: variables that include place of residence defined by regions
- *Household characteristics*: household size, sex of the household head, share of working-age adults in the household, share of adult household members with higher education, and share of employed salaried adults
- *Asset ownership*: bivariate variables that indicate ownership of assets such as cars, tractors, refrigerator, gas stove, washing machine, and so forth
- *Social agent subjective evaluation*: covering different dimensions of household well-being such as household's economic situation, clothing and household condition, or basic hygiene.

The analysis is conducted using the 15th percentile as the eligibility cutoff, as it was a premise of the reform to maintain the size of the program. The eligibility cutoff is defined at the welfare level of the 15th percentile of the household welfare distribution provided by the predicted rating score calculated following the formula in box 3.1. The choice of this cutoff point responded to the fact that the TSA program covers almost 15 percent of the country's households and the government of Georgia (GoG) needed to maintain the coverage constant in a tight fiscal environment and after generous expansions in the previous years. For sensitivity analysis and to facilitate comparisons with other programs, the analysis was also conducted using the 30th percentile cutoff.

Estimated models are compared using three performance indicators. Maximizing targeting accuracy is the main objective of the exercise. This is measured by the following indicators:

- *R-squared or goodness of fit*: in which models are compared to minimize the unexplained errors in the regression, measured by the R-squared statistic
- *Undercoverage*: defined as the number of poor households incorrectly excluded by the formula ("exclusion" or type 1 error) divided by the total number of poor households in the sample, where poor households are defined as being below the 15th consumption percentile
- *Leakage*: defined as the number of eligible households incorrectly included by the formula divided by total number of eligible households ("inclusion" or type 2 error), where incorrectly included households are those above the 15th consumption percentile.

Estimated Models

First, a few models were estimated to decide the best specification—broadly defined. Table 3.2 shows the performance indicators corresponding to six models that tested different specifications (variables used as predictors). All of them have a few commonalities that were agreed to be retained based on previous work, such as the use of four subformulas for different geographical areas (Tbilisi, large cities, small cities, and villages).

- *Model 1* sets the baseline; it is the status quo model, but the coefficients are allowed to change to adjust to changes in consumption over time.
- *Model 2*, following the stepwise practice, keeps variables that are statistically significant (p-value lower than 0.2) in model 1 and tests adding new variables: a dummy for mountain regions, numbers of adult household members in salaried employment,[4] quantitative indicators for quality of dwelling, and other real estate property.
- *Model 3* tests the subjective evaluation variables, by removing them from model 2.
- *Model 4* has neither subjective evaluation variables nor durable household items that were identified as having been concealed. Instead, the size of the owned agricultural land is included. The demographic variables are maintained, although they do not have high significance levels.
- *Model 5* drops variables that are not highly significant (p-value less than 0.05) from model 4.
- *Model 6* replicates model 4 and uses a share of working-age household members instead of salaried employment.

Very specific requirements related to the PMT were shared by the government from the outset of the reform. The Ministry of Labor, Health, and Social Affairs (MoLHSA) and the Social Services Agency (SSA) had very clear suggestions on variables that should be included or excluded from the formula. The discussion around this issue was fed by the understanding that even if in theory

Table 3.2 Undercoverage and Leakage for Models 1–6 at the 15th and 30th Percentiles

	Undercoverage		Leakage	
Models	*15%*	*30%*	*15%*	*30%*
Status quo	62.09	50.52	62.12	50.48
Model 1	48.51	40.25	48.51	40.22
Model 2	47.49	39.34	47.49	39.27
Model 3	48.91	40.44	48.92	40.37
Model 4	47.28	39.54	47.24	39.56
Model 5	48.89	40.75	48.91	40.74
Model 6	47.61	39.57	47.63	39.51

Source: IHS 2013 (additional module data).

durable goods indeed help to differentiate among two poor households, they are concealable, making it easier for the households to cheat the system and deteriorating the targeting accuracy of the PMT model. Therefore, it was agreed that variables corresponding to easily concealable durable goods (mobile phones, washing machines, hygienic items, TVs, and so forth) as well as subjective assessment by the interviewers should not be part of the revised formula. Instead, the formula should concentrate on easily verifiable variables and items that could potentially generate income.

Conversations with government led to choosing model 6 for further refinement. Model 6 was preferred to others by the GoG for the above-mentioned reasons as well as for the total number of variables employed and the overall performance in terms of undercoverage and leakage. Four additional models fine-tune model 6, as shown below. Table 3.3 shows the performance of these models.

- *Model 7* tests whether separate regressions should be run for urban and rural areas.
- *Model 8* tests whether a single regression should be run for the entire sample.
- *Model 9* trims down the top 20 percent of the distribution (Grootaert and Braithwaite 1998; Grosh and Glinskaya 1997; Grosh and Baker 1995; Narayan, Vishwanath, and Yoshida 2006).
- *Model 10* uses a two-stage selection method. The first stage consists of the four regressions by settlement type and are run on the entire sample. From this sample, only households with predicted consumption below the 70th percentile of actual consumption are selected for further analysis. The second-stage consumption is estimated only for the sample selected in the first stage. The households with predicted consumption below the cutoff at the second stage are selected for the TSA.[5]

The additional fine-tuning did not improve the performance of the estimates. Simplifying estimation procedures (using an urban/rural divide or single sample instead of running four separate regressions) came at the cost of reducing targeting accuracy. However, this difference was not so drastic. Instead, the two-stage

Table 3.3 Undercoverage and Leakage for Models 7–10 at the 15th and 30th Percentiles

Models	Undercoverage		Leakage	
	15%	30%	15%	30%
Status quo	62.09	50.52	62.12	50.48
Model 7	47.72	40.35	47.75	40.33
Model 8	48.43	40.52	48.45	40.34
Model 9	50.91	41.53	50.94	41.46
Model 10	46.15	38.76	46.13	38.75

Source: IHS 2013 estimation sample (additional module data).

estimation approach (model 10) proved to give marginally stronger results. However, the SSA considered this model to have larger implementation costs. Thus, model 10 was discarded in deference to practicality.

The estimated models showed results aligned to those of other countries. Table 3.4 compares the estimates of some of the models to those of select studies from other countries, using the eligibility cutoff of 30th percentile of monthly consumption (not adjusting for the needs index). The estimates for Georgia are comparable to those of select international examples. Although this report's estimates are somewhat higher when it comes to undercoverage (Georgia's estimates range from 51 to 53 percent versus 41 to 45 percent in the international comparators), estimates for leakage were slightly better than those of the comparators (Georgia's estimates range from 28 to 30 percent, while those of the other countries varied between 28 and 36 percent).

The difference in performance could be explained by the variation in the level of undercoverage. This diminishes with the rate of coverage of the program, and the coverage rate in Georgia is considerably smaller than those of the comparators. For instance, the coverage rate in Sri Lanka (Narayan, Vishwanath, and Yoshida 2006) is 26 percent for the 30th percentile cutoff. When the cutoff is a basis on the predicted value, the difference in targeting errors becomes negligible. When using the 30th percentile of predicted consumption as the cutoff, targeting errors are about 38–40 percent, while the same levels of undercoverage and leakage (both at 37 percent) are found in Narayan, Vishwanath, and Yoshida (2006). The coefficient of goodness of fit—R-squared—for present models is between 47 and 55 percent, while the same coefficient for international models is in the range of 41–57 percent.

Table 3.4 Comparisons with PMT Models from Other Countries

Models	Undercoverage	Leakage	R-squared
Georgia revised models[a]			
Model 2	52.54	30.16	0.498–0.553
Model 4	53.05	29.82	0.498–0.514
Model 6	53.46	29.90	0.485–0.514
Model 10	51.92	28.35	0.465–0.527
Select international models			
Sri Lanka	43.0	36.0	0.560
Jamaica	41.0	34.2	0.410
Uganda[b]	45.3	27.7	0.505
Bangladesh	42.7	30.2	0.570

Note: All indicators are reported for the 30th percentile cutoff. Sri Lanka comes from Narayan, Vishwanath, and Yoshida 2006; Jamaica from Grosh and Baker 1995; Uganda from Houssou et al. 2007; Bangladesh from Sharif 2012. PMT = proxy means test.
a. Results without correction for needs index.
b. Computed at 32.36 percent poverty rate.

Incidence of Targeting and Distribution

All models maintain the progressive pattern of targeting as in the status quo. Nevertheless, model 6 has a more desirable pattern relative to the rest, in terms of coverage and leakage. The status quo model targets approximately 62 and 23 percent of the first and second deciles, respectively, and around 4 and 3 percent of the richest two deciles, respectively. Model 6 covers 84 percent and 33 percent of the first and second deciles and around 1 percent in the richest two deciles. From the total number of beneficiaries predicted by the new model, about 78 percent of households are from the bottom two consumption deciles and about 1.2 percent from the highest two deciles. For the existing model these figures are correspondingly 57 percent and almost 5 percent, respectively. Figure 3.1 shows the distribution of eligible beneficiaries for the four models under examination.

Performance indicators have reasonable confidence intervals. The reliability of the targeting accuracy, undercoverage, and leakage for the models was assessed estimating errors using bootstrapping. Results reported in table 3.5

Figure 3.1 Distribution of TSA-Eligible Population, by Different Models

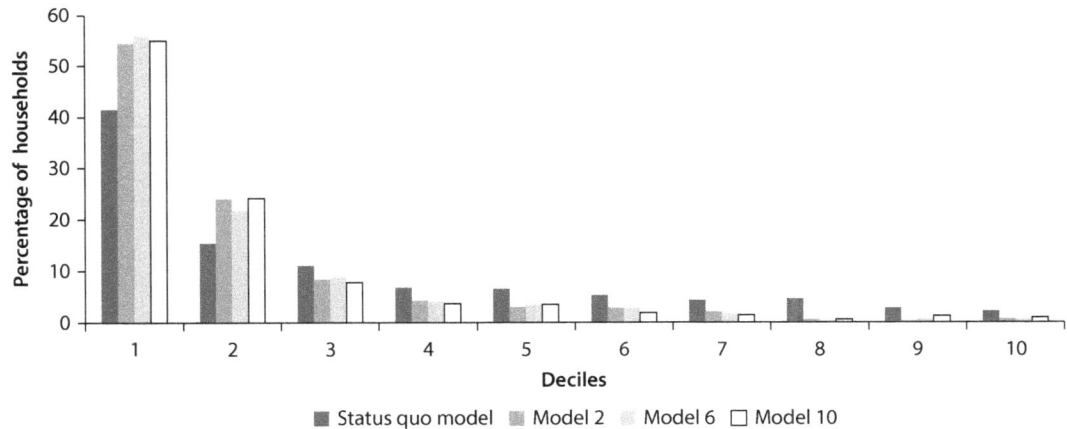

Source: IHS 2013 estimation sample (additional module data). TSA = Targeted Social Assistance.

Table 3.5 Confidence Intervals for Targeting Accuracy, Undercoverage, and Leakage

	Targeting accuracy		Undercoverage		Leakage	
	Coef.	C.I.	Coef.	C.I.	Coef.	C.I.
Status quo model	81.3	79.77; 83.00	62.1	56.90; 67.27	62.1	53.71; 70.56
Model 2	85.7	84.39; 87.15	47.4	42.38; 52.59	47.4	42.60; 52.38
Model 6	85.7	84.34; 87.12	47.6	42.46; 52.77	47.6	42.85; 52.42
Model 10	86.1	84.78; 87.57	46.1	40.99; 51.31	46.1	41.25; 51.02

Source: IHS 2013 (additional module data).
Note: C.I. = confidence interval of the statistic; Coef. = coefficient of the statistics.

Continuous Improvement • http://dx.doi.org/10.1596/978-1-4648-0900-2

correspond to 1,000 draws at a 95 percent confidence level.[6] The consumption prediction power of the newly developed models is high: in 85 percent of cases, households' predicted consumption is correctly ranked above or below the 15th percentile of real consumption. Conversely, for those households below the 15th percentile of real consumption, about 47 percent of them will have consumption above the 15th percentile of estimated consumption. This is similar to the actual result: 47 percent of households below the 15th percentile of estimated consumption actually have consumption above the 15th percentile of real consumption.

Validation Exercise

The validation exercise provides further evidence with which to support the chosen model. Using the validation sample coming from Q4 of the IHS, table 3.6 compares the targeting accuracy results for the two main indicators: undercoverage and leakage. The analysis does not reveal any dramatic change in the targeting errors that could potentially question the validity of the model. The confidence intervals estimated for the validation sample further prove the validity of the results. Although confidence intervals are a bit larger (see table 3.7 in comparison to table 3.5), the qualitative statements remain.

Table 3.6 Performance Indicators for Estimation and Validation Sample

Models	Undercoverage			Leakage		
	Estimation	Validation	Change	Estimation	Validation	Change
Status quo model	62.09	69.15	7.06	62.12	68.98	6.86
Model 2	47.49	54.69	7.20	47.49	54.39	6.90
Model 4	47.28	53.53	6.25	47.24	53.40	6.16
Model 6	47.61	53.53	5.92	47.63	53.40	5.77
Model 10	46.15	52.85	6.70	46.13	52.76	6.63

Source: IHS 2013 (additional module data).
Note: Estimation refers to the estimation sample of Q3 2013, and validation sample to that of Q4 2014. Q = quarter.

Table 3.7 Confidence Intervals for Targeting Accuracy, Undercoverage, and Leakage for Validation Sample

	Targeting accuracy		Undercoverage		Leakage	
	Coef.	C.I.	Coef.	C.I.	Coef.	C.I.
Status quo model	79.36	76.24; 82.48	69.15	60.02; 78.29	68.98	59.12;78.83
Model 2	83.71	80.89; 86.53	54.69	44.90; 64.47	54.39	44.55; 64.24
Model 6	84.00	81.17; 86.83	53.53	43.66; 63.40	53.40	43.38; 63.42
Model 10	84.19	81.47; 86.91	52.85	43.09; 62.61	52.76	42.82; 62.71

Source: IHS 2013 (additional module data).
Note: C.I. = confidence interval of the statistic; Coef. = coefficient of the statistics.

Summary

The revised PMT formula of the TSA underwent a few updates but still maintained the main features of the existing methodology. As previously stated, to refine the PMT of the consumption index, the major priorities of the MoLHSA and the SSA were the following:

1. Improve leakage and undercoverage results given the changing economy.
2. Remove the easily concealable durable goods, as there was a belief that households have concealed them.
3. Include new easily verifiable and potentially income-generating items.
4. Reduce the total number of variables used.
5. Remove the subjective assessment of the social workers.

Based on these criteria, MoLHSA selected model 6 as a new methodology for the TSA formula of the consumption index. The government wanted to include as many easily verifiable variables as possible, as it believed that this would reduce cheating and wrongful computation of scores. Also, the model was overall performing better than the rest and administratively would not require additional costs that could have negatively affected the budget of the program.

As a result, there is a small increase in the eligibility cutoff of the TSA vulnerability score from 57,000 to 65,000. Despite the nominal change in the threshold, the level of nationwide coverage slightly increased from 12.6 percent of Georgia's population to 13.4 percent.

Going forward, the GoG should continue with its practice of seeking improvements in the PMT formula of the consumption index. However, given the excellent levels of targeting accuracy for the level of coverage, further improvements might require quite a deal of experimentation. On the one hand, GeoStat should regularly collect new candidate variables for the household declaration, to be alert of those that could be incorporated into the design. On the other hand, a line of work in the poverty field that seems promising and that could potentially be applied to PMTs is the use of "small area estimates." Recent research indicates that poverty estimates for very small geographic areas, based on rich population census data, provide highly accurate estimates. Before engaging in this, it is advisable that Georgia produce poverty maps using the data coming from the 2014 population census.

The second recommendation is to maintain an efficient registration system that facilitates households to go in and out of the TSA program. The well-known shortfall of a PMT methodology is that it is a static model and is able to capture the well-being of a household only in a specific period of time, based on durables ownership. Even if assessing asset holdings aims to capture aspects of permanent income, the PMT does not take into consideration the fact that families extensively move in and out of poverty, and that they might not be able to protect themselves from transient shocks. For example, as figure 2.5 in chapter 2 suggests, only 40 percent of households remained in the first quintile in 2013, the rest have moved, some even to the fifth quintile. Conversely, many households move down to the bottom quintile. Such movement means that the households in Georgia are very vulnerable. Often reassessment of the TSA vulnerability score helps to capture some of this income mobility, if this mobility affects the vulnerability score. This needs to be studied, as there is no longitudinal survey that measures poverty and the variables in the household declaration. In any case, it is very likely that the TSA score does not capture the mobility as reassessments occur every four years or in case of life events (death, birth, migration, and so forth).

A third recommendation is to further improve the system of social protection and labor, to avoid asking more of the TSA than what it can deliver. Improving the system of social protection does not necessarily mean increasing social spending but it does mean making it more efficient by coordinating programs to cover different needs of the population that could not be covered by a single program, and optimizing the delivery from the government to maximize efficiency gains. For example, when we think about systems of social protection and labor, we can think that households that are more likely to be in and out of the TSA might need further support in terms of health, education, and nutrition for their children, in order to avoid transmitting vulnerabilities to the next generation. Another aspect that is usually considered by the analysis of systems of social protection and labor is crossing data from employment services—now being developed in Georgia—with those from social assistance to ensure that those who are benefiting from a program like the TSA are encouraged to look for work but also to support those who find a job by extending their benefits from assistance until their position in the labor market is solid, via in-work benefits. Chapter 10 further discusses how to start thinking about systems of social protection.

Notes

1. See World Bank (2012, 2014) for a discussion of the performance of the Targeted Social Assistance program, including a comparison to services in other countries in the region.
2. The difference in the cutoff values is due to a combination of reasons: for example, differences in the scale of the predicted consumption variables computed using two different PMT formulas and potential improvements in the level of welfare of Georgia's population since the last PMT model was estimated.
3. For example, out-of-sample validation was used by Johannsen (2006) to identify poverty in Peru, and by Houssou et al. (2007) in the context of Uganda.
4. See "Glossary" for the formal definition of salaried employment.
5. The targeting efficiency is calculated taking into account the whole sample.
6. The definition of bootstrapping is included in appendix C ("Glossary").

References

Berulava, George. 2014. "PMT Estimation for TSA Reform." Project Report, UNICEF.

Grootaert, C., and J. Braithwaite. 1998. "Poverty Correlates and Indicator-Based Targeting in Eastern Europe and the Former Soviet Union." Poverty Reduction and Economic Management Network, Environmentally and Socially Sustainable Development Network, World Bank, Washington, DC.

Grosh, M., and J. Baker. 1995. "Proxy Means Tests for Targeting Social Programs: Simulations and Speculation." Working Paper 118, Living Standards Measurement Study, World Bank, Washington, DC.

Grosh, M., and E. Glinskaya. 1997. "Proxy Means Testing and Social Assistance in Armenia." Draft, Development Economics Research Group, World Bank, Washington, DC.

Houssou, Nazaire, Manfred Zeller, Gabriela Alcaraz V., Stefan Schwarze, and Julia Johannsen. 2007. "Proxy Means Tests for Targeting the Poorest Households: Applications to Uganda." European Association of Agricultural Economists, No. 7946, 106th Seminar, Montpellier, France, October 25–27. http://ageconsearch.umn.edu/bitstream/7946/1/sp07ho01.pdf.

IHS (Integrated Household Survey). 2013. GeoStat, Tbilisi. http://www.geostat.ge/?action=meurneoba&mpid=1&lang=eng.

Johannsen, J. 2006. "Operational Poverty Targeting in Peru—Proxy Means Testing with Non-Income Indicators." Working Paper 30, International Poverty Center, United Nations Development Programme, New York.

Narayan, A., T. Vishwanath, and N. Yoshida. 2006. "Sri Lanka Welfare Reform." In *Poverty and Social Impact Analysis*. Washington, DC: World Bank.

Sharif, Iffath A. 2012. "Can Proxy Means Testing Improve the Targeting Performance of Social Safety Nets in Bangladesh?" *Bangladesh Development Studies* 35 (2): 1–43.

World Bank. 2012. *Georgia Public Expenditure Review: Managing Expenditure Pressures for Sustainability and Growth*. Washington, DC: World Bank. https://openknowledge.worldbank.org/handle/10986/12315.

———. 2014. *Georgia Public Expenditure Review: Diagnostics of Public Investment Management System*. Washington, DC: World Bank. https://openknowledge.worldbank.org/handle/10986/19302.

———. 2015. "Georgia Poverty Assessment: Poverty Reduction and Shared Prosperity since the Crisis." Note prepared under the FY15 South Caucasus Programmatic Poverty Assessment (P151474), World Bank, Washington, DC.

CHAPTER 4

Revision of the Needs Index

Introduction

The needs index is a unique element of the Targeted Social Assistance (TSA) targeting formula that adjusts the family final score by the needs of the individual family members. This adjustment is needed because the proxy means test (PMT) formula is calculated using total monthly consumption, as opposed to consumption per capita or per adult equivalent. The needs index calculates the needs of different categories of consumers and individuals relative to the subsistence minimum of a healthy 30- to 39-year-old man.[1] Table 4.1 shows the groups of the population considered in the needs index. The categories differ by sex, age, and social or health status. In a way, the needs index can be thought of as an adult equivalent adjustment. The advantage of using the needs index rather than directly proxying consumption per adult equivalent when estimating the PMT is that it allows one to maintain demographic characteristics of the household among the explanatory variables in the PMT estimation—and thus in the formula—and that the needs of each group can be adjusted easily over time without reestimating the PMT alone.[2] The way the "subsistence minimum" is calculated draws on the methodology developed by Georgia's National Statistics Office (GeoStat) to adjust by adult equivalent.[3] This revision of the needs index was timely as it had never been updated since the TSA was introduced in the country in 2006.

The index comprises two major categories of needs: caloric and noncaloric. Caloric needs are those covering food and caregiving services; noncaloric needs are those related to transportation, medical services, special means,[4] and other needs. The caloric needs are expressed in calories (kcal) and the noncaloric ones in Georgian currency, the lari (GEL). All needs are then summed to obtain one final coefficient for each category. Every household member is assigned the maximum coefficient depending on the categories that this person is classified into. Appendix B shows in separate tables the caloric needs and the associated coefficients for each category of consumer and for each type of need.

Table 4.1 Groups of Population Used in the Needs Index

Status/age	All				Male				Female			
	(0–3)	(4–6)	(7–12)	(13–17)	(18–29)	(30–39)	(40–59)	(60+)	(18–29)	(30–39)	(40–59)	(60+)
Healthy	1	1	1	1	1	1	1	1	1	1	1	1
Child with disability	1	1	1	1	0	0	0	0	0	0	0	0
Person with disability group 1	0	0	0	0	1	1	1	1	1	1	1	1
Person with disability group 2	0	0	0	0	1	1	1	1	1	1	1	1
Refugee	1	1	1	1	1	1	1	1	1	1	1	1
Bedridden	1	1	1	1	1	1	1	1	1	1	1	1
Single pensioner	0	0	0	0	1	1	1	1	1	1	1	1
Pregnant	0	0	0	1	0	0	0	0	1	1	1	0
Breastfeeding woman	0	0	0	1	0	0	0	0	1	1	1	0
Single mother	0	0	0	1	0	0	0	0	1	1	1	0
Orphan	1	1	1	1	0	0	0	0	0	0	0	0

Note: 1 indicates that the combination of row and column forms a group; 0 indicates otherwise.

More precisely, the needs for each category is the sum of food needs (K_F), caregiver needs (K_C), medical service needs (K_{MS}), transportation needs (K_T), special means needs (K_{SM}), and other needs (K_O):

$$N = K_F + K_C + K_{SM} + K_T + K_{MS} + K_O. \tag{4.1}$$

One of the objectives of the revision was to simplify the needs index whenever possible. The new needs index, N, now combines a few categories of needs: the service needs component (K_S) is added to transportation needs (K_T), other needs (K_O), and medical service needs (K_{MS}) for a healthy (30- to 39-year-old) male. That is, $K_S = K_T + K_O + K_{MS}^{(30-39)M}$.

Thus, the new needs index is calculated using the following formula:

$$N = K_F + K_C + K_{MS} + K_T + K_{SM} + K_O + K_S - K_S$$
$$= K_F + K_C + K_{MS} + K_T + K_{SM} + K_O + K_S$$
$$- \left(K_T + K_O + K_{MS}^{(30-39)M} \right) \tag{4.2}$$
$$= \underbrace{K_F + K_C + K_{SM}}_{\text{caloric}} + \underbrace{K_S + \left(K_{MS} - K_{MS}^{(30-39)M} \right)}_{\text{noncaloric}}$$

In equation 4.2, *F* is food needs, *C* is caregiver needs, *MS* is medical service needs, *T* is transportation needs, *O* is other needs, and *SM* is special means needs.

The subsistence minimum for the healthy working-age male is set at GEL 149.6 per month.[5] This subsistence minimum is slightly above the one set by GeoStat for the average of the third and fourth quarters (Q3 and Q4) in 2013, when the data were collected,[6] but it is lower than that prevalent in December 2015 at GEL 162.4. A total of 70 percent of the subsistence minimum is attributed to caloric needs and the remaining 30 percent to noncaloric needs. It is assumed that a 30- to 39-year-old healthy male does not require any care-giving services and has no special means needs. The noncaloric 30 percent of the subsistence minimum is distributed among transportation, medical services, and other needs. Of the noncaloric needs, the updated index has attributed 25 percent to medical services (of which, 48 percent is for medicines and 52 percent is for monitoring), 20 percent for transportation services, and 55 percent for other expenditures.

Programs financed by the government are not excluded from the needs index. Even though some needs like kindergarten expenses, textbook expenses, and universal health care are covered through government programs, the Ministry of Labor, Health, and Social Affairs (MoLHSA) and the Social Services Agency (SSA) have decided not to exclude these expenses from the needs. Since such programs often change over time, the government expressed an interest in maintaining them in the needs index to make sure that these necessities would be captured, even if the programs no longer existed.

Calculation of the Caloric Needs

The caloric needs make up 70 percent of the total of the subsistence minimum for a healthy man. This is equivalent to 2,230 kcal (per day per month) for the reference individual.[7] There are two subgroups of consumption items: food and care needs. The coefficient for food needs (K_F) is

$$K_F = 0.7 \times \frac{X \times (\text{days per month})}{2{,}230 \times (\text{days per month})} = 0.7 \times \frac{X}{2230}, \qquad (4.3)$$

where *X* is the calories per day that a person needs. If a person belongs to two or more different categories with different food needs, the higher of the two possible food needs apply. This is the so-called overlapping principle that was used in the previous methodology as well. The caloric needs for each category of the population are shown in table B.1 and the estimated food coefficients in table B.2 (appendix B).

Care needs are calculated as the food needs of a caregiver during the working hours. Care needs (K_C) are calculated for special functioning contingent (SFC) groups that have a limited capacity for full functioning due to age, health, or social conditions and that require additional rehabilitation and reintegration measures. The coefficient is calculated using the volume of energy consumption (2,000 kcal per day) of a person (mainly woman) employed on an hourly basis: $\frac{x}{24} \times 2{,}000$, where x is working hours. This approach was used in the previous methodology and the overlapping principle applies here as well. The caloric needs for this group are shown in table B.3 and associated care coefficients in table B.4.

Calculation of the Noncaloric Needs

Thirty percent of the subsistence minimum goes to noncaloric needs. These needs are split between transportation needs, medical service needs, special means needs, and others. The reference point is a 30- to 39-year-old healthy man who does not have any medical service needs. Thus, the coefficients for the other groups of needs (measured in GEL) are calculated as $\frac{x}{149.6} \times 0.30$, where x is the monetary value in GEL of the noncaloric need. Of this rubric, 20 percent is for transportation, 25 percent for medical services,[8] and the residual 55 percent for other needs.[9]

Nevertheless, some categories of the population have different splits among the different rubrics of noncaloric needs. For example, for children ages 0–3 and 4–6 years old and for the bedridden, transportation needs are considered zero. For people in the SFC categories, all noncaloric needs cannot be fully covered by 30 percent of the subsistence minimum. For these categories, the additional medical service needs are added to the standard medical service needs (25 percent of noncaloric needs in subsistence minimum of healthy male). The special means needs are added to a null baseline, since a healthy male does not have such special means needs. In this case, the overlapping principle is not considered appropriate when calculating service needs, as the only difference comes with the transportation costs. Instead the minimum value is used.

The *special means* needs of noncaloric needs includes expenses on special inventories, personal hygiene items, textbooks and other school items, and adaptation facilities or equipment for certain categories of SFC. This category includes the items that, if unavailable, would make an individual's functioning either impossible or severely limited. The following additional special means are considered for different categories of SFC: diapers (for children 0–3); walking and playpens (children 0–3); kindergarten (children 0–6); school-related expenses (children 6–17); and hearing aids, aids for those with impaired sight, walking canes, crutches, walking frames, wheelchairs, and orthopedic equipment for persons with disabilities. Since estimation of the needs of disabled children is not possible, their special means needs were equalized with disability group 2. When estimating the final coefficients, the overlapping principle is not considered appropriate, and instead the sum of the two values is used. Tables B.7 and B.8 show the needs values (in GEL) and the associated coefficients.

The final *medical service needs* consist of medicine, monitoring, and rehabilitation needs. In the case of one person being in two different categories, the overlapping principle is used.[10] The methodology assumes 48 percent of total medical service expenditures is spent on medicines and the remaining 52 percent on monitoring. The absolute value of the expenditure on medicine is evaluated using the National Center for Disease Control health expenditure survey of 2011 (NCDC 2011). The amount is corrected for inflation using the GeoStat consumer price index indicator for medicines from 2011 to the end of 2013. It should be noted that this includes not only the healthy category, but also the average for the whole population.

The MoLHSA has provided detailed data on the losses of insurance companies administering the state health insurance program. According to these data, the average payment per person diminishes by 4 percent when persons with disabilities are excluded. So the assumption is that the average yearly expenditure of each healthy person is actually approximately 96 percent of the average yearly expenditure of the healthy population. The medicine needs for each category are estimated in accordance with the health risk coefficients of each category. The abovementioned data also provide information on the insurance company's average expenditure on medicines for different categories. The alternative measure of medicine needs is calculated from the data, and the average of the two methods is considered as the reliable measure. Monitoring needs are assumed to be 52 percent of all medical service needs, excluding rehabilitation needs, with medicine needs comprising the remaining 48 percent of all medical services, excluding rehabilitation needs.

For each subgroup of the population, the monitoring needs are calculated by multiplying all medicine needs of the respective category by $\frac{52}{48}$. One additional assumption is required for pregnant women. Pregnant women need intensive monitoring and less medicine; thus the needs are assessed based on five prenatal visits involving visits to a doctor, examinations, and ultrasounds. The monitoring needs coefficients can be found in table B.9.

The rehabilitation needs methodology was only slightly modified. In contrast to medicine needs, the data for the rehabilitation needs of a disabled child are available. These needs are estimated using yearly budgeted rehabilitation expenses for disabled children. Expenditures for other groups are estimated using the same proportions as previously: the rehabilitation needs of the disabled child are equal to the rehabilitation needs of the second disability group, are half of the rehabilitation needs of the first disability group, and are 60 percent of the rehabilitation needs of the bedridden. With this revision, the coefficients were updated for each type of disability, as described in table B.10.

The final needs index is a sum of the coefficients for food, caregiver, service, special means, and medical service needs as indicated in equation 4.2. Table 4.2 shows the final coefficients associated to each category group of table 4.1. As expected, people with disabilities receive a higher needs index, followed by children, refugees, single pensioners, and, lastly, single mothers.

Table 4.2 Needs Coefficients, N

Status/age	All				Male				Female			
	(0–3)	(4–6)	(7–12)	(13–17)	(18–29)	(30–39)	(40–59)	(60+)	(18–29)	(30–39)	(40–59)	(60+)
Healthy	1.24	1.16	1.04	1.21	1.04	1.00	1.04	1.13	0.93	0.92	0.95	1.04
Child with disability	1.58	1.59	1.50	1.70	0	0	0	0	0	0	0	0
Person with disability group 1	0	0	0	0	1.64	1.60	1.56	1.50	1.50	1.50	1.50	1.50
Person with disability group 2	0	0	0	0	1.56	1.51	1.47	1.41	1.41	1.41	1.41	1.41
Refugee	1.40	1.29	1.15	1.30	1.14	1.10	1.05	1.13	0.99	0.99	0.99	1.12
Bedridden	1.65	1.58	1.46	1.68	1.58	1.53	1.49	1.43	1.42	1.40	1.38	1.38
Single pensioner	0	0	0	0	1.33	1.29	1.25	1.18	1.17	1.16	1.14	1.12
Pregnant	0	0	0	1.32	0	0	0	0	1.11	1.11	1.11	0
Breastfeeding woman	0	0	0	1.21	0	0	0	0	1.08	1.09	1.13	0
Single mother	0	0	0	1.44	0	0	0	0	1.14	1.14	1.14	0
Orphan	1.36	1.20	1.04	1.21	0	0	0	0	0	0	0	0

Source: Pkhakadze, Kvantaliani, and Tsakadze 2015, background paper for this report.

Summary

The needs index captures the caloric and noncaloric needs of particular groups of people as compared to a healthy adult male. The different groups are distinguished by age, gender, social status, and health. Each subset of the population has varying necessities and expenditures, which are important to capture in the ultimate coefficient. While the rubric calls for a 70:30 split for caloric and noncaloric and a 48:52 split for medicine and monitoring needs, these weights are now adjusted according to the groups' defining features.

The revision of the needs index was an important contribution of this exercise as it had not been revised since 2006, although the needs of many groups have changed. Nowadays, technology changes and recently gained knowledge can generate more needs for children but can alleviate the cost of special needs for some people with disabilities.[11] Moreover, the support of the government has changed radically with the introduction of universal health care.

Children got an important increase in the needs index. One of the main reasons for this increase from the original index was that kindergarten costs were omitted by mistake. Additional elements that added to the needs of this group were an increase in the monitoring costs of children 0–3 years old and a rise in the price of textbooks.

On the other hand, the coefficients for people with disabilities decreased. Many of the adjustments came from the use of optimal coefficients that could catch cases where expenses were exaggerated. This applies to particular illnesses, for example, psychological therapy was overestimated for single pensioners.

Internally displaced persons (IDPs) were excluded from the needs index. It was argued that if a person has no disability or other special status, then the caloric and noncaloric needs are the same for IDP or any other person. On the other hand, the household consumption index (the numerator of the PMT formula) can estimate if the consumption is not enough to satisfy the needs of IDPs.

Notes

1. From Georgian law regarding "the rule for calculation of the subsistence minimum."
2. For example, the introduction of universal health care clearly affects the needs of the elderly and disabled, as their medicines are now covered by the program and the person needs to cover only out-of-pocket expenses.
3. See GeoStat, "Subsistence Minimum Calculation Methodology for a Working Male," http://geostat.ge/cms/site_images/_files/english/methodology/Subsistence%20 Minimum%20Calculation%20Methodology%20for%20Working%20Age%20 Male%20ENG.pdf.
4. *Special means* refers to all the additional expenses needed by different groups of the population, from books for children of school age to special equipment for persons with disabilities. More details are provided later in this chapter.
5. The previous needs index used the subsistence minimum for 2004 of GEL 130. The subsistence minimum is yet another parameter that authorities could modify to affect the level of generosity.
6. The average of Q3 and Q4 of 2013 was GEL 148.9, ranging between GEL 144.8 and 155.1.
7. This is based on the caloric needs of different age groups. According to GeoStat the minimum caloric needs for the working-age healthy male is 2,300 kcal. However the needs index looks at the age group 30–39. The caloric need for this age group as defined by previous methodology is 2,230 kcal per day.
8. This assumes that a healthy young man has no special means need.
9. Tables B.5 and B.6 show the noncaloric service needs (in GEL) for all the categories of individuals and the associated coefficients. Keep in mind that $K_S = K_T + K_O + K_{MS}^{(30-39)M}$.
10. The final values and coefficients of the medical service needs can be found in tables B.11 and B.12.
11. Table B.13 shows the percentage change in the index for each category group of the population.

References

NCDC (National Center for Disease Control). 2011. *Health Care: Statistical Yearbook.* Tbilisi. http://www.ncdc.ge/AttachedFiles/ENG688.pdf.

Pkhakadze, Nikoloz, Varlam Kvantaliani, and Vasil Tsakadze. 2015. "Needs Index Revision—Project Report." International School of Economics at Tbilisi University.

CHAPTER 5

The New Scheme of TSA Benefits and the Child Benefit Program

Introduction

The Targeted Social Assistance (TSA) reform not only reviewed the proxy means test (PMT) of the consumption index and updated the needs index, it also modified the structure of benefits of the TSA and established an associated program. In this chapter the TSA benefit structure modifications and the creation of the Child Benefit Program (jointly the TSA+CBP reform hereafter) are introduced together because they have common elements, such as using the TSA vulnerability score for targeting beneficiaries, being financed from the same budget, and being implemented by the same agency. By having two complementary programs with a common targeting tool, the Social Services Agency (SSA) is now making a step toward a more comprehensive and efficient system of social protection and labor.

A differentiation of TSA benefits according to the level of vulnerability score was established. It creates four categories or tiers, and the tiers' combined benefit allotments are equivalent to the current TSA coverage (table 5.1). In addition, the equalization of the benefits for each member of the household is expected to reduce the incentive among members of a household to apply separately to the TSA. The new cutoffs in the revised benefit structure were set in accordance with the following requests from the government of Georgia (GoG): (1) households below 57,000 score should not receive less than before the reform, (2) total population coverage should not be decreased or increased, (3) all household members should receive similar amounts, and (4) the total monthly budget should not be increased substantially.[1]

The CBP was introduced during the reform and uses the TSA targeting formula. This transfer program provides funds to families registered with the TSA that have a score of up to 100,000 and that have children under 16 years of age. Despite being two separate and distinct programs, the TSA and the CBP could be perceived as one package, as the size of the transfer provided to those under the 65,000 cutoff was calculated taking into account the CBP benefit. Box 5.1

Table 5.1 Structure of Benefits: Comparing Current and New TSA Programs

Tier	Prereform TSA			Postreform TSA			Child benefit (per child)
	Prereform TSA score	Core benefit (for first HH member)	Variable benefit (per each additional member)	Postreform TSA score	Core benefit (for first HH member)	Variable benefit (per each additional HH member)	
1	⎫	60	48	0–30,000	60	60	10
2	⎪ 0–57,000	60	48	30,001–57,000	50	50	10
3	⎬	60	48	57,001–60,000	40	40	10
4	⎭	60	48	60,001–65,000	30	30	10
5	⎫ 57,000+	0	0	65,001–100,000	0	0	10
Not beneficiary	⎭	0	0	Over 100,000	0	0	0

Note: Benefits given in GEL per month. GEL = Georgian lari; HH = household; TSA = Targeted Social Assistance.

Box 5.1 Child Benefit Program Criteria

- Benefits are for children under the age of 16.
- Households with vulnerability scores up to 100,000 are eligible. Households with scores 65,000–100,000 receive Child Benefit Program solely.
- The transfer is GEL (Georgian lari) 10 per child, payable every month.

Source: Decree No. 215 of the Government of May 18, 2015, which amends decree No. 145.

---

describes the main features of the CBP. Part of the program is financed with savings coming from the differentiated benefit structure of the TSA, but it requires additional budget support. The combination of the new benefit structure for the two programs TSA+CBP resulted in the five-tier scheme described in table 5.1, in comparison with the situation before the reform. The reader should bear in mind that only households with children in tiers one to four will collect both the TSA and the CBP.

Thus, depending on the level of vulnerability and the demographic composition of the household, winners and losers (both in terms of TSA participation and the size of the TSA transfer) will be rendered. Table 5.2 summarizes the benefit levels for the most common household configurations as well as the percentage of households expected to fall in each cell. It is clear that in terms of size of transfer, tier 1 is the group of households that will clearly win. Those in tiers 2 to 4 will be losers, with those in tier 4 losing the most. In tier 2, only childless households will receive a lower transfer. However, their loss only moves them back in time to their situation two years ago, to the level of benefits received up until 2013.

Some of the TSA newly ineligible households will be partially compensated for the loss, because they will receive the CBP transfer. For example, for households with many children in tier 2 and tier 3, the loss in the TSA transfer will be offset by the gain of the CBP. For example, a family in tier 2 with two adults and

Table 5.2 Theoretical Benefit Levels Based on Prereform and Postreform Benefit Structures and Percentage of the Population Affected by the Change

				TSA benefit only (GEL)					Postreform Child benefit (GEL)	Population				
HH size	Adults	Children	Prereform benefit structure (GEL)	Tier 1 <30,000	Tier 2 30,000– 57,000	Tier 3 57,000– 60,000	Tier 4 60,000– 65,000	Tier 5 65,000– 100,000	(0–100,000)	Tier 1 <30,000	Tier 2 30,000– 57,000	Tier 3 57,000– 60,000	Tier 4 60,000– 65,000	Tier 5 65,000– 100,000
1	1	0	60	60	50	40	30	0	0	0	4,763	304	2,428	19,463
2	2	0	108	120	100	80	60	0	0	576	16,872	2,566	4,294	41,163
2	1	1	108	120	100	80	60	0	10	633	0	1,645	0	4,402
3	3	0	156	180	150	120	90	0	0	3,569	20,949	1,441	3,662	50,247
3	2	1	156	180	150	120	90	0	10	0	8,069	1,441	3,620	15,215
3	1	2	156	180	150	120	90	0	20	2,286	4,474	0	0	2,225
4	4	0	204	240	200	160	120	0	0	649	15,365	6,711	6,846	39,436
4	3	1	204	240	200	160	120	0	10	7,330	17,511	2,181	4,594	33,660
4	2	2	204	240	200	160	120	0	20	8,526	13,876	10,082	4,552	36,423
4	1	3	204	240	200	160	120	0	30	0	0	0	0	1,132
5	5	0	252	300	250	200	150	0	0	2,773	6,775	0	3,727	26,549
5	4	1	252	300	250	200	150	0	10	664	14,984	1,583	1,439	32,908
5	3	2	252	300	250	200	150	0	20	8,475	19,407	0	4,851	41,375
5	2	3	252	300	250	200	150	0	30	5,336	2,706	0	0	11,839
5	1	4	252	300	250	200	150	0	40	2,763	2,161	0	2,043	13,419

Note: Population percentages calculated using Integrated Household Survey (IHS) 2013 estimation sample (additional module data). Tiers are determined by TSA vulnerability score as described in table 5.1.
GEL = Georgian lari; HH = household; TSA = Targeted Social Assistance.

two children would have almost no reduction in the total TSA transfer, from GEL (Georgian lari) 204 to GEL 200. However, if the CBP is added, the total transfers TSA+CBP will increase relative to the prereform, from GEL 204 to GEL 220 (see chapter 7).

The new scheme of benefits is expected to result in increases in benefits for the poorest groups and reductions in benefits for those closer to the eligibility threshold. In the poorest tiers—tier 1 and tier 2 as defined in table 5.1—some households are expected to receive an increase in benefits of up to 38 percent (tier 1) and 18 percent (tier 2), depending on the household demographic composition. Households with more children have larger gains than households with fewer children. Still, in tier 2 there are pockets of benefit losers: these are childless households. Among this tier, one-person and two-person households are of special concern, since they are likely to comprise elderly people, whose ability to receive support from other income sources may be limited. Some of the newly ineligible are also compensated later by the later modification to the needs index (see chapter 9).

The TSA+CBP reform contains elements—change in eligibility formula, change in structure of benefits, and introduction of CBP—that will result in different combinations of winners and losers. Some households will be winners because they can now enter the program, others because they receive a larger transfer, either by the TSA or the TSA in combination with the CBP. Others will be losers because their benefits will decrease to pre-2013 levels. In the next two chapters, there is more detailed analysis of each of these elements, with attention to the performance of the TSA+CBP package. Notice that the analysis of winners and losers is confined to the TSA program and does not evaluate changes in total welfare coming from other programs and services.

Fiscal Implications

The introduction of the TSA+CBP reform package will require an increase in the program budget by 14 percent. Almost all of the increase can be attributed to the CBP. The TSA will cost 2 percent more than previously, and most of the increment comes from extending benefits to the CBP beneficiaries. The combined package will increase the total budget to GEL 26.4 million from the 2014 level of GEL 23.1 million, based on the survey data.

The additional budget buys increased coverage of families via the CBP, which contributes to reducing child poverty. The 9 percent increase in the TSA+CBP budget buys a considerable expansion of coverage and makes policy sense (figure 5.1). The reform predicts halving extreme poverty among children, from around 7.1 to 3.23 percent based on UNICEF's measure of child poverty (see chapter 2 and "Glossary" for definitions). According to the Integrated Household Survey (IHS) 2013 additional module, 7.1 percent of the child population lived under extreme poverty (58 percent higher than the population extreme poverty rate of 4.5 percent). By introducing the new methodology, the extreme poverty rates are estimated to fall to 4.4 and 3.7 percent for children and the overall population, respectively. The only way to equalize the extreme

Figure 5.1 Budget Implications of the Reform

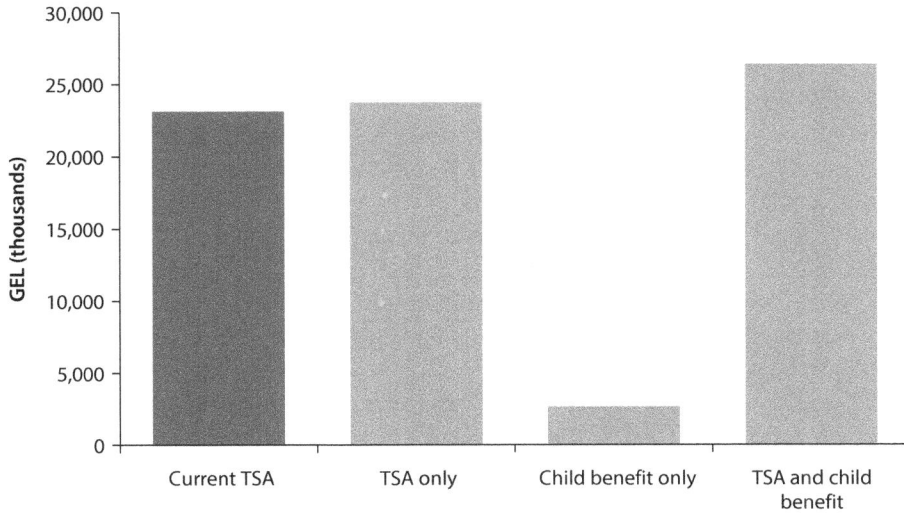

Note: CBP includes children 0 to 16 years old. CBP = Child Benefit Program; GEL = Georgian lari; TSA = Targeted Social Assistance.

child poverty rate with the general population poverty rate is to introduce a well-targeted child benefit (according to the model, even GEL 10 per child per month can reduce both rates to 3.2 percent). However, it should be noted that (1) the extreme poverty threshold is half of the subsistence minimum and (2) covering the children below the 65,000 TSA score would not give the same results. More analysis needs to be done in terms of the broader impact of the program on a variety of outcomes (poverty, but also employment, education, health, and nutrition) and the potential comparison with other allocations of funds. Ultimately, however, the decision is a favorable one. As a result, the government is already planning jointly with UNICEF a sound evaluation of the impact of the CBP.

Summary

The reform comprised the following elements: a change in eligibility formula, a change in the structure of benefits, and the introduction of CBP. As expected, these types of reforms yield winners and losers of the TSA program. Some households will be winners because they become eligible to the TSA program, others because they receive a larger transfer (either from the TSA, the CBP, or both). Other households will be losers because they become ineligible to the TSA or because the benefits received will decrease to the levels of 2013.

As previously discussed, the change in PMT formula improved targeting, leakage and undercoverage results, and accuracy. The reform will also create a new structure of benefits: four tiers of coverage based on level of vulnerability. Instead of all beneficiaries receiving the same amount (which was the case before), differentiated groups of beneficiaries will receive proportional amounts according to need. This scheme of benefits should also be instrumental in maintaining low work disincentives as corroborated by the World Bank study (Santos et al. 2015). Moreover, the new CBP will provide additional support for families with children under 16 and who score below 100,000. Since the TSA covers only households that score below 65,000, a new tier of beneficiaries will be added—tier 5: households with children and a score of 65,000–100,000. While tier 5 families will not receive TSA benefits, they will have financial help from CBP.

With these policy changes, winners and losers of the TSA will be rendered, depending on their level of vulnerability and their households' demographic compositions. The new scheme of benefits results in increases in benefits for the poorest groups and reductions in benefits for those closer to the eligibility threshold. That being said, less vulnerable families with children who suffer benefit reductions due to the revisions in the eligibility formula may recover part of their loss by receiving the CBP. Moreover, a whole new tier of vulnerable families will be qualified for SSA assistance. As for budgeting, total allotments given by the new benefits structure will be equivalent to that of the prereform scheme. However, the CBP will require additional funding. In total, the TSA+CBP reform package will require an increase in the program budget by 14 percent, from GEL 23.1 million to GEL 26.4 million.

The combination of the scheme of benefits of the TSA and the CBP can be perceived as a hybrid along the way to a comprehensive and efficient social protection system. On the one hand, the gradual reduction of benefits serves to maintain the low work disincentives of the TSA program, but it also relies on an underlying assumption that poorer families have larger needs than relatively less poor ones. Based on this assumption and given that the PMT is usually not accurate enough to statistically differentiate the level of poverty for narrowly defined groups (as those that give place to the four tiers), an alternative and probably more accurate approach would be to identify the specific needs of the population to serve and to provide a transfer or service directed to that need. This is exactly what the CBP does: it identifies families with children under 16 as a group with a specific need.

A natural next step is to continue the identification of needs of this group. As the needs are identified and served through specific programs, the total transfers to households will result from a staggered (short) list of programs instead of a narrowly defined range in the TSA vulnerability score. Chapter 10 proposes an analytic framework for Georgia to start thinking about how to approach the development of a system of social protection and labor.

Note

1. The total budget will increase due to the implemented compensation measures. However, this was not forecasted by the GoG, and the decision of adjusting the measures to ensure fiscal sustainability has been postponed until the elections of October 2016 are completed.

References

IHS (Integrated Household Survey). 2013. GeoStat, Tbilisi. http://www.geostat.ge/?action=meurneoba&mpid=1&lang=eng.

Santos, I., B. Kits, A. Isik-Dikmelik, and O. Smith. 2015. *The Impact of Targeted Social Assistance on Labor Market in Georgia*. World Bank Report 98707. Washington, DC: World Bank.

Winners and Losers of the TSA Program

Introduction

Chapter 6 examines the effect of the revision of the Targeted Social Assistance (TSA) formula on the targeting performance and the identification of the winners and losers of the TSA reform, before the introduction of compensation measures. It analyzes two types of winner-loser dichotomies. The first group, *extensive margin winners or losers*, are those who win eligibility to the program and those who lose it. The second group, *intensive margin winners or losers*, are those who remain eligible and are winners or losers based on increases or decreases in transfer amount (see box 6.1 for a summary of the definitions).

Note that persons and households benefit from other transfers besides the TSA. A limitation of this report is that it does not examine winners and losers in terms of total transfers received from all programs and services. Ideally, a comprehensive winners and losers analysis should account for the total transfers received, the needs (access and costs of services) of the groups, and their opportunities. Simply looking at whether they gain or lose eligibility to a single program is not enough to assess the well-being of the group with respect to its past or in relation to other vulnerable groups. Moving toward the delivery of social assistance in a systemic way will help stakeholders understand the relative well-being of the various vulnerable groups.

The transition from the pre- to the postreform program presents significant challenges that need to be addressed. Nearly half of current beneficiaries become losers—either extensive or intensive losers as defined above. Twenty-six percent of current beneficiaries would become altogether ineligible in the absence of compensation measures. In absolute terms, this means that about 120,000 people would lose eligibility to the TSA (counting all members residing in affected households), and of these only 20,000 will qualify for the Child Benefit Program (CBP) created as part of this reform (see chapter 5). Also, over 164,000 would experience a decline in benefit level. Of the 28 percent of current beneficiaries

Box 6.1 Types of TSA Winners and Losers

- *Always eligible* are those who remain eligible for Targeted Social Assistance (TSA), that is, those who were eligible before and after the reform.
- *Always ineligible* are those who remain ineligible for the TSA, that is, those who were ineligible before and after the reform.

Among those who are affected by the reform we identify winners and losers. There are two ways current beneficiary households can lose as a result of the TSA reform.

- *Extensive loss* is experienced by people who lose eligibility to the TSA under the new proxy means test (PMT) formula (they may be called *newly ineligible*).
- *Intensive loss* is experienced by those who remain eligible (always eligible) to the TSA but receive a smaller benefit as a result of changes in the benefit structure.

Winners, too, can be classified in two types:

- *Extensive gain* is experienced by those who were ineligible under the current targeting but become eligible under the new formula (they may be called *newly eligible*).
- *Intensive gain* is experienced by those who remain eligible (always eligible) but receive higher benefit amounts after the reform.

that would experience a partial reduction in benefits, 12 percent would lose more than half of their prereform benefit amount.

The CBP does provide additional protection to the vulnerable, but likely not enough. Although the predictions on poverty suggest that the CBP benefits will protect some of the poor and will decrease child poverty, the value of CBP transfers may often be insufficient to provide adequate levels of protection due to their small size. Moreover, the devaluation of the GEL (Georgian lari) that occurred after the approval of the program in December 2014 already dilutes part of the value of the transfer. The expected impact of this program is described in more detail in chapter 7.

Coverage of the TSA remains unaltered by design.[1] One of the objectives from the outset was to maintain the level of coverage of the TSA. The objective responds to different political needs. On the one hand, the government is able to maintain its commitment to pay more attention to social issues. On the other, the TSA—jointly with other transfers—has played a critical role in reducing poverty since 2008, and with the economic slowdown of 2014 and the devaluation of the GEL, it is critical now to sustain the size of the program. Thus, to maintain coverage at 12.6 percent, the eligibility threshold to the TSA was raised from 57,000 to 65,000 in the vulnerability score. It should be noted that the increase in the threshold is not associated with an expansion of the program, but rather is intended to maintain the coverage.

The revised eligibility formula leads to some reshuffling of beneficiaries. Under the revised formula and using comparable thresholds, 26.0 percent of

Table 6.1 Transition Matrix: People Moving in and out of the TSA Program

| | Postreform TSA status | | | |
| | TSA beneficiary | | TSA nonbeneficiary | |
Prereform TSA status	HH with children	HH w/o children	HH with children	HH w/o children
Nonbeneficiary	114,948	31,602	369,142	2,654,621
Beneficiary	251,862	87,249	21,267	97,736

Source: Calculations based on Integrated Household Survey (IHS) 2013 estimation sample (additional module data).
Note: Only third quarter included. Persons receiving TSA live in a household with a vulnerability score lower than 57,000 for prereform eligibility formula and scores below 65,000 for postreform eligibility formula. HH = household; TSA = Targeted Social Assistance.

prereform beneficiaries (119,003 persons with scores under 57,000 in the old formula) will lose eligibility to the TSA—they are called *extensive margin TSA losers* or simply *TSA losers*, hereafter. At the same time, 146,550 persons (or 31.9 percent of prereform beneficiaries) will enter the program—they are called *extensive margin TSA winners* or *newly eligible* for short. Table 6.1 shows in detail the transition matrix for people in and out of the TSA as a result of the revision of the formula. Some of the TSA losers, it should be noted, will gain eligibility to the CBP as discussed in chapter 7, so the net loss becomes smaller. The reshuffling responds to the government's objective of supporting families with children while maintaining constant the level of coverage.

Besides the reshuffling, the revised eligibility formula improves the targeting performance by increasing the coverage of the poorer quintile and by reducing the leakage from richer households. More precisely, the coverage of the poorest quintile increases from 47 to 53 percent. While improvements in the coverage of the poor are concentrated in the second decile, from 22.5 to 32 percent coverage, the coverage of the households in the first decile also slightly increases, from 71 to 73 percent. Both are very good targeting outcomes (see figure 6.1).

Improvements arise because the revised eligibility formula accomplishes its objective of excluding wealthier households while replacing them with poorer ones. The percentage of TSA beneficiaries under the reform are relatively concentrated in the second decile (figure 6.2). Among the excluded households, 42 percent come from above the poorest quintile, while among the newcomers, 77 percent belong to that group (see figure 6.3).

TSA winners and losers are not equally distributed across space, but the reshuffling within regions is relatively balanced. Map 6.1 shows the percentage of winners and losers by region. Mtskheta-Mtianeti has the highest share of newly ineligibles (losers), while Kvemo Kartli has a negligible number of losers. As can be seen, most of the regions with the darker shade also have the darker dots, suggesting that the reshuffling occurs within regions too. An exception is Kvemo Kartli, where there are more new extensive margin winners than losers before compensation measures.

Consistently, TSA extensive winners have lower total expenditure per adult equivalent (PAE) than TSA extensive losers, at every point in the

Figure 6.1 Coverage of the TSA, Before and After the Reform

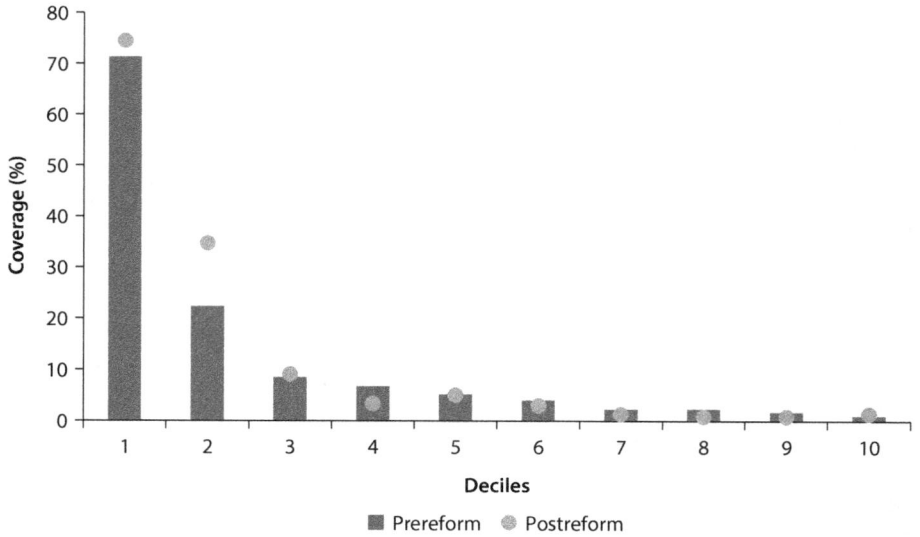

Source: Calculations based on IHS 2013 estimation sample (additional module data).
Note: Deciles are computed using consumption pre-TSA transfer and per adult equivalent (PAE). Persons eligible live in a
household with a vulnerability score lower than 57,000 for prereform eligibility formula and scores below 65,000 for
postreform eligibility formula. TSA = Targeted Social Assistance.

Figure 6.2 Distribution of TSA Beneficiaries, Before and After the Reform

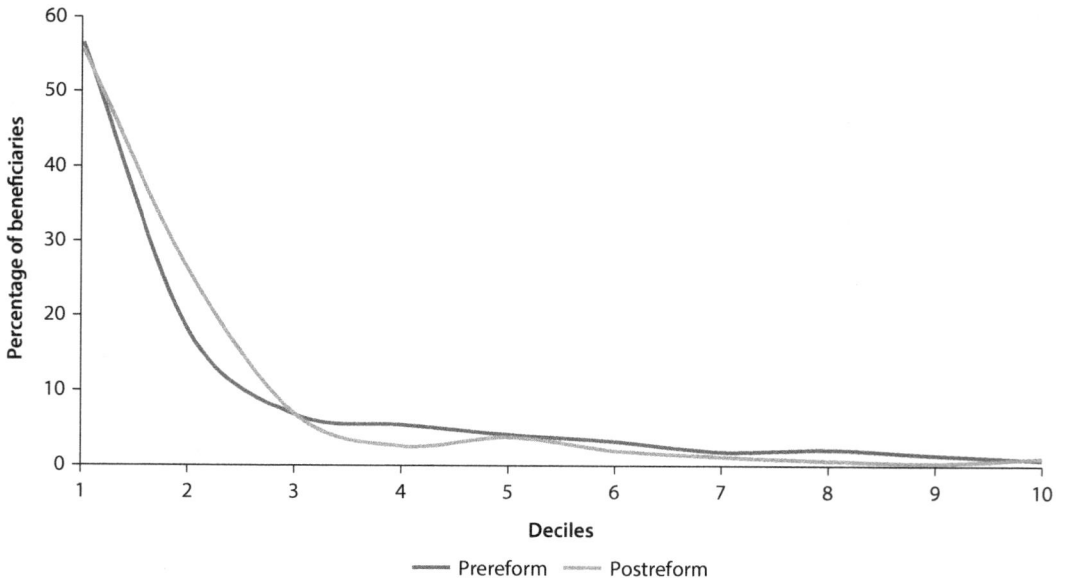

Source: Calculations based on IHS 2013 estimation sample (additional module data).
Note: Deciles are computed using pre-TSA transfer consumption PAE. Beneficiaries are persons living in households receiving TSA. PAE = per adult
equivalent; TSA = Targeted Social Assistance.

Figure 6.3 Distribution of Extensive Winners and Extensive Losers

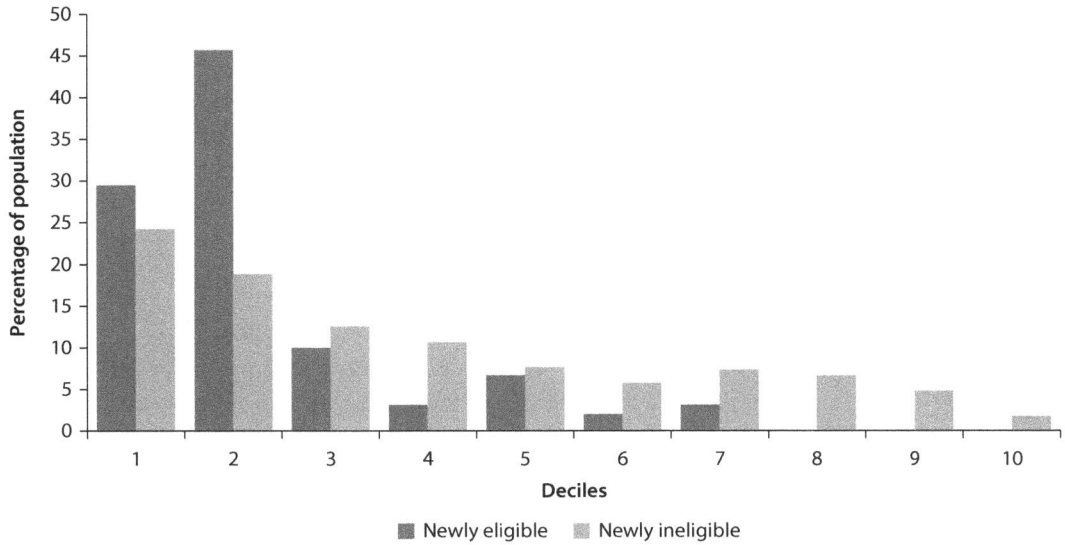

Deciles

■ Newly eligible   ■ Newly ineligible

Source: Calculations based on IHS 2013 estimation sample (additional module data).
Note: Deciles are computed using consumption pre-TSA transfer and PAE. Newly eligible are persons living in households that gain eligibility to the TSA, and newly ineligible are persons living in households that lose eligibility to the TSA with the reform. PAE = per adult equivalent; TSA = Targeted Social Assistance.

Map 6.1 Percentage of TSA Winners and Losers, by Region

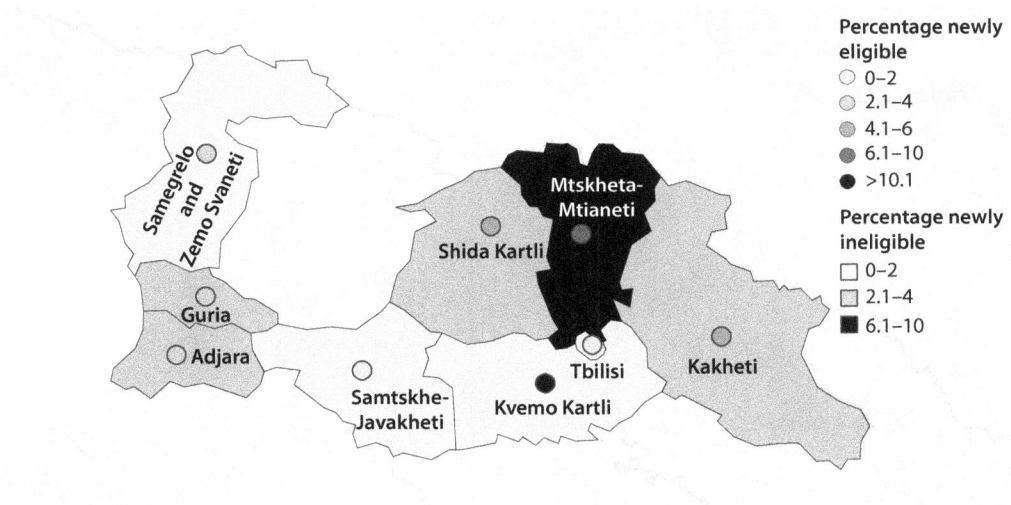

Note: Percentages are calculated from the population. Information from Racha-Lechkhumi-Kvemo Svaneti is merged with Imereti in our dataset, and therefore not reported. TSA = Targeted Social Assistance.

welfare distribution. The proxy means test (PMT) proxies consumption based on observable characteristics that cannot be manipulated by the beneficiary to increase his or her probability of eligibility for the program. First, noneligible households spend more than eligible households; always-ineligible households spend twice as much as newly eligible (TSA winners) and always-eligible households. Second, as shown in figure 6.4, the total expenditure PAE is lower for those who are entering the program than for those leaving it (with the exception of the third decile, which is not statistically different). Moreover, greater differences are observed in the lower deciles. For instance, TSA loser households in the poorest decile spend twice as much as TSA winners (GEL 108 against GEL 51 per month PAE, respectively).

Within each decile, TSA winners not only consume less in total—suggesting more vulnerability—but also consume less food, beverages, and tobacco than TSA losers. For example, TSA extensive margin losers and those households that continue to be eligible (always eligible), spend 49 percent and 46 percent, respectively, on food, beverages, and tobacco as a percentage of total consumption (figure 6.5). TSA extensive margin losers consume 55 percent (or GEL 28 per month PAE) more in these items than always-eligible households. Only expenditure on clothing and education as a percentage of total cash consumption is slightly lower for TSA extensive margin losers than for the rest of the population. Note, however, that TSA extensive margin winners spend a larger share in the rubric "other" than always eligible and losers, which could be worrisome if

Figure 6.4 Consumption of Winners versus Losers by Decile

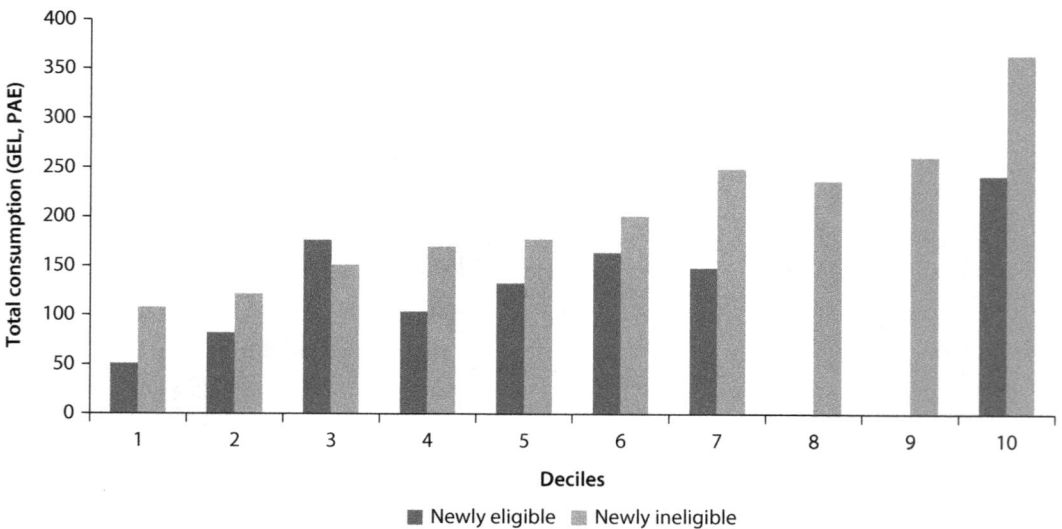

Newly eligible ■   Newly ineligible ■

Source: Calculations based on IHS 2013 estimation sample (additional module data).
Note: Deciles from total pre-TSA consumption PAE in GEL. Population-weighted averages. Newly eligible are persons living in households that gain eligibility to the TSA, and newly ineligible are persons living in households losing eligibility to the TSA with the reform. GEL = Georgian lari; PAE = per adult equivalent; TSA = Targeted Social Assistance.

Figure 6.5 Disaggregation of Consumer Spending per Adult Equivalent

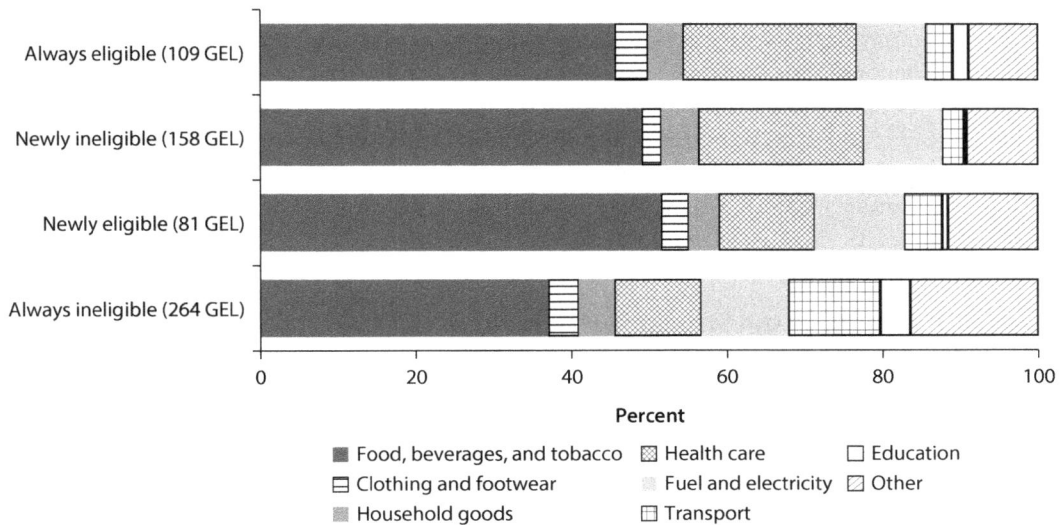

Source: Calculations based on IHS 2013 estimation sample (additional module data).
Note: Weighted data at the household level. Total cash expenditure in parenthesis, in 2013 GEL. Note that these categories refer to basic needs of the households. Excludes nonconsumption expenditures (agriculture, transfers, saving and lending, and property acquirement). See box 6.1 for the definitions of winners and losers.

Table 6.2 Income Elasticity to Spending in Different Types of Goods, by TSA Status

Disaggregation	Always ineligible	Newly eligible	Newly ineligible	Always eligible
Food, beverages, and tobacco	0.931	1.328	1.018	1.072
Clothing and footwear	1.653	1.009	*0.720*	1.130
Household goods	1.397	1.440	1.063	0.924
Health care	1.191	2.339	2.300	2.331
Fuel and electricity	0.755	0.699	0.815	0.560
Transport	2.677	2.044	1.542	1.504
Education	1.711	*−0.223*	*−0.169*	0.796
Other	1.059	1.084	0.888	1.054

Source: Calculations based on IHS 2013, all quarters included.
Note: Elasticities are calculated using a weighted ordinary least squares (OLS) regression of the dependent variable (logarithm of the total pre-TSA consumption PAE) in the explanatory variables for each type of consumption category, also in logs. Logs of zero values are replaced for Log(0.0001). Total pre-TSA consumption is interpreted as a proxy of total income. Italics denote estimates that are not significant. PAE = per adult equivalent; TSA = Targeted Social Assistance.

the additional transfer is not directed toward its intended uses: food, health, and education.

If income increased for TSA newly eligible and always-eligible beneficiaries, consumption on health care would increase more than proportionally, relative to TSA newly ineligible and TSA always-ineligible. Table 6.2 displays the income elasticity of demand for each category of consumption goods. It shows that an increase of 1 percent of income is associated with a more than proportional increase on food consumption of 32 percent and 7 percent for newly eligible and always-eligible households, respectively. And the elasticities for health care are even higher. However, the values for health care should be interpreted with caution, as spending in health can increase or decrease with income. For example, it could also be possible that, as income increases, the proportion of the income spent in health becomes relatively smaller, maybe due to access to better health insurance. Other high-income countries show the opposite result: wealthier families spend relatively more on health than poor families spend. This is very much linked to the type of health insurance and health services available in different countries.

Change in the Structure of Benefits of the TSA

The revised benefit structure is progressive in that it awards larger transfers to poorer households. The prereform benefit structure allocates GEL 60 to the first adult in the household and GEL 48 to each subsequent person (regardless of age). The revised benefit structure introduces a more complicated benefit calculation formula as the transfer depends on the vulnerability score, but it also simplifies allocation by distributing the same amount to every member in the household. The amount of the transfer varies from GEL 60 to GEL 30 per household member, with an additional GEL 10 per child from the CBP. The details of the benefit structure are presented in table 5.2 in chapter 5. The fact that each household member contributes to the total transfer in the same proportion will discourage large households from artificially splitting to receive a bigger transfer.

Even if the poor will be relatively better off overall, some current poor beneficiaries will experience a loss. Figure 6.6 shows that, as expected, total consumption PAE before the reform was lower for those who will receive higher benefits than for those who will experience a benefit loss. The persons in the poorest deciles are the ones who now receive the largest transfer, while those in the other deciles are more likely to see a reduction in the amount received—for instance, households close to the threshold will receive a smaller transfer (23 percent lower than the prereform transfer).

However, the type of consumption rubric does not change significantly between intensive margin winners and intensive margin losers. Figure 6.7 presents the proportion of spending allocated to each category, which varies by a maximum of 2 percentage points between the two groups. Food, beverages, tobacco, and health care expenditures account for more than 66 percent of the total spending in both cases. Differences in mean levels are sizable, however. While households that will lose benefits spend GEL 117 per month, households that win benefits spend GEL 101.

For most of the intensive margin losers, the loss will be a small percentage of the transfer, but for a few, the loss will be sizable. Figure 6.8 shows the kernel distribution for the losses and gains (in percentage points of the original transfer) as a result of the reform. As it can be seen, the largest accumulation of the mass of the distribution occurs just below zero, and there is some mass for loses

Figure 6.6 Cumulative Distribution of Consumption for TSA Intensive Margin Winners and Losers

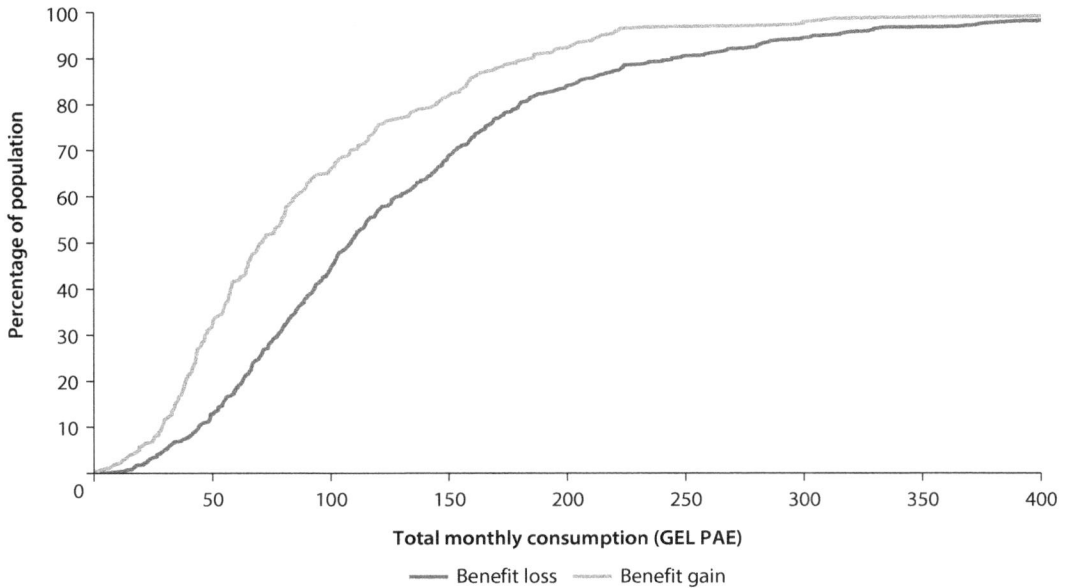

Source: Calculations based on IHS 2013 estimation sample.
Note: Population-weighted estimates based on persons living in households eligible for TSA. GEL = Georgian lari; PAE = per adult equivalent; TSA = Targeted Social Assistance.

Figure 6.7 Composition of Consumption among Eligible Households, Intensive Margin Winners and Losers

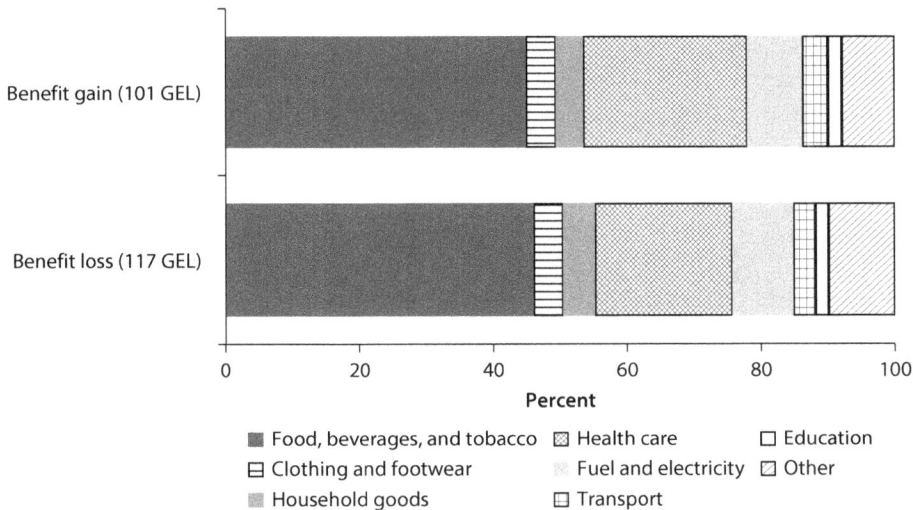

Source: Calculations based on IHS 2013.
Note: Household weighted estimates based on persons living in households eligible for TSA. Total cash expenditure PAE in parenthesis, in 2013 GEL. GEL = Georgian lari; PAE = per adult equivalent.

Figure 6.8 Distribution of Intensive Margin Winners and Losers, by Size of Loss or Gain

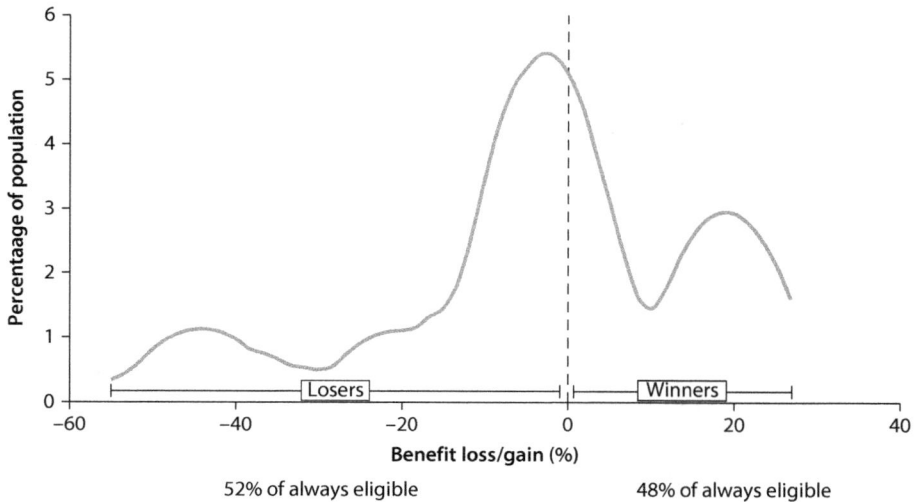

52% of always eligible   48% of always eligible

Source: Calculations based on IHS 2013 estimation sample (additional module data).
Note: Population-weighted results based on persons living in TSA-eligible households. Losses and gains are expressed as a percentage of total transfer before the reform. TSA = Targeted Social Assistance.

around 50 percent. Thus, while 35 percent of the always eligible lose less than 15 percent of the transfer, fewer than 10 percent lose more than 40 percent of the transfer. Alternatively, the gains are more concentrated in smaller values. No intensive margin winner obtains more than a 26 percent increase, and most of the winners gain around 20 percent.

There are more intensive winners than losers in the bottom decile, while the opposite is true in the second-to-bottom decile. Figure 6.9 shows the distribution of intensive winners and losers by decile of monthly consumption PAE. As expected, among all TSA recipients the entire action is observed in the bottom two deciles. Consistent with the objective of the benefit structure, most of the intensive margin winners are in the bottom decile, while more intensive margin losers than winners are closer to the eligibility threshold, both in the second and third decile.

Winners and Losers in Terms of Social Categories

There are sectors of the population that are entitled to other social benefits beyond the TSA in Georgia. The IHS identifies a wide range of social categories that are considered vulnerable and/or entitled to benefits under Georgia's social assistance system. Some of these categories are rather specific, and the number of observations corresponding to them in the IHS sample is small, making it necessary to group them into larger, conceptually homogeneous categories. Thus, this report combines "disabled persons" and "persons with specific health needs."[2] Another category analyzed for this purpose is "single nonworking pensioner." The definition

Figure 6.9 Distribution of Winners and Losers

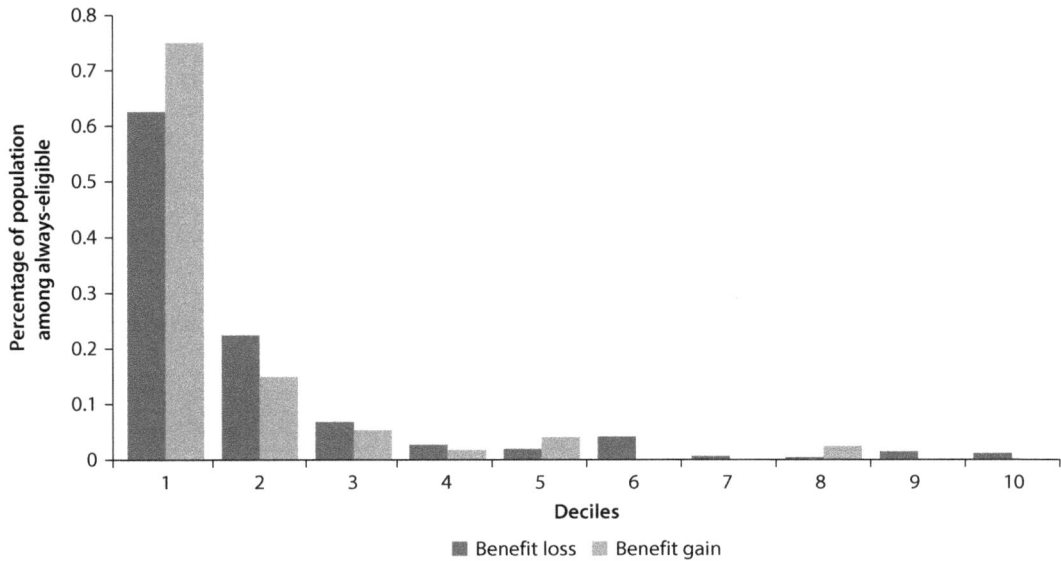

Source: Calculations based on IHS 2013 estimation sample (additional module data).
Note: Deciles from total pre-TSA consumption PAE. Population-weighted estimates based on persons living in TSA-eligible households.
PAE = per adult equivalent; TSA = Targeted Social Assistance.

of that group allows for certain discrepancies, thus complicating the situation for the social agents who establish the membership of people belonging to this group.[3]

The single, nonworking pensioners group constitutes an important share of the newly ineligible persons before compensation measures. Table 6.3 shows the coverage rates within each social group. As seen in the table, coverage rates were slightly reduced for all groups, but for single nonworking pensioners coverage is drastically reduced, from 34 to 6 percent. Disqualification of single nonworking pensioners is not compensated with the admission of other pensioners—in fact, almost no single nonworking pensioners will be newly eligible (less than 1 percent, as seen in table 6.4). It is worth mentioning that even with the prereform eligibility formula the number of single nonworking pensioners would have gone down if the pension levels were adjusted. The pension amount in the prereform formula was maintained at GEL 80 even when the actual pension was already increased to GEL 110 for those 60–67 years old, and GEL 125 for those above 67. The postreform methodology further adjusts to reflect the actual pension at GEL 160 per pensioner. This analysis does not disentangle how much is due to the revision of the PMT and how much is due to increases in Old Age Pensions.

Nevertheless, all social groups, with the exception of IDPs, are extensive margin losers. Second to single nonworking pensioners, the group that faces greater chances of losing eligibility is persons with disabilities. Coverage for this group is estimated to fall from 28 to 20 percent (see table 6.3). Note that this group represents 17 percent of those that are newly ineligible, while they represent only

Table 6.3 Prereform and Postreform TSA Coverage, by Social Categories

	Coverage rate (%)	
Social category	Prereform	Postreform
Disabled persons	27.54	20.30
Persons with specific health needs	20.59	16.53
Single nonworking pensioners	34.47	6.35
IDPs	8.47	17.74

Source: Calculations based on IHS 2013 estimation sample (additional module data).
Note: Population-weighted estimates based on persons living in TSA-eligible/noneligible households.
IDPs = internally displaced persons; TSA = Targeted Social Assistance.

Table 6.4 Proportion of Social Categories within Each Group of Winners and Losers
percent

Social category	Always ineligible	Newly eligible	Newly ineligible	Always eligible		Total of the population
				Benefit loss	Benefit gain	
Disabled persons	3.88	5.23	16.94	11.45	7.89	4.91
Persons with specific health needs	5.09	7.62	14.05	9.95	8.11	5.86
Single nonworking pensioners	1.31	0.50	15.21	1.82	0.00	1.70
IDPs	3.37	17.82	4.47	3.12	1.13	3.88

Source: Calculations based on IHS 2013 estimation sample (additional module data).
Note: Columns one to five show the percentage of each social group within the total of each winners and losers group. For example, 16.94 percent of the newly ineligible are disabled persons. IDPs = internally displaced persons.

5 percent of the total population (table 6.4). In other words, they are overrepresented among newly ineligibles. A similar story can be told for individuals with serious health needs. The coverage rate for this group will fall, and they are overrepresented among the newly ineligibles relative to the size of this group in the total population.

Nevertheless, for each of these groups, there are fewer intensive margin losers at the bottom of the distribution than at the top. Figure 6.10 shows that the distribution of beneficiaries after the reform is more skewed toward the bottom (the points are always above the bars for the bottom two deciles with the exception of IDPs). This suggests that many extensive losers will be coming from the third decile and above.

For all social groups, the numbers of individuals experiencing a reduction in benefits are slightly higher than those of individuals experiencing an increase in benefits. Figure 6.8 shows that the number of people facing benefit losses and benefit gains are almost equal. Thus, since table 6.4 shows that each of the social groups is overrepresented among those with benefit loss than among those with benefit gain, it can be inferred that there will be more people facing benefit losses than gains in each group. For example, while 12 percent of those that will see a benefit loss are disabled, only 8 percent of those that will see a benefit gain belong to that group. Notice that none of the single nonworking elderly are expected to receive higher benefits. For each social group, figure 6.11 shows that

Figure 6.10 Distribution of Prereform and Postreform Beneficiaries for Select Social Categories

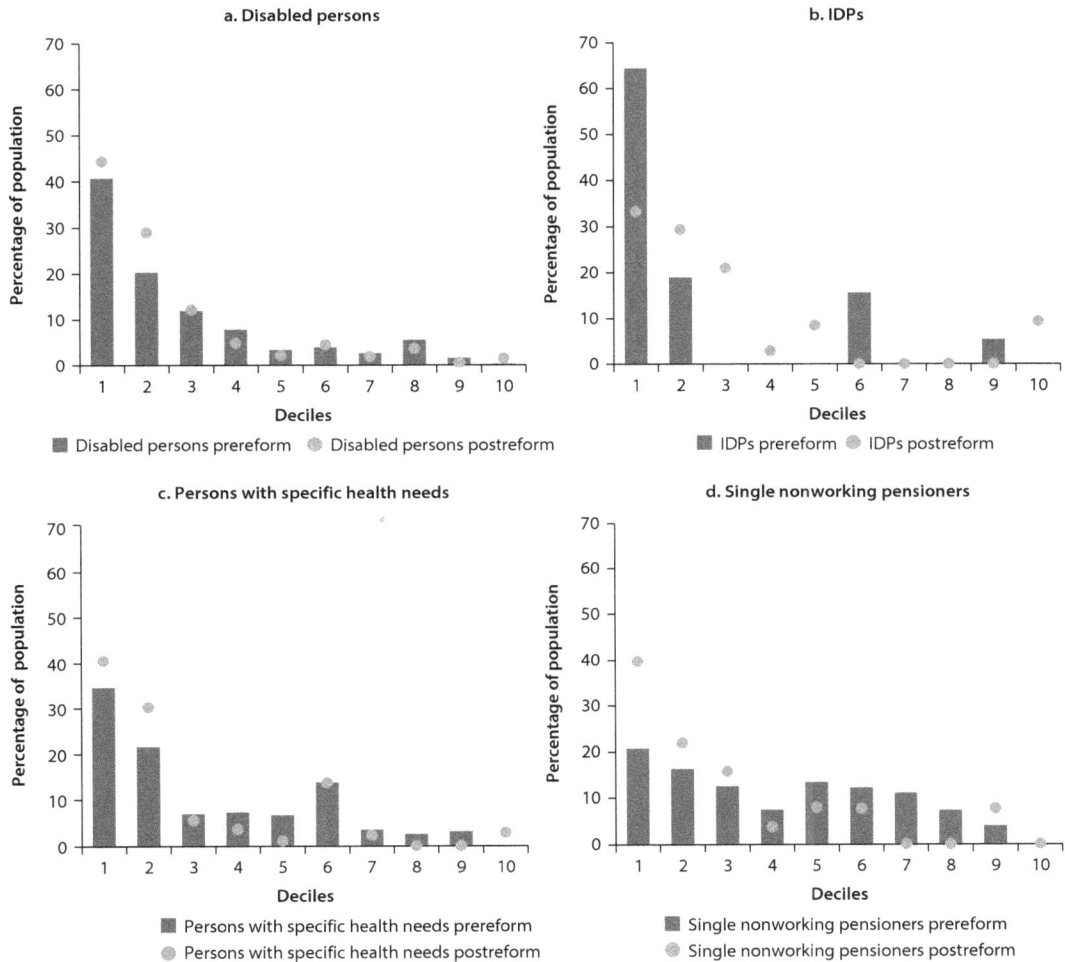

a. Disabled persons

Disabled persons prereform ● Disabled persons postreform

b. IDPs

IDPs prereform ● IDPs postreform

c. Persons with specific health needs

Persons with specific health needs prereform
● Persons with specific health needs postreform

d. Single nonworking pensioners

Single nonworking pensioners prereform
● Single nonworking pensioners postreform

Source: Calculations based on IHS 2013.
Note: Pre-TSA transfer consumption PAE deciles. Population-weighted estimates based on persons living in households eligible/noneligible to TSA. Postreform refers to the new eligibility formula and benefits before compensation measures. IDPs = internally displaced persons; PAE = per adult equivalent; TSA = Targeted Social Assistance.

there is considerable reshuffling within each quintile. However, for disabled people and persons with specific health needs, more winners than losers appear in the second quintile.

The posttransfer distribution of the disabled changes a little and remains pro-poor. The composition of beneficiaries of these two social categories postreform becomes somewhat more pro-poor, with 44 percent of beneficiaries concentrated in the bottom decile, rather than 39 percent prereform (see figure 6.10, panel a). For the persons with specific health needs, the story seems to be similar, but the slim number of observations does not allow one to draw reliable conclusions (figure 6.10, panel c).

Continuous Improvement • http://dx.doi.org/10.1596/978-1-4648-0900-2

Figure 6.11 Distribution of Intensive Margin Winners and Losers for Social Groups

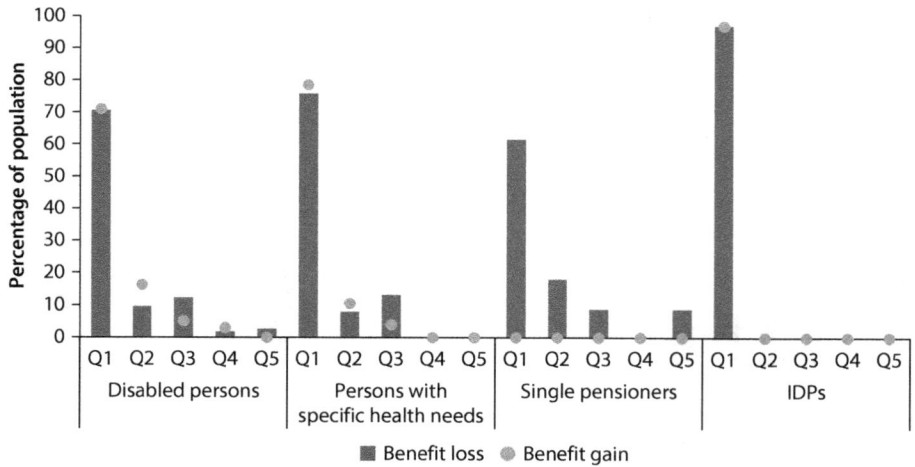

Source: Calculations based on IHS 2013.
Note: Pre-TSA transfer consumption PAE quintiles. Population-weighted estimates based on persons living in elgibible/noneligble TSA households. IDPs = internally displaced persons; PAE = per adult equivalent; Q = quintile; TSA = Targeted Social Assistance.

While the coverage of single nonworking pensioners is much lower under the updated beneficiary structure, the postreform distribution is more pro-poor, with 38 percent coming from the poorest decile (versus 20 percent prereform). In other words, the revised PMT is more likely to disqualify those single elderly who are better off (figure 6.10, panel d). When the intensive margin is examined, most of the benefit losses correspond to single pensioners in the bottom quintile, while there are no single pensioners with benefit gains (figure 6.11). Since single pensioners are the big losers, this report also examines the potential implications in terms of consumption. Panel a of figure 6.12 shows that consumption is lower for pensioners that will enter the program and higher for those that will become ineligible.

Compensation measures to protect the TSA losers were adopted by the government. Often, although not always, governments adopt compensation measures to protect losers from a reform. The government of Georgia introduced two compensation measures in August 2015, and they are discussed in chapter 9.

Winners and Losers in Terms of Demographic Characteristics

This section examines the effect of the change in targeting formula on various types of households, defined by their demographic characteristics.

Based on the government's objective, the big winners are households with children. More gains are identified in chapter 7 as TSA recipients and other households in tier 5 will qualify for CBP. Among the newly eligible, half of them come

Figure 6.12 Composition of Consumption Expenditure PAE for Single Nonworking Pensioners

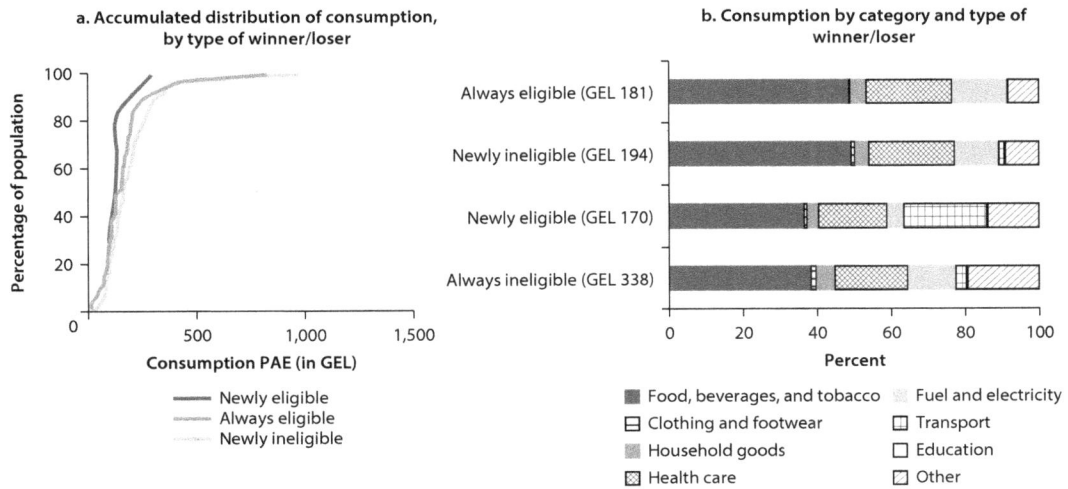

a. Accumulated distribution of consumption, by type of winner/loser

b. Consumption by category and type of winner/loser

Always eligible (GEL 181)
Newly ineligible (GEL 194)
Newly eligible (GEL 170)
Always ineligible (GEL 338)

Legend:
- Newly eligible
- Always eligible
- Newly ineligible

- Food, beverages, and tobacco
- Clothing and footwear
- Household goods
- Health care
- Fuel and electricity
- Transport
- Education
- Other

Source: Calculations based on IHS 2013.
Note: Weighted data at the household level based on persons living in households eligible/noneligible to TSA. Total cash expenditure in parentheses is PAE. GEL = Georgian lari; PAE = per adult equivalent; TSA = Targeted Social Assistance.

from families with one or two children and 29 percent from families with three or more children. Conversely, 70 percent of the newly ineligibles come from families without children and only 6 percent have three or more children. The same pattern is observed for the intensive margin winners and losers (see table 6.6 at the end of this section).

Most of the families with children that enter the program come from the second decile. Figure 6.13, panel c, shows the distribution of beneficiaries for families with children before and after the reform. After the reform, a smaller percentage of beneficiary households with children goes to the bottom decile. However, this result is driven by the fact that there is a higher number of beneficiary households with children in the second decile (not resulting from a fall in the absolute number of beneficiary households in the bottom decile).

Other winners in terms of demographic groups are rural households. Although there are more extensive margin losers than winners among urban households (coverage of urban households goes down from 9.5 percent to 7.2 percent), there is a considerable reshuffling. This is indicated by the large percentages of rural newly eligible and ineligibles compared to its share of the total population: 77 percent of winners and 72 percent of losers are rural households, compared to their proportion of 50 percent of the total population (see tables 6.5 and 6.6).

No conclusions can be drawn for male- and female-headed households. While the percentage of male-headed households that are newly eligible is similar to the representation of this group in the total population (71 versus 74 percent, respectively), many more female-headed households become ineligible for the TSA program relative to their share in the total population

Figure 6.13 Distribution of Prereform and Postreform Beneficiaries, by Select Demographic Groups and Decile

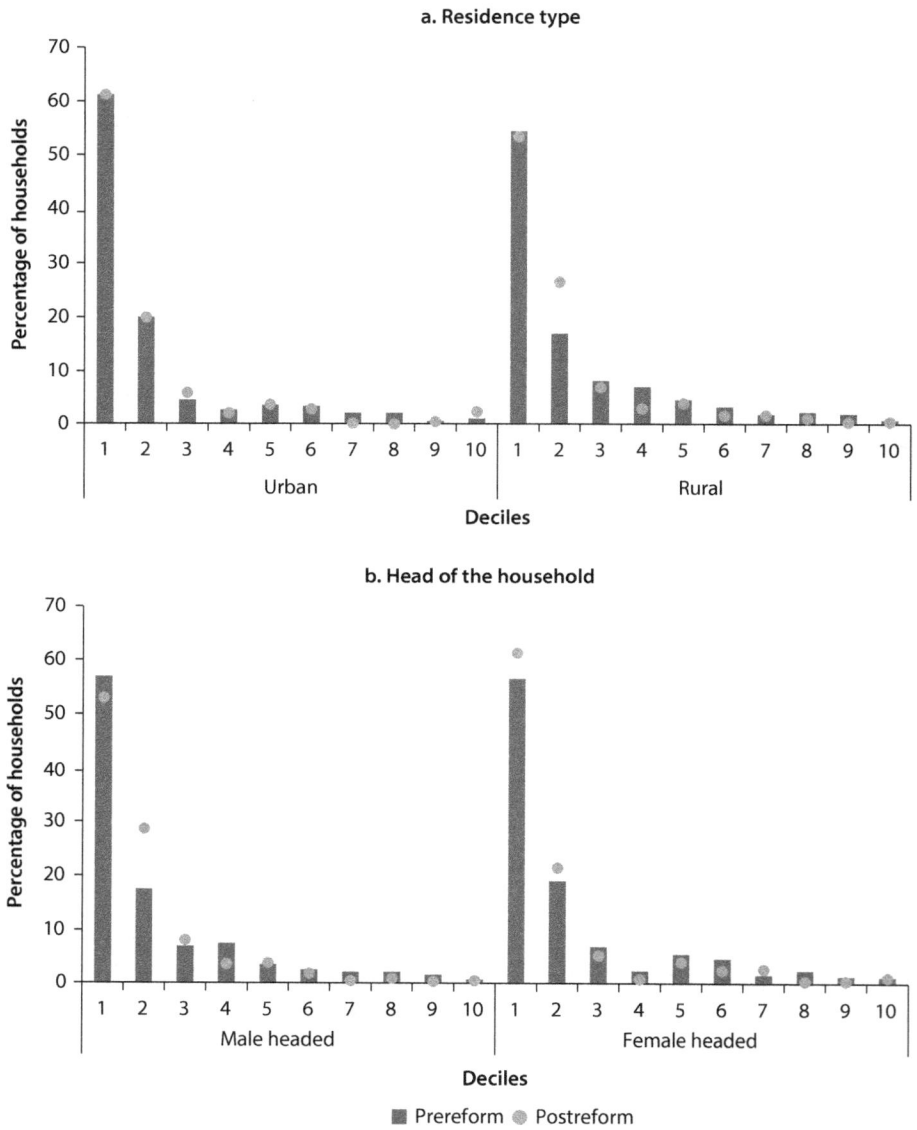

a. Residence type

b. Head of the household

■ Prereform ● Postreform

figure continues next page

Figure 6.13 Distribution of Prereform and Postreform Beneficiaries, by Select Demographic Groups and Decile (continued)

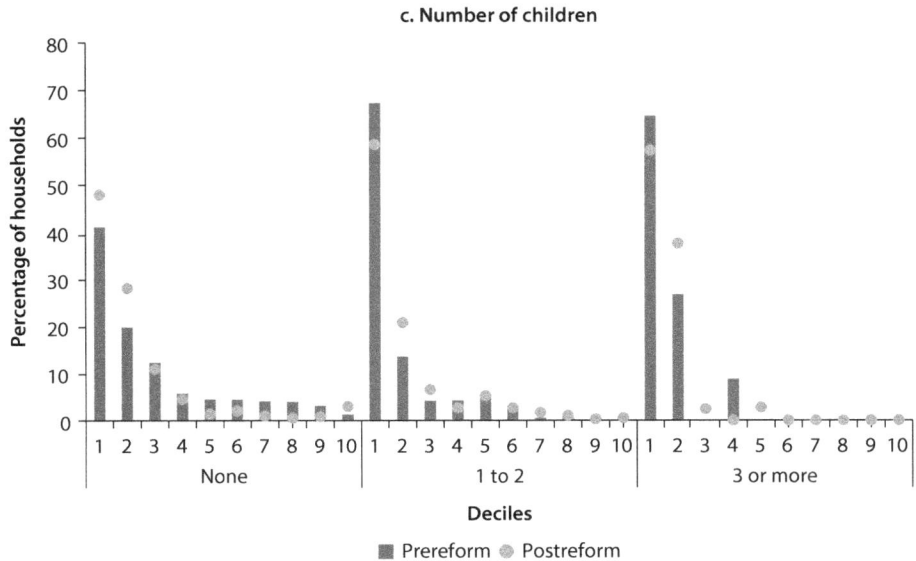

c. Number of children

Source: Calculations based on IHS 2013.
Note: Winners and losers defined within demographic group following definitions of box 6.1. Pre-TSA consumption PAE deciles. PAE = per adult equivalent; TSA = Targeted Social Assistance.

Table 6.5 Current and Postreform TSA Coverage, by Demographic Categories

Demographic category	Prereform coverage (%)	Postreform coverage (%)
Residence type		
Urban	9.48	7.19
Rural	18.68	13.53
Female head of household		
No	11.51	9.21
Yes	19.59	12.81
Number of children		
None	14.28	6.56
1 or 2	12.89	14.64
3 and more	20.69	29.16
Highest level of education for any member of household		
Lower secondary or less	34.60	22.98
Upper secondary	26.07	18.58
Secondary vocational or professional	16.84	12.41
Higher +	4.14	3.60

Note: TSA = Targeted Social Assistance.

Table 6.6 Distribution of Winners and Losers (Intensive and Extensive Margin), by Demographic Group

percent

Demographic categories	Always ineligible	Newly eligible	Newly ineligible	Always eligible Benefit reduction	Always eligible Benefit increase	Total
Residence type						
Urban	52.7	23.4	28.3	38.4	34.1	49.2
Rural	47.3	76.6	71.7	61.6	65.9	50.8
Female-headed household						
No	75.7	71.2	62.2	59.6	66.6	73.9
Yes	24.3	28.8	37.8	40.4	33.4	26.1
Number of children						
None	45.3	21.6	78.5	42.6	7.6	43.8
1 or 2	47.8	50.8	17.0	51.8	63.8	47.8
3 and more	6.9	27.6	4.5	5.6	28.6	8.5
Highest level of education for any member of household						
Lower secondary or less	1.9	10.2	7.7	8.2	2.0	2.7
Upper secondary	18.5	48.5	46.8	42.9	47.5	23.1
Secondary vocational	24.2	25.2	36.3	28.0	34.2	25.2
University	55.5	16.1	9.2	20.8	16.2	48.9

Source: Calculations based on IHS 2013.
Note: Winners and losers defined within demographic group following definitions of box 6.1.

(38 versus 26 percent, respectively).[4] However, this result should be taken with caution for two reasons. First, "female-headed household" in Georgia does not mean single-female-adult households. In many cases, the head is the female elder living in the household, and this is not the main breadwinner. Second, the definition of headship used by the IHS might be different than that of the TSA registration. Caution in interpretation is needed given that the group of female-headed households overlaps with single-elderly pensioners, who were identified as more likely to be newly ineligible.

Overall, when examining the intensive margin winners and losers, most of the results coming from the average are driven by the changes in the bottom quintile of the welfare distribution. As expected, since most of the households in the TSA are in the bottom quintile, information presented in figure 6.14 corroborates that the results described in the preceding paragraph come from reshuffling in the bottom quintile, especially for rural and female-headed households.

Examining Potentially Overlapping Effects

So far, the analysis has focused on each household characteristic in isolation. However, there are overlaps among groups of interest, and some of the observed bivariate relationships could describe a single phenomenon. For instance,

Figure 6.14 Distribution of Intensive Margin Winners and Losers for Rural and Female-Headed Households, by Quintile

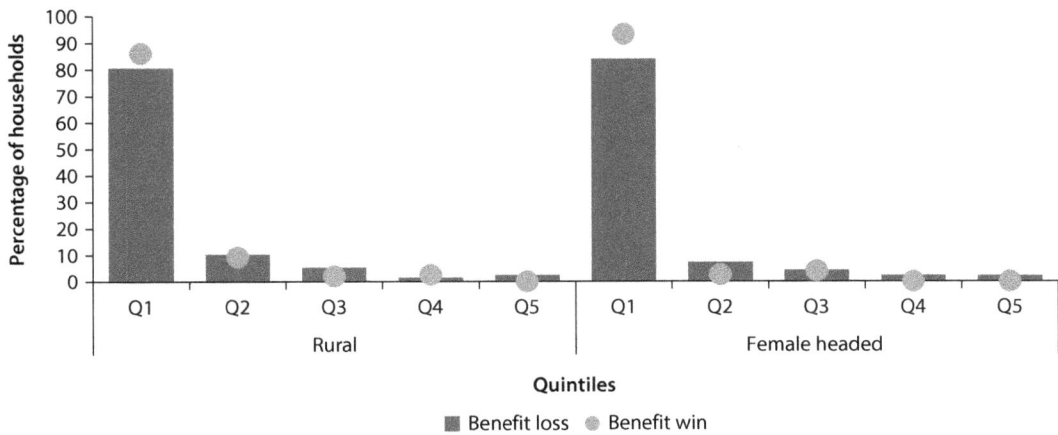

Source: Calculations based on IHS 2013.
Note: Winners and losers defined within demographic group following definitions of box 6.1. Pre-TSA consumption PAE deciles.
PAE = per adult equivalent; Q = quintile; TSA = Targeted Social Assistance.

disabled beneficiaries are also likely to be single nonworking pensioners;[5] female-headed households are also likely to be single pensioners.[6] This section examines marginal contributions of various characteristics using regression analysis. The regressions are used to describe the underlying associations only and are not intended to show causality. In particular, they seek to identify the variables that are correlated with (1) the probability of losing eligibility under the new targeting methodology and (2) the probability of having reduced benefits if remaining eligible. One set of regression results excludes controls for pre-TSA consumption level of the household, while the other includes them.

The probability of becoming ineligible is higher for single nonworking pensioners, households without children, and households whose members hold upper secondary and vocational secondary or professional degrees. In the regressions, the effect on the disability indicator indicates that the disabled are no more likely to be excluded once the presence of single pensioners and persons with specific health needs is accounted for. This does not mean that concerns about the impact of the change in the targeting methodology on the disabled should be discounted. In fact, it suggests that while being a single pensioner is more closely linked to the chance of losing eligibility, many of the single pensioners also suffer from disabilities—that is, they exhibit multiple and overlapping vulnerabilities.

It is not clear whether the revised eligibility formula removes from the program those households who have the capacity to provide for themselves (households with nonemployed adults). More analysis is required to draw conclusions on the correlation with the presence of an unemployed adult in the household, because the variable is significant in all cases but of opposite value depending on the estimation model (negative in the linear probability model but positive in the logit). If it were corroborated that households with spare labor are less likely to lose eligibility—even after accounting for the number of children in these households and consumption levels—then there is a concern, as the program retains those households who have the capacity to provide for themselves while removing those who cannot.

These conclusions are altered when controlling for the level of consumption. Table 6.8 repeats the estimates of table 6.7 but adds as controls the quantile of distribution of the household. None of the results change.

Summary

This reform maintains constant coverage and reshuffles beneficiaries. As a result, the revision of the PMT formula creates winners and losers, both in terms of eligibility to the TSA program and in terms of the size of transfer. The group that bears the burden of the reform is the single pensioners. While the TSA served 21,299 single-pensioner persons, after the reform it is expected to benefit only 3,922 persons. The other category of households affected is that of disabled and

Table 6.7 Regression Results for Probability of Losing Benefits, without Consumption Controls

	HH no longer eligible[a]		HH receives reduced benefit[b]	
	OLS	Logit	OLS	Logit
Independent variables				
Urban	−0.062	0.611	0.010	1.073
HH has a disabled member	−0.078*	0.586*	−0.168**	0.380**
HH has a person with specific health needs	0.013	1.094	−0.148*	0.465*
Single nonworking pensioner	0.358***	7.484***	−0.123	0
HH has an IDP	0.102	1.779	0.086	1.648
Female-headed HH	−0.111**	0.488**	−0.038	0.777
HH has no children	0.378***	9.724***	0.467***	13.678***
Education				
Upper secondary	0.090	2.368	−0.224*	0.247*
Secondary vocational	0.157**	3.402**	−0.235*	0.239*
University +	0.045	1.263	−0.048	0.709
Nonemployed adult	−0.152***	0.376***	−0.203**	0.304**
Constant	0.184**	0.136***	0.838***	8.402**
Number of observations	409	409	232	221
R-squared	0.303	0.274	0.262	0.217

Note: The table displays regression results for probability of losing benefits and receiving reduced benefit among those who remain eligible, without consumption controls (marginal effects reported). Pseudo R-squares shown for logit models. *Education* refers to maximum educational attainment of any HH member. HH = household; IDP = internally displaced person; OLS = ordinary least squares.
a. 1 if newly ineligible and 0 if always eligible.
b. 1 if reduced benefit and 0 if increased benefit.
Significance level: *$p<0.1$, **$p<0.05$, ***$p<0.01$.

Continuous Improvement • http://dx.doi.org/10.1596/978-1-4648-0900-2

Table 6.8 Regression Results for Probability of Losing Benefits, with Consumption Controls

	HH no longer eligible[a]		HH receives reduced benefit[b]	
	OLS	Logit	OLS	Logit
Independent variables				
Urban	−0.033	0.699	0.005	1.052
HH has a disabled member	−0.093**	0.487**	−0.179**	0.351**
HH has a person with specific health needs	−0.001	0.977	−0.156**	0.439**
Single nonworking pensioner	0.288***	8.507***	−0.141	
HH has an IDP	0.121	2.216	0.100	1.799
Female-headed HH	−0.091**	0.459**	−0.028	0.856
HH has no children	0.329***	9.191***	0.461***	13.446***
Education				
Upper secondary	0.138*	4.682**	−0.196	0.267
Secondary vocational	0.170**	5.497**	−0.232*	0.221*
University +	0.055	1.310	−0.026	0.731
Nonemployed adult	−0.096**	0.516**	−0.185**	0.336**
Consumption quintile				
Q2	0.229**	3.984**	0.060	1.739
Q3	0.290***	6.832***	0.245	4.530*
Q4	0.412***	25.55***	−0.159	0.457
Q5	0.280***	5.767***	0.317***	
Constant	0.060	0.0410***	0.795***	6.984**
Number of observations	409	409	232	217
R-squared	0.370	0.350	0.277	0.228

Note: This table displays regression results for probability of losing benefits and receiving reduced benefit for those who remain eligible, with consumption controls (marginal effects reported). Empty cells signify that these variables were not included in the regression. Pseudo R-squares shown for logit models. *Education* refers to maximum educational attainment of any HH member. HH = household; IDP = internally displaced person; OLS = ordinary least squares; Q = quintile.
a. 1 if newly ineligible and 0 if always eligible.
b. 1 if reduced benefit and 0 if increased benefit.
Significance level: $*p<0.1, **p<0.05, ***p<0.01$.

persons with specific health needs, with 25,006 persons losing TSA benefits. On the other side of the spectrum, families with children are clear winners. While 80 percent of the newly eligible households have children, 70 percent of the newly ineligible have no children.

There are overlaps between certain groups of interest, and some of the observed bivariate relationships could describe a single phenomenon. For instance, disabled beneficiaries are also likely to be single nonworking pensioners, and female-headed households are also likely to be single pensioners. Also, the effect on the disability indicator in the ordinary least squares (OLS) and logit regressions indicates that the disabled are not more likely to be excluded once the presence of single pensioners and specific health needs is accounted for.

Continuous Improvement • http://dx.doi.org/10.1596/978-1-4648-0900-2

Besides reshuffling beneficiaries, the revision of the PMT increases targeting accuracy and maintains pro-poor distribution among narrowly defined population groups. As expected from the discussion in this chapter, when analyzing the winners and losers, most of the reshuffling still manages to bring more people from the bottom of the welfare distribution within each category analyzed into the TSA program. Most of these gains within categories come from households in the second decile or even the second quintile.

The improvements in targeting due to the reform as seen in the simulations are likely to be attenuated during implementation. It must be kept in mind that the comparison drawn here is between the current TSA performance, which already reflects inaccuracies and errors related to implementation, and the theoretical (ideal) performance of the revised targeting model. When implemented, the revised PMT model is likely to perform worse than these estimates due to a number of possible factors, including (1) lower than expected take-up (since not all poor are likely to register for the scheme); (2) errors in collection of applicant data by social agents, combined with potential bottlenecks in the grievance and case-management system; and (3) possible instances of misrepresentation and manipulation of data by household members, and so on. Nevertheless, these effects are expected to be very small given that management processes function very well.

Compensation measures were needed and adopted for some social categories. The analysis points to the disproportionate disqualification of the disabled, persons with specific health needs, and single nonworking pensioners. Even when accompanied by a parallel admission of persons from these categories to other programs and benefit increases to some of the existing beneficiaries, these "losers" produced by adjustments to the targeting methodology should be carefully considered, because the individuals in these categories are commonly regarded as socially vulnerable. Compensation measures are discussed in chapter 9.

Notes

1. Coverage is defined as the share of beneficiaries in the total population. Unless explicitly stated otherwise, coverage figures consider direct and indirect beneficiaries, that is, *all* members of beneficiary households.

2. *Disabled persons* include (1) persons with sharply expressed disability (group one), (2) persons with significantly expressed disability (group two), (3) persons with a moderately expressed disability (group three), (4) children with disability (under the age of 18), (5) blind persons (disability of the first group), (6) ill persons (including persons confined to bed), (7) persons who cannot move without assistance, (8) mentally ill persons registered in an outpatient clinic, and (9) mentally ill persons not registered in an outpatient clinic. *Persons with specific health needs* include (1) persons who require urgent surgery for treatment of life-threatening disease, (2) persons who require permanent medicine and/or outpatient treatment against life-threatening disease, (3) persons who require a nurse, (4) pregnant women (20 weeks and over), and (5) breastfeeding mothers (with a child under the age of one year).

Continuous Improvement • http://dx.doi.org/10.1596/978-1-4648-0900-2

3. As per Decree of the Government of Georgia No. 145 of July 28, 2006, Article 8, *single pensioner* is defined as a pensioner (by age or by disability) who has a permanent address but does not have a breadwinner (as defined by the Civil Code of Georgia, articles 1212, 1218, 1223, 1224, 1225, 1226, 1227, 1228, 1229); or became homeless for a number of reasons and does not have a permanent address, lives with a separate household, but does not participate in the household affairs and there is proof that the household does not take care of the person.

4. Being labeled a female- or male-headed household does not necessarily mean that the designated female or male is the main breadwinner for the family. The surveys used in this study leave it up to family to decide who they declare as a household head. In half of the cases these might be the oldest member of households, in the rest, the breadwinner.

5. However, once a person reaches the age of retirement he or she is no longer assessed for disability. Thus, with the current data it cannot be determined if a disabled person is also a single pensioner.

6. To be more precise, in the total population, the female-headed single-pensioner households represent 73 percent of all single pensioners' households, but only 5 percent of all female-headed households.

References

IHS (Integrated Household Survey). 2013. GeoStat, Tbilisi. http://www.geostat.ge/?action =meurneoba&mpid=1&lang=eng.

UNICEF (United Nations Children's Fund). 2010. "Education in Georgia—Country Profile." UNICEF, New York.

CHAPTER 7

Winners from the CBP

Introduction

Chapter 7 examines the performance of the Child Benefit Program (CBP). It focuses on coverage, distribution of beneficiaries and benefits, and resulting winners and losers of the reform. Clearly, all CBP beneficiaries will be winners, as the program did not exist in 2013. Thus, this chapter links the results to those of chapter 6 to understand if this transfer alleviates the losses of households affected by the revision of the eligibility formula of the Targeted Social Assistance (TSA) program.

The CBP will provide support to 265,400 children. As shown in table 7.1, many of these children live in households that will receive TSA support after the reform (366,810 persons in households with TSA and children) while many others live in households that will not (390,409 persons in households without TSA and children). With the introduction of the new program, the support from the Social Services Agency (SSA) spreads in smaller amounts to a larger number of households.

Who's Winning from the Child Benefit Program

Only 20 percent of prereform beneficiaries will not qualify for either program, TSA or CBP, based on estimations before the introduction of compensation measures. This 20 percent comprises mostly households with adults. By design, the reform benefits families with children, and only 3 percent of prereform beneficiaries with children will not qualify for any program.

Not only does the targeting performance of the TSA improve, but the combination of programs remains pro-poor. Figure 7.1 shows the coverage of the TSA and CBP by decile before and after the reform. It shows that coverage of TSA recipient households with children increases after the reform, especially in the bottom quintile, and also in the third decile (green bar is taller than striped bar). On top of this, the CBP will add support to families with children, and most of it goes to the bottom half of the distribution. However, this program has some

Table 7.1 Child Benefit Program Beneficiaries and TSA Eligibility Before and After the PMT Reform

| | Postreform TSA vulnerability score (and eligibility) | | | | | |
| | Score 0–65,000 | | Score 65,000–100,000 | | Score 100,000+ | |
Prereform TSA eligibility status	TSA with children	TSA w/o children	No TSA with children	No TSA w/o children	No TSA with children	No TSA w/o children
Nonbeneficiary	114,948	31,602	369,142	127,895	1,283,804	1,242,922
Beneficiary	251,862	87,249	21,267	61,809	4,357	31,570

Source: Calculations based on Integrated Household Survey (IHS) 2013 estimation sample (additional module data).
Note: TSA eligible with vulnerability score under 65,000 with the new PMT formula. PMT = proxy means test; TSA = Targeted Social Assistance.

Figure 7.1 Coverage of CBP and TSA Beneficiaries

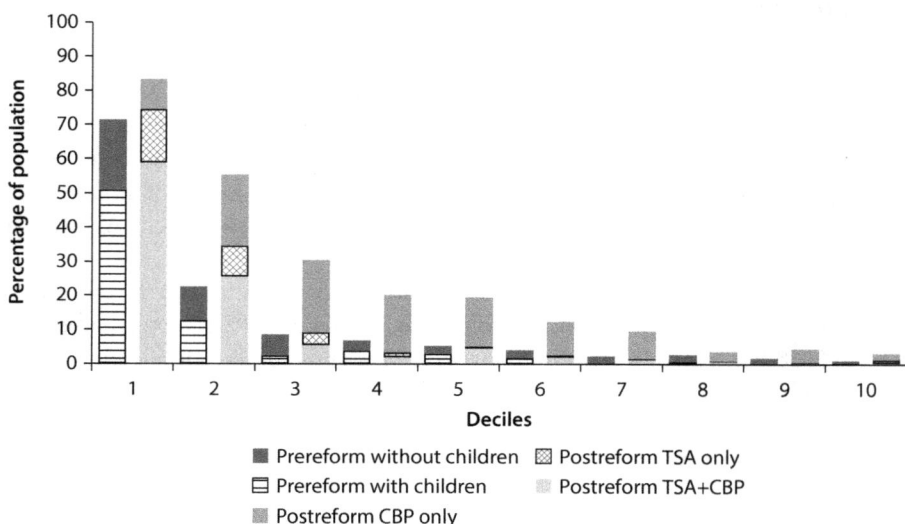

Source: Calculations based on IHS 2013 estimation sample (additional module data).
Note: Deciles from total pre-TSA consumption per adult equivalent (PAE). Population-weighted estimates. CBP = Child Benefit Program; TSA = Targeted Social Assistance.

leakage in the top deciles, even with the improvements of the revised eligibility formula.

The distribution of beneficiaries of the CBP is more spread along the deciles in the bottom half of the distribution. Since the CBP is distributed using a less restrictive threshold, by definition its targeting accuracy will be lower. However, this is relative as the threshold is set higher. Also, programs that are not narrowly targeted to the poor are not less accurate if they are reaching the intended group. Figure 7.2 shows that the distribution of beneficiaries of the CBP is less skewed to the bottom than that of the TSA—either pre- or postreform. Still, consumption of households with CBP is more similar to those of the TSA than those that are left out of the TSA or the CBP (figure 7.3).

Figure 7.2 Distribution of CBP and TSA Beneficiaries Before and After the Reform

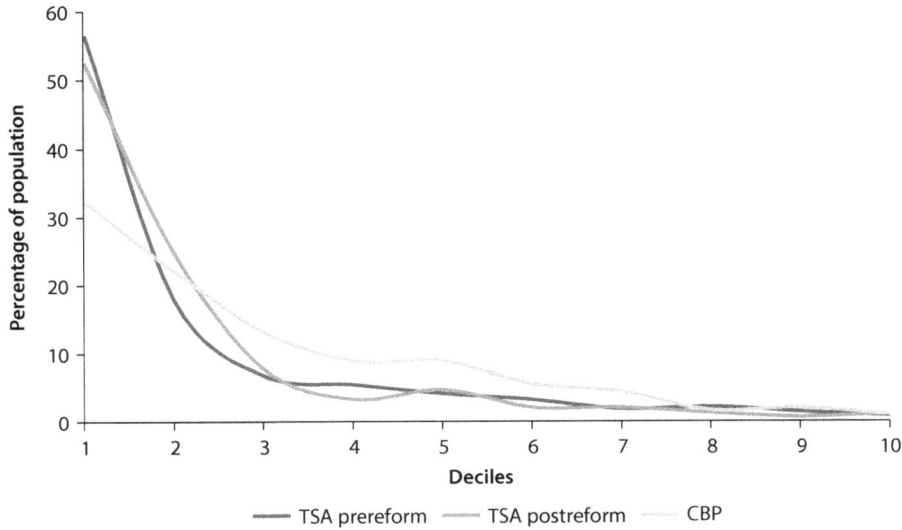

Source: Calculations based on IHS 2013 estimation sample (additional module data).
Note: Deciles from total pre-TSA consumption PAE. Population-weighted estimates based on persons living in households eligible/noneligible to TSA. CBP = Child Benefit Program; PAE = per adult equivalent; TSA = Targeted Social Assistance.

Figure 7.3 Cumulative Distribution of Consumption for Different TSA Vulnerability Scores (per Adult Equivalent)

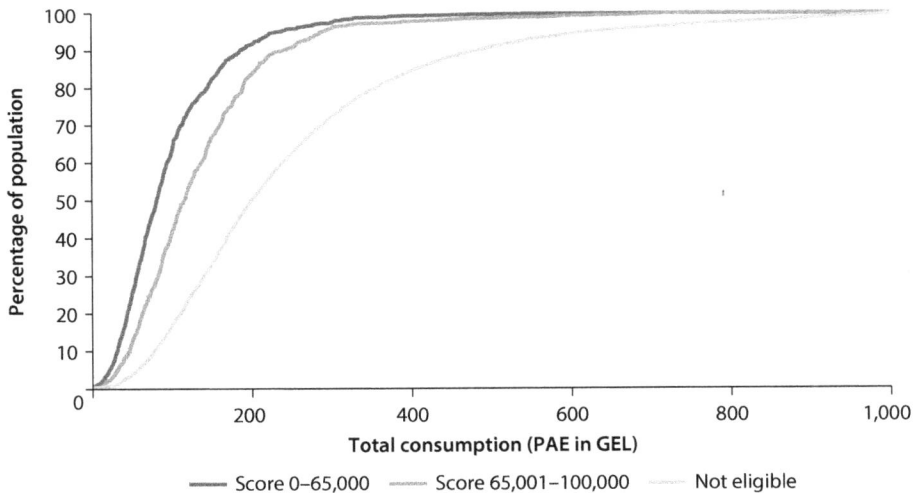

Source: Calculations based on IHS 2013.
Note: Deciles from total pre-TSA consumption PAE. Population-weighted estimates based on persons living in households eligible/noneligible to TSA. GEL = Georgian lari; PAE = per adult equivalent; TSA = Targeted Social Assistance.

Figure 7.4 Disaggregation of Consumption Spending by TSA Score

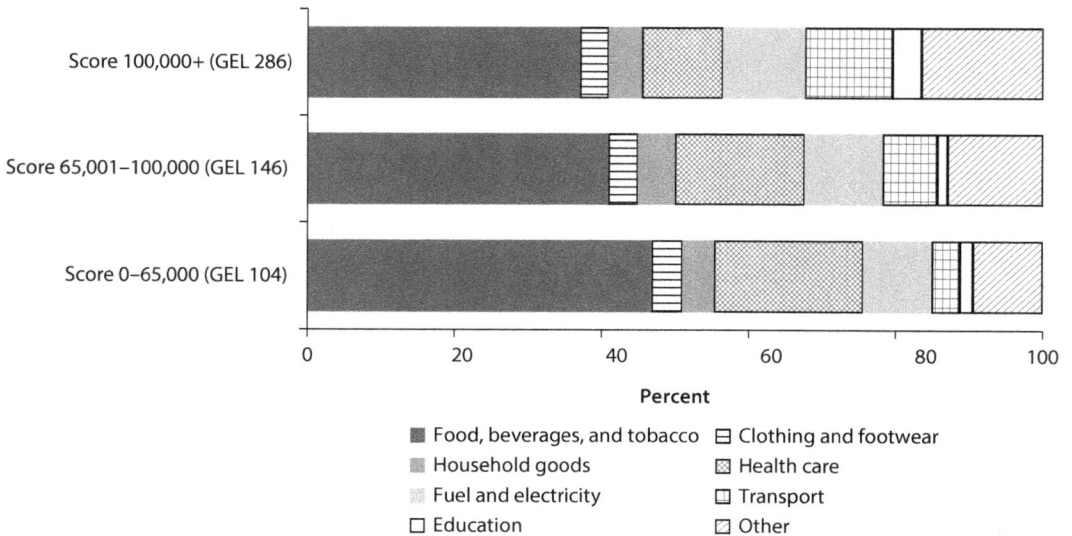

Note: Weighted data at the household level. Total cash expenditure in parentheses. GEL = Georgian lari; TSA = Targeted Social Assistance.

Some CBP beneficiaries are less vulnerable than TSA beneficiaries but are much more vulnerable than those left out of both programs. When looking at the expenditure per adult equivalent (PAE), it is clear that those receiving solely CBP (score 65,001–100,000 with children) are better off than those receiving the TSA (score 0–65,000, with or without children). However, they are still far away from the rest of the population (score 100,000+). The average monthly spending PAE of those with scores of 0–65,000 is GEL (Georgian lari) 104 per month, while for those with scores of 65,001–100,000 it is 44 percent higher (GEL 146). See figure 7.4 for more details.

Note that those who receive only CBP allocate resources differently than those with lower scores. Households with scores of 65,001–100,000 spend 6 percent less of their budgets on food, beverages, and tobacco. As household income increases, a larger proportion of income is allocated to expenditures on other types of consumption. For example, these households increase spending on transportation and nonclassified goods. Furthermore, as household income increases, relatively less is allocated on food, beverages, tobacco, and health. For example, eligible households allocate 47 percent of their income on food spending while noneligible assign 37 percent.

Summary

With the revisions, the TSA program will be better at targeting and covering households with children. To further the SSA objective of providing additional support for vulnerable families, the CBP will spread small amounts of support to a larger number of households. Together, the programs are pro-poor and focus their attention on the bottom half of the consumption distribution curve.

The CBP is able to help two main groups of vulnerable families: those who qualify for TSA and those who do not. The first group of "winners" are simultaneously TSA and CBP beneficiaries. For these households, the CBP gives an additional help to alleviate the financial hardships that come with raising children.

The second group of vulnerable families—in the third, fourth, and fifth deciles of the pre-TSA consumption distribution—may not be in conditions of extreme poverty, but they are still in need of help. Even though they are not as poor as those that qualify for TSA (as they have TSA scores of 65,001–100,000), they still lag far behind the rest of the population in terms of having the resources to meet familial needs. The CBP can be an important tool for addressing the age-specific vulnerabilities of children and the needs for the families with children. Moreover, many of these families would have been made newly ineligible for the TSA program after the reform; the CBP will help them cope with the transition. About 20 percent of the newly ineligible TSA beneficiaries will receive CBP.

Reference

IHS (Integrated Household Survey). 2013. GeoStat, Tbilisi. http://www.geostat.ge/?action =meurneoba&mpid=1&lang=eng.

From Theory to Practice: Pretesting

Introduction

Chapter 8 discusses the results of the pretest of the reformed eligibility formula (by reestimation of the proxy means test [PMT] methodology and needs index) and the benefits schemes. Many of the lessons drawn from the preliminary analysis of winners and losers were applied to formulate the framework of the pretesting. Namely, special attention was given to the following nine groups: (1) households with children, (2) pensioners, (3) people with disability, (4) internally displaced persons (IDPs), (5) households in the mountain regions, (6) pensioners with disabilities, (7) people with disabilities living in mountain regions, (8) pensioners living in mountain regions, and (9) people with disabilities living in mountain areas.

The government of Georgia moved quickly into the implementation phase of the Targeted Social Assistance (TSA) program reform. The pretesting was done between March and April 2015, once the law with the new eligibility formula was passed in December 2014. This was done with the objective of starting the reassessment of households by June 2015. The plan is to assess about a tenth or a twelfth of the beneficiaries each month and to use the new formula for those that are new to the registry. The pretest is critical to uncover potential problems that could not be accurately estimated in the distributional analysis based on household survey data, and to identify implementation issues either in the training of the social agents or in delivering the revised household declaration registry. Many times, the pretesting does not bring new information, especially if the preparatory work has been thorough. Nevertheless, this is part of the due diligence, and not catching potential implementation issues could be costly, not only administratively but also politically.

The pretest sample comes from the Social Services Agency database of the TSA applicants that have applied for the benefits since June 1, 2010, comprising 407,307 households. Using a two-stage cluster sampling, 4,560 households were selected. Full interviews were conducted in 3,565 households. The lowest response rate was observed in Tbilisi's urban area (63.6 percent) and the highest was in village-type settlements (85.6 percent). Tbilisi's low response rate

Table 8.1 Pretest Response Rate, by Areas Used in the PMT Formula

Strata type	Sampling volume	Number of responses	Response rate (%)
Capital (urban part)	720	458	63.6
Big cities	960	668	69.6
Other urban-type settlement	1,280	1,069	83.5
Village type	1,600	1,370	85.6
Total	4,560	3,565	78.2

Note: Based on administrative pretesting data of March–April 2015. PMT = proxy means test.

entails a potential bias, as it is most likely that better-off households refused to participate in the pretest. See table 8.1 with the response rates for all areas.

Results from Pretesting

The main winners of the reform are large families, in particular families with children. As expected from the prereform distributional analysis on winners and losers (chapters 6 and 7),[1] the pretesting confirmed that the largest groups negatively affected by the change are single pensioners and adults with disabilities (Berulava 2015). The results of the pretest also showed the discrepancy in coverage rates of the capital city. The reason is related to the low response rate; higher differences in the mean values of indicators are likely to come from richer households that were not part of the pretesting, that is, households participating in the interview were poorer than the average registered household. This fact demands that readers use caution when interpreting the results from the pretesting in Tbilisi. Nevertheless and overall, the pretest confirms findings of the projections conducted while the methodology was being developed.

The number of people covered will remain practically unchanged. Even though the overall number of beneficiaries does not change much, there is a reshuffling among groups who will be targeted by the revised eligibility formula. Table 8.2 shows the numbers of beneficiaries for each of the groups of interest coming from the pretesting sample. While there is an 8 percentage point increase in the coverage of children and IDP populations, there are reductions in the coverage of pensioners (16 percentage points) and adults with disabilities (14 percentage points). Noticeably, the results arising for IDP populations in the pretesting differ from those of the household survey. While results from the household survey (table 6.3 in chapter 6) indicated that the total number of IDPs covered before and after the reform would increase, the results from the pretesting provide a more accurate estimate of this important gain for this group (table 8.2). The gain is as large as that identified for families with children, who without doubt are the big winners of the reform. This difference very likely comes from the fact that in the pretesting the sample was derived from the household declaration registry, and certain groups, such as IDPs, tend to register themselves for assistance more than others.

Table 8.2 TSA Beneficiaries for Select Groups of Population, Before and After the Reform

Category	Prereform formula		Newly recalculated prereform formula		Postreform formula	
	Number	Percent	Number	Percent	Number	Percent
Population	441,114	33.8	332,928	25.5	433,220	33.2
Children	102,024	39.9	81,432	31.8	122,792	48.0
Pensioners	79,447	34.0	49,873	21.3	40,766	17.4
Adults with disability	53,505	49.4	46,764	43.2	38,283	35.3
IDPs	34,515	41.8	23,912	28.6	41,081	49.1
Mountain	61,865	33.4	42,135	22.7	57,592	31.1
Pensioners and disabilities	17,917	47.0	15,663	41.1	9,944	26.1
Pensioners, disabilities, and mountain	1,637	39.6	1,505	36.4	1,401	33.9
Pensioners and mountain	12,394	33.6	6,195	16.8	5,367	14.6
Disabilities and mountain	5,463	41.6	5,060	38.6	4,717	35.9

Note: All groups of population are registered in the Social Services Agency's database for vulnerable families. *Pensioners* refers to the Old Age Pension recipients. Percentages represent current TSA beneficiaries in the corresponding category. *Pensioners and disabilities* refers to pensioners who have disabilities. IDPs = internally displaced persons; TSA = Targeted Social Assistance.

The new methodology favors larger families. The average family size of beneficiary households identified by the new PMT formula is 3.85, while family sizes for the status quo formula as well as for recalculated status quo are 3.07 and 3.24, respectively. Such changes also led to a 31 percent increase of mean monthly TSA amount per household.

The new formula performs better than the recalculated status quo (preform) formula when comparing coverage by regions. The new formula—either when it increases the number of potential beneficiaries compared to the status quo scores or when it decreases the coverage—still performs better compared to the recalculated status quo. Most of the gains are observed in Tbilisi, Guria, Mtskheta-Mtianeti, Samegrelo, Samtskhe-Javakheti, and Kvemo Kartli (table 8.3). In other regions where the coverage goes down, the new formula still performs better than the recalculated status quo, except in Racha.

The largest groups made ineligible by the revision of the eligibility formula are pensioners and adults with disabilities. Table 8.4 shows the number of current TSA beneficiaries that lose eligibility according to the pretesting for each of the groups of interest. The pretesting corroborates the findings from the previous chapters as pensioners—especially those living in mountain areas—is the group that is affected the most by the reform. However, it is interesting to note that part of the loss in terms of eligibility already comes from the newly recalculated status quo formula, not from the revision of the methodology (51 and 63 percent, respectively, for pensioners living in mountain areas).

The new formula shows lower rates than the recalculated status quo of withdrawal for the population in all regions except for Racha and Guria (table 8.5). At the same time, Guria will have a higher number of beneficiaries than the status quo or the newly recalculated status quo. However, the same cannot be said about Racha. Again, these regional patterns might arise in the pretesting because the number of observations is larger compared to the household survey.

Table 8.3 TSA Beneficiaries for Regions, Before and After the Reform

Region	Prereform formula		Newly recalculated prereform formula		Postreform formula	
	Number	Percent	Number	Percent	Number	Percent
Tbilisi	94,842	41.72	81,128	35.69	96,738	42.55
Guria	11,885	21.40	13,917	25.05	15,787	28.42
Racha	8,913	60.06	7,465	50.30	7,849	52.89
Kakheti	57,404	43.19	47,829	35.98	54,066	40.68
Imereti	82,686	30.97	56,138	21.02	69,752	26.12
Mtskheta-Mtianeti	10,042	34.33	5,740	19.63	15,199	51.96
Samegrelo	34,050	25.36	22,113	16.47	35,040	26.10
Samtskhe-Javakheti	4,771	26.59	3,830	21.34	5,190	28.92
Kvemo Kartli	27,686	29.58	23,772	25.40	33,622	35.93
Shida Kartli	63,969	47.77	41,830	31.23	56,038	41.84
Ajara	44,861	22.61	29,160	14.70	43,933	22.15

Note: Percentages represent current TSA beneficiaries in the corresponding category. Information for Racha-Lechkhumi-Kvemo Svaneti is merged with Imereti in the study dataset and therefore not reported. TSA = Targeted Social Assistance.

Table 8.4 Current TSA Beneficiary Population Becoming Newly Ineligible to TSA, by Newly Recalculated Pre- and Postreform Formula

Category	Newly recalculated prereform formula		Postreform formula	
	Number	Percent	Number	Percent
Population	142,501	32.30	99,948	22.66
Children	27,117	26.58	6,782	6.65
Pensioners	35,415	44.58	46,049	57.96
Adults with disability	10,942	20.45	18,601	34.77
IDPs	15,000	43.46	9,372	27.15
Mountain	21,720	35.11	15,129	24.45
Pensioners and disabilities	4,374	24.42	8,731	48.73
Pensioners, disabilities, and mountain	131	8.02	558	34.13
Pensioners and mountain	6,296	50.81	7,871	63.52
Disabilities and mountain	615	11.27	1,453	26.61

Note: Percentages represent current TSA beneficiaries in the corresponding category. *Pensioners and disabilities* refers to pensioners who have disabilities. IDPs = internally displaced persons; TSA = Targeted Social Assistance.

The new formula also has the highest incoming population, compared to the recalculated status quo. This is especially true for IDPs and children, which show the highest percentage of newcomers—38.8 percent and 22.4 percent, respectively (see table 8.6). As discussed in table 8.2, it is worth noting that IDPs are now identified as winners of the reform.

With the introduction of the new eligibility formula, the total funds required for the TSA and the CBP financing will increase by approximately GEL (Georgian lari) 1,400,000 (or by 6 percent) and amount to GEL 24,298,441 per month. All regions, with the exception of Racha, Imereti, and Shida Kartli, will

Table 8.5 Current TSA Beneficiary Population Newly Ineligible to TSA across Regions, by Newly Recalculated Pre- and Postreform Formula

Region	Newly recalculated prereform formula		Postreform formula	
	Number	Percent	Number	Percent
Tbilisi	21,778	9.58	19,797	8.71
Guria	989	1.78	1,407	2.53
Racha	1,969	13.27	2,601	17.53
Kakheti	16,344	12.30	11,487	8.64
Imereti	27,508	10.30	23,988	8.98
Mtskheta-Mtianeti	4,796	16.40	1,534	5.25
Samegrelo	15,376	11.45	10,652	7.93
Samtskhe-Javakheti	1,670	9.31	726	4.05
Kvemo Kartli	6,411	6.85	4,560	4.87
Shida Kartli	28,632	21.38	14,578	10.89
Ajara	17,024	8.58	8,614	4.34

Note: Percentages represent current TSA beneficiaries in the corresponding category. Information for Racha-Lechkhumi-Kvemo Svaneti is merged with Imereti in the study dataset and therefore not reported. TSA = Targeted Social Assistance.

Table 8.6 Beneficiary Population Newly Eligible to the TSA Program, by the Newly Recalculated Pre- and Postreform Formula

Category	Newly recalculated prereform formula		Postreform formula	
	Number	Percent	Number	Percent
Population	34,314	10.31	92,054	21.25
Children	6,525	8.01	27,550	22.44
Pensioners	5,841	11.71	7,368	18.08
Adults with disabilities	4,200	8.98	3,378	8.83
IDPs	4,396	18.39	15,937	38.80
Mountain	1,991	4.73	10,856	18.85
Pensioners and disabilities	2,120	13.54	757	7.62
Pensioners, disabilities, and mountain	0	0	322	23.02
Pensioners and mountain	98	1.58	845	15.75
Disabilities and mountain	213	4.21	708	15.01

Note: Percentages represent current TSA beneficiaries in the corresponding categories. Pensioners and disabilities refers to pensioners who have disabilities. IDPs = internally displaced persons; TSA = Targeted Social Assistance.

get higher amounts of financing according to the new formula (see table 8.7). The highest rates of growth go to Mtskheta-Mtianeti (61.6 percent), Guria (39.6 percent), and Kvemo Kartli (29.7 percent).

On average, the TSA amount received by each household will increase by almost GEL 50 (31 percent increase) per month, which implies a transfer of GEL 210 for the average household. The highest amounts of assistance received will be in households in Ajara (GEL 255.78), followed by Kakheti (GEL 219.71), Racha (GEL 214.73), Tbilisi (GEL 215.85), and Mtskheta–Mtianeti (GEL 212.7) (see table 8.8).

Continuous Improvement • http://dx.doi.org/10.1596/978-1-4648-0900-2

Table 8.7 TSA+CBP Benefits by Region, per the Newly Recalculated Pre- and Postreform Formula (in GEL)

Region	Prereform formula	Newly recalculated prereform formula	Postreform formula
Tbilisi	4,928,574	4,200,426	5,604,627
Guria	613,754	714,373	856,938
Racha	467,070	392,807	431,539
Kakheti	2,989,103	2,471,378	3,045,463
Imereti	4,312,200	2,910,851	3,826,315
Mtskheta-Mtianeti	523,333	295,873	845,674
Samegrelo	1,778,273	1,142,303	1,915,304
Samtskhe-Javakheti	248,307	199,221	296,046
Kvemo Kartli	1,451,982	1,240,370	1,883,391
Shida Kartli	3,309,746	2,163,480	3,114,253
Ajara	2,272,757	1,482,705	2,478,891
Total	22,895,099	17,213,787	24,298,441

Note: Percentages represent current TSA beneficiaries in the corresponding categories. Information for Racha-Lechkhumi-Kvemo Svaneti is merged with Imereti in the study dataset and therefore not reported. CBP = Child Benefit Program; GEL = Georgian lari; TSA = Targeted Social Assistance.

Table 8.8 Mean Household TSA Benefit by Region per Status Quo Scores and the Newly Recalculated Pre- and Postreform Formula (in GEL)

Region	Prereform formula	Newly recalculated prereform formula	Postreform formula
Tbilisi	157.23	164.58	215.85
Guria	170.20	184.97	209.26
Racha	142.96	136.83	214.73
Kakheti	153.50	168.94	219.71
Imereti	150.75	161.54	208.57
Mtskheta-Mtianeti	152.02	174.78	212.70
Samegrelo	148.34	169.49	186.20
Samtskhe-Javakheti	154.71	155.79	179.20
Kvemo Kartli	141.60	149.89	182.32
Shida Kartli	166.03	166.84	206.96
Ajara	228.44	214.38	255.78
Total	159.59	167.50	210.69

Note: Percentages represent current TSA beneficiaries in the corresponding categories. Information for Racha-Lechkhumi-Kvemo Svaneti is merged with Imereti in the study dataset and therefore not reported. GEL = Georgian lari; TSA = Targeted Social Assistance.

Summary

The pretesting confirmed all the predictions coming from the analysis based on household survey data and shed additional light on the impact of the reform on minority groups such as the IDPs and on the regional distribution of benefits. Winners and losers identified in chapters 6 and 7 coincide with those observed during the pretesting. Pensioners are the big losers and families with children the big winners. Because the pretesting allowed oversampling of minority groups and regional coverage, more accurate estimates were obtained for these groups. Thus, the pretesting showed that IDPs will benefit from the TSA reform. At the same time, the pretesting helped to identify that mountain areas were performing as expected.

The other main objective of the pretesting was to uncover potential implementation issues that social agents could face working with the new registry. No issue appeared during the pretesting in this regard.

Note

1. In chapters 6 and 7 the analysis is conducted on the total population, while in the pretest survey only those households registered in the Database of Socially Vulnerable Families are interviewed.

Reference

Berulava, George. 2015. "Pre-testing Results of the New Methodology." Project Report, UNICEF.

CHAPTER 9

Compensation Measures

Introduction

Chapter 9 discusses the measures that Georgia introduced to minimize the adverse impacts of the Targeted Social Assistance (TSA) reform. This discussion is framed within the good practice guidance and the scattered international evidence in this matter.

Reforms generating winners and losers are usually accompanied by associated measures to maximize the impact of the reform: (1) enhancement or mitigation measures, (2) complementary measures, or (3) compensation measures. Mitigation measures take into account the context so that the design and implementation of the reform minimize the negative impact on the poor.[1] Complementary measures are those that are not directly related to the core objective of the reform but will affect the total well-being of the person. For example, complementary measures to a TSA reform that create losses among pensioners could be to raise the minimum social pension.

Compensation measures are introduced when adverse effects of a reform are unavoidable, and their goal is to directly compensate losers. The reason for compensating losers could be to minimize the impact of the reform on poverty or on inequality. But the reasons may also be related to political economy issues, especially if the losers have the capacity to organize themselves and threaten the reform itself or its sustainability.

The design of compensatory schemes has to be cost-effective and aligned with the main objective of the reform. First, the compensation measures should not distort the objective of the reform. In other words, the compensation measures should not create biases or distortions in the incentives to the point of invalidating the implementation of the reform or the objectives set at the outset of the reform. Second, the cost of the compensation scheme should be lower than the expected benefits of the reform, especially in the long run. Third, the policy maker should take into account the opportunity cost of the resources used to finance the compensation scheme—resources that could otherwise be used elsewhere, even to provide support to the losers through other policies.

It is also very important to carefully consider the sequencing of the reform, including the timing of the compensation measures and how the several measures are communicated to the population. It is advisable to build support for the reform among key stakeholders from the outset to facilitate the implementation and communication of the reform. All these aspects are critical for the sustainability of the reform process.

International evidence on compensation measures varies and depends very much on the context and the political objectives. For example, when Brazil was designing the program Bolsa Familia there was a need to migrate beneficiaries from a multiplicity of small programs at the municipal and the state levels to the federal program. The federal government decided to set a threshold high enough to include all previous beneficiaries (mitigation measures). In the few cases where the family still would not qualify for eligibility under the new federal higher threshold, families were automatically transferred to the new program anyway (compensation measures).[2] In this case, the design incorporated the mitigation measures, and there was no need to introduce compensation measures.

Other countries, although considering compensation measures when designing a reform, prefer to face the political cost of having losers rather than increase the fiscal spending on the programs. For example, Romania has been working on introducing a revised targeting system that will be used by three social programs.[3] During the design stage, various options of grandfathering—mechanisms through which the newly ineligible remain in the program or receive a separate "grandfathering transfer" indefinitely or for a limited time—were considered by the government of Romania. In particular, one of the options examined consisted of having a separate transfer for newly ineligible households for a limited period of time. Having analyzed all these options, the government of Romania decided to face the political cost of the reform and not introduce any compensation measure.

The government of Georgia decided to establish compensation measures to minimize the negative impact on single nonworking pensioners—the group that is affected the most negatively by the reform. The compensation measure introduced in August 2015 was an increment of the needs coefficient (caloric and noncaloric) of the pensioners in the needs index. In this way, the final well-being score would decrease for this group, and more of them will remain eligible. Table 9.1 shows the increment in the needs coefficient for single pensioners, which is about 50 percent for each age group.[4]

Another compensation measure introduced modifies the measurement of the utility consumption to minimize the total number of losers. As utility spending has a significant weight in the proxy means test (PMT) formula, the government will take out only the household's out-of-pocket spending, after the subsidy.[5] This benefit affects only families that apply to the Social Services Agency (SSA) for it.[6] For example, the municipality of Tbilisi provides a utility subsidy in the amount of GEL (Georgian lari) 500 to families with qualification scores below 70,000.[7]

Table 9.1 Needs Index Coefficient for Single Pensioners and Other Age Groups Before and After Compensation Measures

Status/age	Male				Female			
	(18–29)	(30–39)	(40–59)	(60+)	(18–29)	(30–39)	(40–59)	(60+)
Before	1.33	1.29	1.25	1.18	1.17	1.16	1.14	1.12
After	1.99	1.94	1.88	1.80	1.76	1.74	1.71	1.80

Source: Based on Social Services Agency reports.

Figure 9.1 Budget Implications of the TSA Reform and Compensation Measures

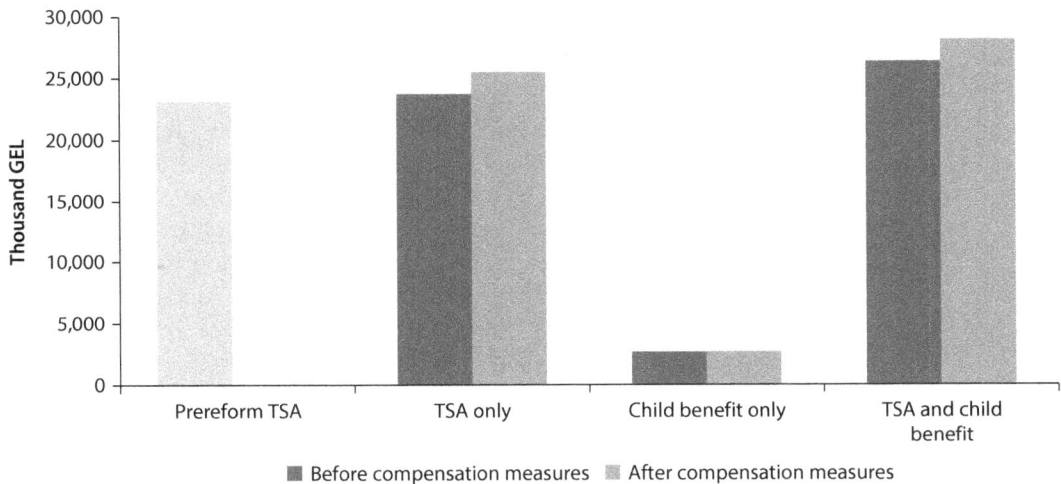

Source: Calculations based on Integrated Household Survey (IHS) 2013 estimation sample (additional module data).
Note: Persons eligible with vulnerability score lower than 57,000 for prereform eligibility formula and with scores below 65,000 for postreform eligibility formula. GEL = Georgian lari; TSA = Targeted Social Assistance.

The compensation measures will result in an increase in public expenditures of GEL 1.77 million. Figure 9.1 shows the budget changes before and after the compensation measures. As expected, the budget implications are driven mostly by the increase in the coverage of the TSA, and not by changes in coverage in the Child Benefit Program (CBP). The question going forward is whether the compensation is the best use of the additional resources dedicated to social assistance. For example, these resources could also be channeled to those that are now brought into the TSA through other programs. In particular, if the target group of compensation measures is single pensioners, it should be considered whether the same overall transfer could be done through social pensions, for example by raising the minimum social pension. This could help to (1) have a more direct link between the transfer and the group of beneficiaries and avoid having people benefit from more than one program and (2) diminish leakages at the middle and top of the welfare distribution.

Winners and Losers After Compensation Measures

After the compensation measures there are fewer losers of the reform and more winners. The new measures increased the number of beneficiaries of the program and did not generate any newly ineligible to the TSA. As a result, and compared with the situation before the reform, the number of newly eligible is expected to increase and the number of newly ineligible is expected to decrease. Table 9.2 shows that the number of newly eligible TSA beneficiaries rises from 146,550 to 155,939 (about a 6.4 percent increase in the number of newly eligible), and the number of newly ineligible TSA beneficiaries shrinks from 119,003 to 91,037 persons (about a 24 percent decrease). In other words, the compensation measures bring in 9,389 new beneficiaries and prevents 27,966 prereform beneficiaries from having to leave the program.

Targeting accuracy diminishes but efficiency improvements are maintained, especially at the bottom of the distribution. As expected, the introduction of the compensation measures increases coverage in all deciles. Targeting accuracy after compensation measures is still better than the prereform targeting situation—the coverage in the bottom two deciles increases, and coverage decreases in all the other deciles. Figure 9.2 shows the coverage of the TSA by decile for the prereform, postreform before compensation measures, and postreform after compensations measures. Clearly, coverage increased all along the distribution compared with the situation after the reform but before compensation measures. (Note that in figure 9.2 all the circles are above the triangle marks.) More important, the coverage after the compensation measures is above the prereform levels only at the very bottom of the distribution (bottom two deciles).

The measures bring into the program people from the middle (and to a lesser extent from the top) of the welfare distribution. Figure 9.3 shows the distribution of newly eligible and newly ineligible beneficiaries by deciles, before and after the introduction of the compensation measures. The number of newly eligible beneficiaries coming from the bottom deciles decreases, while it increases at the middle and top of the distribution. Instead, more of the newly ineligible now come from the bottom of the distribution. This, in a way, is causing the distortion of the targeting accuracy of the program. This is why this report recommends that the compensation measures be eliminated gradually over time.

Table 9.2 Winners and Losers Before and After Compensation Measures

	Postreform TSA status			
	Before compensation measures		After compensation measures	
Prereform TSA status	Nonbeneficiary	Beneficiary	Nonbeneficiary	Beneficiary
Nonbeneficiary	3,023,763	146,550	3,014,374	155,939
Beneficiary	119,003	339,111	91,037	367,077

Source: Calculations based on IHS 2013 estimation sample (additional module data).
Notes: Persons eligible with a vulnerability score lower than 57,000 for prereform eligibility formula and with scores below 65,000 for postreform eligibility formula. Deciles are computed using consumption pre-TSA transfer and PAE. PAE = per adult equivalent; TSA = Targeted Social Assistance.

Figure 9.2 Coverage of TSA Before and After Compensation Measures

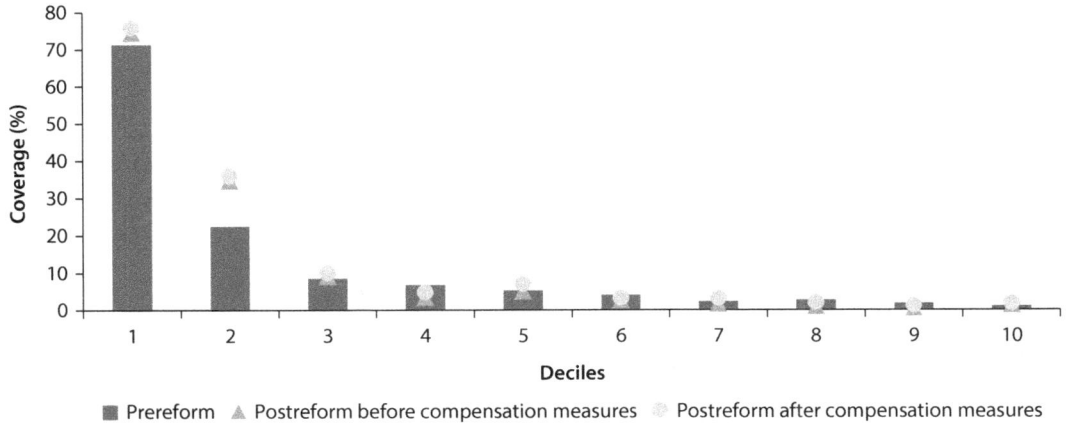

Source: Calculations based on IHS 2013 estimation sample (additional module data).
Note: Deciles are computed using consumption pre-TSA transfer and PAE. Persons eligible with a vulnerability score lower than 57,000 for prereform eligibility formula and with scores below 65,000 for postreform eligibility formula. PAE = per adult equivalent; TSA = Targeted Social Assistance.

Figure 9.3 Distribution of Extensive Winners and Extensive Losers Before and After Compensation

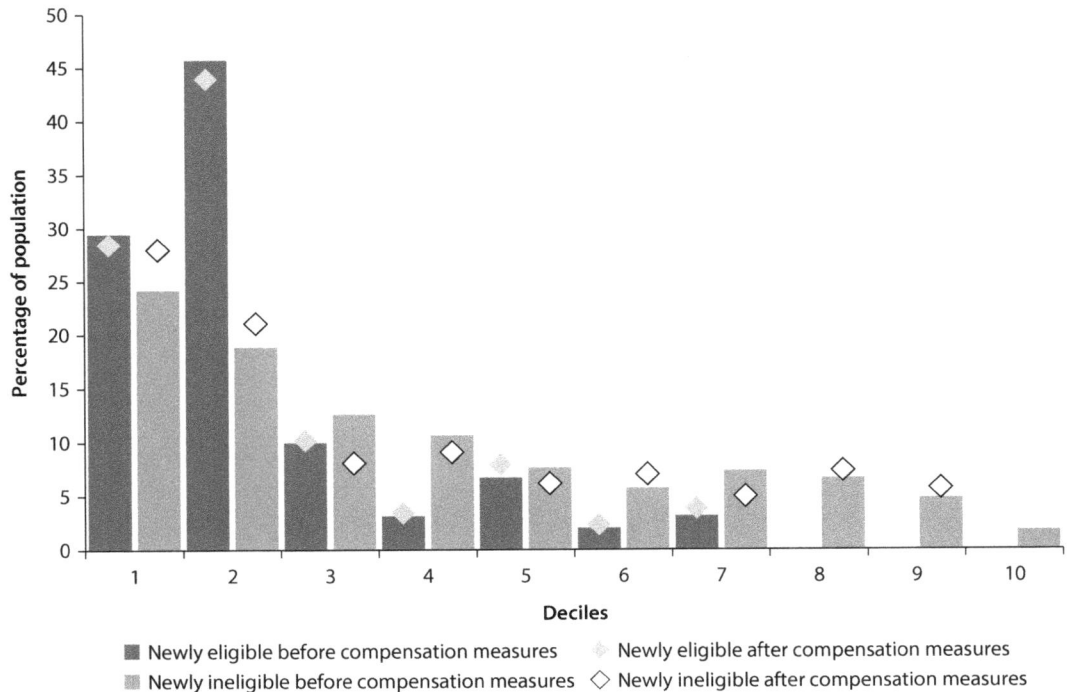

Source: Calculations based on IHS 2013 estimation sample (additional module data).
Note: Deciles are computed using consumption pre-TSA transfer and PAE based on persons living in eligible/noneligible TSA households. PAE = per adult equivalent; TSA = Targeted Social Assistance.

The compensation measures also bring more intensive margin winners and reduce the number of intensive margin losers. Figure 9.4 shows the distribution of intensive margin winners and losers. The after-compensation measures curve is below the before-compensation measures curve for negative values and above it for positive values. Now there is a smaller percentage of intensive margin winners and a higher percentage of intensive margin losers. This is explained by the fact that those who are "recovered" as TSA beneficiaries with the compensation measures are close to the eligibility threshold that is associated to a lower transfer.[8] The percentage of intensive margin losers has increased from 52 to 55 percent after the introduction of such measures.

The objective of leaving a higher number of single pensioners in the TSA program is achieved. Table 9.3 shows that the coverage of all socioeconomic groups increased. In particular, responding to the objective of the compensation measures, the coverage of the single elderly pensioners increased the most, from 6.35 to 23.7 percent. There is a small increase in coverage of internally displaced persons (IDPs). This increase may not be materialized later on, as those closer to the threshold are likely to prefer the IDP benefit to the TSA transfer, as the former is larger for those with a high vulnerability score. Notice that the IDP benefit is GEL 45, while the TSA transfer for those close to the eligibility threshold is GEL 30 per person.

The single nonworking pensioners and other social groups that are brought back in the TSA have relatively better levels of welfare. Figure 9.5 shows the distribution of single pensioners' beneficiaries by decile. After the compensation measures, the percentage of single pensioners at the bottom decile diminishes. The same result is observed for disabled persons or seriously ill persons.

Figure 9.4 Distribution of Intensive Margin Winners and Losers, by Size of Gain or Loss

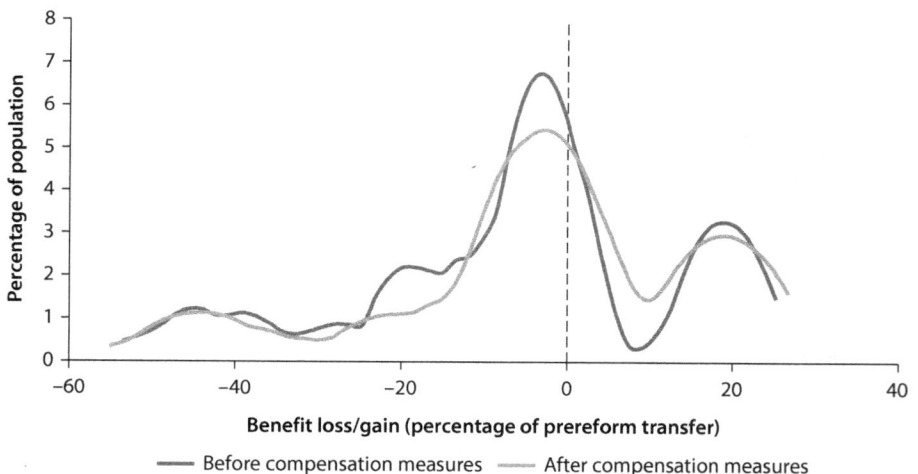

Source: Calculations based on IHS 2013 estimation sample (additional module data).
Note: Population-weighted results. Losses and gains are expressed as a percentage of total transfer before the reform. Before compensation measures, 52 percent of always eligible are extensive margin losers, and after the measures the number is 55 percent.

Table 9.3 Current and Postreform TSA Coverage Before and After Compensation Measures, by Social Categories

Social category	Coverage rate (%)		
	Prereform	Postreform before compensation measures	Postreform after compensation measures
Disabled persons	27.54	20.30	25.62
Persons with specific health needs	20.59	16.53	20.55
Single nonworking pensioners	34.47	6.35	23.70
IDPs	8.47	17.74	18.51

Source: Calculations based on IHS 2013 estimation sample (additional module data).
Note: Population-weighted estimates. The analysis is done at household level, and there is some overlap in the categories used. As discussed in chapter 6, some single nonworking pensioners can also be persons with specific health needs. Thus, the number of persons that could be out of any of these groups ranges between 20,394 and 22,805, depending on the overlap of the categories. IDPs = internally displaced persons; TSA = Targeted Social Assistance.

Figure 9.5 Distribution of Pre- and Postreform Beneficiaries for Single Nonworking Pensioners

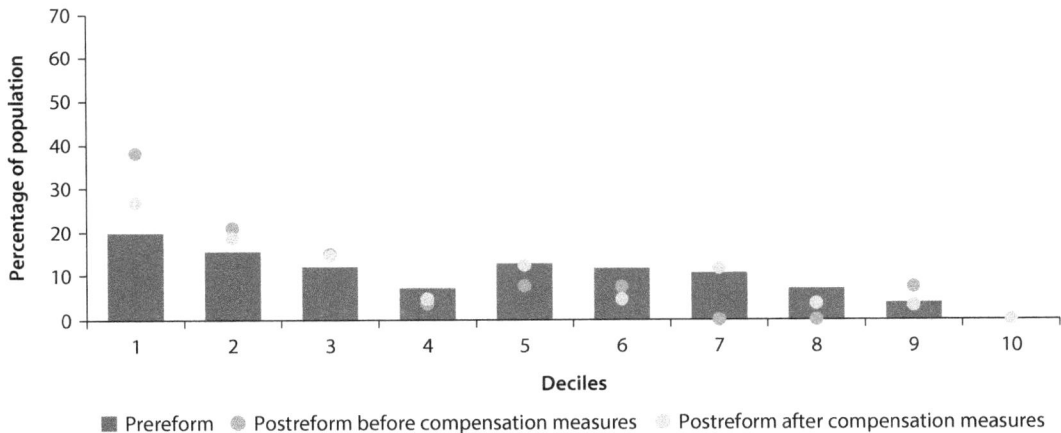

Source: Calculations based on IHS 2013 estimation sample (additional module data).
Note: Persons eligible with vulnerability score lower than 57,000 for current PMT formula and with scores below 65,000 for new PMT. Deciles are computed using consumption pre-TSA transfer and PAE. PAE = per adult equivalent; PMT = proxy means test; TSA = Targeted Social Assistance.

Summary

With the introduction of compensation measures, the aim of maintaining a higher number of single pensioners in the TSA program is achieved at a cost of almost GEL 2 million. The pensioners and other social groups that are brought back in the TSA have relatively better levels of welfare than those that were already in the program. These measures will result in an increase in public expenditures of GEL 1.77 million associated with the cost of the TSA program.

After the compensation measures there are fewer losers and more winners. The measures increase the number of beneficiaries of the program and do leave very few prereform beneficiaries of the TSA out. Although targeting accuracy with the compensation diminishes when compared with precompensation measures, improvements are maintained, especially at the bottom of the distribution. The compensation measures bring into the program people from the middle (and even to a lesser extent from the top) of the welfare distribution. There are also more intensive margin winners and the number of intensive margin losers is reduced.

The compensation measures, although achieving the objectives, could be improved to increase their alignment with the objective of the reform at the outset and for fiscal sustainability. This report recommends that the design and the resources dedicated to the compensation measures be further analyzed. Other options that could be further explored are the following:

- Split the single pensioner groups into various age categories to reflect more accurately their needs in the adjusted coefficient in the needs index.
- Introduce a program directed to single pensioners, similar to the CBP.
- Consider returning to the Old Age Pension with age cutoffs.

It is important that the amount of the compensation measures is assessed, as the new coefficients in the needs index for single elderly pensioners have risen highly compared to their prereform value. Both for fiscal sustainability and to avoid undoing the correction in the bias that the targeting formula had toward this group, the government of Georgia should consider gradually phasing out this compensation measure.

Notes

1. For more details on mitigation, complementary, and compensation measures see World Bank 2003. For example, a reform on electricity that increases the electric tariff may adversely affect the poor. The analysis of the context may show that poor households may face difficulties in accessing the grid and thus the *mitigation measure* could be a subsidy of the fixed cost of connecting to the grid. If the main objective of expanding the electrical grid was to increase the production in a certain region, *complementarity measures* could further assist firms in that region in growth, providing such things as simplification of business registration or tax exemptions. Finally, *compensation measures* are those that are introduced to minimize unavoidable negative effects of the reform.

2. For more details on the Brazilian program see Lindert et al. 2007.

3. These are guaranteed minimum income, family benefit, and heating benefit.

4. 2015 Amendment to the Decree of the Government of Georgia No. 758 establishing the methodology for assessing socially vulnerable families.

5. In other words, the amount of the subsidy is subtracted from the total spending in utilities.

6. 2015 Amendment to the Decree of the Government of Georgia No. 141/n of May 20, 2010, establishing the rules for assessing the socioeconomic situation of socially vulnerable families.

7. Decree No. 18–57 of Tbilisi City Council, December 19, 2014.

8. The "recoveries" are those who would have become newly ineligible in the absence of compensation measures but after the compensation measures are retained in the TSA program.

References

IHS (Integrated Household Survey). 2013. GeoStat, Tbilisi. http://www.geostat.ge/?action =meurneoba&mpid=1&lang=eng.

Lindert, Kathy, Anja Linder, Jason Hobbs, and Bénédicte de la Brière. 2007. "The Nuts and Bolts of Brazil's Bolsa Família Program: Implementing Conditional Cash Transfers in a Decentralized Context." SP Discussion Paper 0709, World Bank, Washington, DC.

World Bank. 2003. "A User's Guide to Poverty and Social Impact Analysis." Poverty Reduction Group and Social Development Department, World Bank, Washington, DC.

CHAPTER 10

Toward a Comprehensive and Efficient System of Social Protection and Labor

Continuous improvement is better than delayed perfection.
—Mark Twain

Introduction

The Targeted Social Assistance (TSA) program is an efficient tool for lifting people out of poverty. The TSA program reduces poverty incidence by about 6 percentage points. The program has performed well since its inception in 2006. More important, there has been continuous improvement. In 2010, the formula was revised, and in various ways for various groups the level of benefits was raised.[1] This reform is an other example of the attention the government of Georgia (GoG) pays to this important program and the interest in keeping it efficient and relevant.

In parallel to the technical work review in this report, the GoG has been implementing the reforms since the end of 2014. The new decrees on the revision of the TSA and on the establishment of the Child Benefit Program (CBP) were passed in December 2014 and May 2015, respectively. The lessons from winners and losers were used to identify the groups that were stratified in the pretesting of the new household declaration and eligibility formula in March 2015; as well as the groups for which the GoG then implemented protective measures and, in the case of persons that needed to transition out of the TSA program, compensation measures.

Going forward, the GoG should work along two parallel tracks: continuing improvement of the TSA program and shifting the attention from an efficient social assistance program to an efficient social protection and labor system. Continuous improvement has been a principle guiding the management of the TSA and this should not change, as it is one of the main reasons why the TSA is a good practice example for middle-income countries, particularly those with high poverty incidence. Now it is time that Georgia devote more efforts to achieve the same level of efficiency of the TSA program in its social protection and labor system. Currently, there is little knowledge on how many programs there are, who the populations they serve are, and how they overlap and coordinate. Developing a system is crucial for a country like Georgia, where spending on social issues is relatively low compared to spending in similar countries (in terms of economic development and poverty), so it can make the most out of its investment. In what follows, this chapter presents recommendations for Georgia along these two tracks.

Implementation of the Reform

The GoG has been working in close collaboration with UNICEF from the outset of the reform effort, and later also with the World Bank Group (WBG), in implementing the results drawn from the analysis reported here. In 2013 UNICEF signed a memorandum of understanding with the Ministry of Labor, Health, and Social Affairs (MoLHSA) and Georgia's Social Services Agency (SSA) to assist in the reform of the TSA. Soon after, both UNICEF and the WBG joined efforts in working with the National Statistics Office of Georgia (GeoStat) in developing an additional module to the Integrated Household Survey (IHS) to retrieve information on the household declaration variables of the TSA and its analysis. The output of this effort is described in chapters 2 and 3. The data were indispensable to the reform process. Going forward, the GoG should consider regularly collecting this module in the IHS. Although ideally this would be done every month, it could also be done biennially and provide the necessary information to monitor the program.

Based on the estimates from the proxy means test (PMT) developed for the reform, two new decrees were passed updating the TSA formula and introducing the CBP. In December 2015, soon after the results described in chapter 3 of this report were presented,[2] the GoG worked closely with UNICEF in selecting a PMT model that improved the performance of the TSA program. From early on, part of this dialog evolved around the idea of introducing a program to provide an additional transfer for children. The WBG came on board once the PMT model was selected, as the reform has been included as a trigger of the Inclusive Growth Development Policy Operation.

The PMT estimates showed there was scope for marginal improvements based on a rather similar—though simplified—set of covariates and that the performance was comparable to that of studies for other countries. The analysis described in chapter 3 followed best practices in the field. For example, it worked with two samples (one to estimate the PMT and another to validate the results). It worked with various econometric models—ordinary least squares (OLS), probit, logit, and quantile regressions—tried several basic specifications, and refined them later based on goodness of fit and feedback from the GoG (stepwise approach). The results showed that the performance of the TSA could be improved—even if only marginally—with the revised estimates of the PMT.

The selected model responded to several criteria of interest to the government. Its targeting performance is equal to or better than the runner-up models, including the status quo. The model is simple: it uses OLS, eliminates unnecessary variables, and sticks to the number of adult household members of working age, as opposed to a share of salaried workers, in order to avoid inaccurate reporting of labor statuses in the declaration. The estimated PMT model also performed well when tested using the validation sample.

Most of the gains come from improvements in the second decile. Coverage in the bottom quintile is expected to raise 47 to 53 percent, with marginal improvements in the bottom decile from 71 to 73 percent. Moreover, after the reform, the distribution of benefits becomes even more pro-poor for some groups, such as seriously ill persons or the single elderly.

The update of the PMT resulted in a reshuffling of beneficiaries, creating winners and losers in terms of TSA eligibility. Because coverage remains constant, the revision of the PMT generates an equal number of newly eligible and newly ineligible persons. Survey estimates indicated that 122,721 persons in prereform TSA recipient households would lose eligibility, while 124,343 persons would enter the TSA program before the compensation measures were passed. Given the efficiency gains, most of the newly eligible households come from the bottom and second deciles.

If only TSA participation is considered, the big winners are families with children and the big losers are single elderly households. Although the objective of the revision of the formula was not to generate this reshuffling of beneficiaries, these results were expected, as the TSA funding under the prereform formula was more likely to be directed to poor families without children than poor families with children (figure 1.7 in chapter 1). The distributional analysis coming from the household survey data (chapters 6 and 7) was also used to inform the design of the pretesting. This analysis uncovered internally displaced persons (IDPs) as an additional group of potential winners, with an increase in total beneficiaries of 8 percent (equivalent to families with children). However, this result should be taken with caution as the pretesting was carried on with poor families, of which many are IDPs, while the household survey was representative of the total population of the country, of which IDPs are a minority.

Jointly with the revision of the PMT, the reform introduced a scheme of differentiated levels of benefits for the TSA. Besides helping to avoid work disincentives, the idea of introducing a scheme of benefits was rooted in the fact that the TSA vulnerability score also reflects a household's distance to a minimum level of subsistence, normalized at 100,000 points of the vulnerability score. Ideally, the level of the transfer should allow the household to reach that minimum standard of living. While the idea was to provide a transfer to fill in that distance to the minimum standard of living, it was quickly discarded due to its implementation and financial constraints.

After being confronted with all these challenges, the GoG decided to have a four-tier benefit scheme. The first tier would maintain the level of transfers for those households that remained below the eligibility score of 57,000 but now based on the revised vulnerability score associated with a lower level of welfare. The subsequent three tiers have narrow brackets up to a score of 65,000—which is the score that leaves the coverage constant based on the new formula. The main weakness of this stepped scheme of benefits is that the brackets are too small to statistically significantly differentiate the level of welfare of households.

An alternative approach to this scheme of benefits is to implement layers of benefits associated to particular needs of households, in order to move toward a system of social protection. The introduction of the CBP is a first step in this direction. Based on a unique targeting system, different types and levels of benefits could be allocated to households based on their needs. For example, households with children receive an additional support given the additional expenses during each stage of life, or households living in mountainous areas could receive a supplement to face their higher cost of living (relative to that already accounted for in the formula). This approach is further discussed below, as one of the recommendations for Georgia is to move toward a comprehensive and efficient system of social protection.

The differentiated level of transfers resulting from the TSA scheme of benefits creates another layer of TSA winners and losers. Among always-TSA-eligible households, some will receive higher transfers—especially if the CBP is topped up—while others will receive a lower transfer. Without taking into account the CBP transfer, there are about an equal number of persons in households where transfers will be cut back as in households where transfers would be augmented. Most of the gains are concentrated at around 20 percent of the prereform level, while most of the losses are of less than 10 percent of the prereform level. There is, nevertheless, a small but not negligible group of households that will have to face loses of 50 percent or more.

A typical policy recommendation when implementing reforms like this one—that creates winners and losers—is to accompany it with transient measures that help losers adjust to their new status. Policies could phase out over a short period—perhaps from three to six months—or call for a trajectory of change of the coefficients of the formula (or the score itself) to smooth the transition. Another alternative could be to (temporally) complement the support coming from other programs. The GoG decided to modify the needs index for single elderly pensioners—the big loser group—to maintain them in the program. However, there is not clarity yet as to whether this measure is temporal or not in Georgia.

The Way Forward

Continuing Improvement of the TSA

From a design point of view, the TSA should continue with its commitment to adjust periodically the PMT formula and revise the needs index, and to collect the data for this purpose. To embark on this reform, an additional, tailored module to the IHS was introduced. This module collected the variables of the TSA declaration form that are not part of the core survey. In the future, it would be valuable if this additional module would be collected regularly, for example every two years, to ensure that the ongoing revision of the PMT formula and the needs index becomes routine.

Recent innovations in poverty measurement could be tested in the PMT formula to increase the goodness of fit. One of these is the use of small-area estimation models. To overcome the shortfalls in poverty measurement coming from incomplete and unreliable time series on consumption and price deflators, the field has been working on poverty predictions based on poverty correlates. The methods that use small-area estimation techniques have proved to produce poverty estimates that matched observed data very well, when employing either nonstaple food or nonfood expenditures or a full set of assets as predictors (Christiaensen et al. 2012). In principle, it seems reasonable to think that these techniques could also be applied to the estimation of PMT formulas with equal success.

Another active area in poverty measurement is work on multidimensional poverty. Many countries (for example, Mexico) are introducing multidimensional measures to track poverty and also to articulate the policy dialog among several line ministries (Colombia). These efforts come from the recognition that monetary poverty measures do not always capture all the deprivations that households face (Alkire and Foster 2011). In spite of what consumption theory predicts (Ravallion 2011), deprivations on housing, health, education, and other fundamental aspects of life are not fully captured in the poverty head count nor in the estimation of the PMT. The multidimensional approach would require one to identify verifiable measures that could be associated to these dimensions. Currently Mexico is tackling this problem by developing a multidimensional measure of the PMT. This approach sounds very promising, as it can also be linked to the development of systems of social protection and labor.

Finally, there are two pending issues from this revision of the TSA formula and that rightly are a concern of the government. First, it is needed to straighten the effect of the energy subsidy in the design of the TSA formula. Going forward, the government should explore the following options: (1) transform the formula based on actual consumption of energy (for example, by kilowatts) and avoid using out-of-pocket expenditures as a basis; or (2) incorporate into the utility expenses the value of the subsidy. Second, it is needed to regularly update the value of the minimum subsistence income in the formula. The GoG is working to address both issues.

From a Social Assistance Program to a System of Social Protection

Going forward, Georgia could benefit from the innovative work done so far and move from an efficient social assistance program to an efficient social protection system. Today, Georgia covers the bottom 12 percent of the population with the TSA. However, half the population is registered with the TSA, as other programs use the TSA vulnerability score to target their beneficiaries. Many questions still remain unanswered: Are all these other programs reaching out to all their intended beneficiaries by using the vulnerability score? And going beyond this, is there any coordination among them? Can conditionality clauses help to install/increase coordination? Are they jointly serving all vulnerable populations? These among others are questions that still need to be tackled in Georgia.[3]

Social protection systems can be an efficient tool to fight poverty and inequality. They provide a coordinated set of programs and services that aim to maximize the impact in poverty alleviation and more generally provide equal opportunities for all. The advantage of thinking of social protection as a system is that it allows one to identify and reduce the vulnerabilities across the life cycle of a person.

A system approach helps to exploit coordination and synergies as much as possible to have efficiency gains coming both from targeting and from administration. In most countries, social protection programs are often fragmented and uncoordinated. Fragmentation can create significant inefficiencies, undermining the potential impact of social protection on building resilience and contributing to human development. Isolated programs may be effective in addressing a particular issue but may lead to duplication or contradictory results if not coordinated with other interventions in related sectors. More important, uncoordinated programs usually result in overlapping objectives or parallel structures serving a similar purpose. Initiatives not integrated into national structures and/or strategies result in inefficient allocation of resources and have limited capacity to benefit from economies of scale and be financially and politically sustainable in the long term.

Moreover, fragmentation has implications in terms of limited and scattered coverage, with high inclusion and exclusion errors, where those hardest to reach, the poorest and most excluded, are not covered. In many instances, although programs may have similar eligibility requirements for accessing benefits, limited coordination of administrative and information systems (for example, cross-matching data of beneficiary lists and multiple targeting systems) reduces the likelihood of beneficiaries being able to access available services. Weak referral systems and limited awareness among staff about other programs and benefits become key obstacles to children's, families', and communities' access to essential benefits and services.

However, all the benefits of coordination need to be weighed against the risks, challenges, and costs. First, there are risks of excessive centralization. A flaw of integrated systems is that errors can quickly propagate across programs. For example, if there is a single registry of beneficiaries working across programs and an individual is not included in that registry, he or she may not have access to a number of benefits. This can serve to compound exclusion or segregation. Centralization can also limit the ability to adapt effectively to the needs of particular regions or groups. Systems can be less than flexible in their ability to adapt to changing economic circumstances and to react rapidly to crises. Second, there are costs of coordination such as transaction costs, given the involvement of various agencies or line ministries. Last, there are the challenges arising from complex political economy issues.

UNICEF and the WBG have a common understanding on the key steps to operationalize a system approach to social protection. Rawlings, Murthy, and

Winder (2013) describe in detail how the social protection strategies of both UNICEF and the World Bank are based on common ground geared toward building a social protection system.[4] First, the movement toward a more integrated system needs to be gradual and accompanied by sound analytic work and relevant data to monitor progress. Second, the operationalization must occur at different levels: policy, program, and administration. At the policy level, a government needs to define a long-term vision that aligns the social protection system to broader political and economic goals of the country. This is usually reflected in a national social protection strategy that defines goals and priorities for the country, given the fiscal space and the socioeconomic context. At the program level, this approach focuses on integrating, harmonizing, and coordinating programs to eliminate duplications, maximize synergies, and exploit interactions. At this level, the coordination could and must go beyond programs delivered by a single ministry or agency. Finally, at the administrative level, it should facilitate the functioning of the programs. For example, it should focus on whether there has to be a single unique social assistance registry, maybe with a common targeting tool, and a developed identity. Monitoring and evaluation of programs can also be coordinated to facilitate the administration and the measurement of interactions.

The development of the system should be based on the existent programs and policies and in coordination with other services provided by the country. The horizontal coordination should focus at a minimum on other supply-side services and benefits such as education, child protection and nutrition, and health, but also on those services coordinated by other ministries such as energy subsidies and taxes, which are usually in the agenda of ministries of finance or other line ministries.

The recommendation to move toward a social protection and labor system is to start by analyzing the existing programs and identifying the needs of the population. The WBG has developed an interesting framework for Latin American countries that could be used in Georgia, as the country conceptualizes its social assistance strategy for 2016. Figure 10.1 visualizes the elements of a social protection and labor system.

The analysis of the demand for services and programs can be done using a life-cycle approach. At different moments in life, people face different risks. Persons live in families and communities, which in turn face their own idiosyncratic risks. Families and communities have different needs of programs and services depending on their stage of life and their overall level of vulnerability and that of the country. The government thus needs to develop a system of programs to respond to these different needs. This system can respond to the specific levels of vulnerabilities of families and communities and/or by type of risk. Figure 10.2 shows the different stages in life and the risks associated to them.

Before performing a demand-for-services analysis, it is fundamental to identify target populations. They could be identified in terms of the risks at each stage of life and their overall level of vulnerability. It is important to evaluate not only the risks themselves but also how they relate to one another, including their

Figure 10.1 Framework for Taking Stock of a Social Protection and Labor System

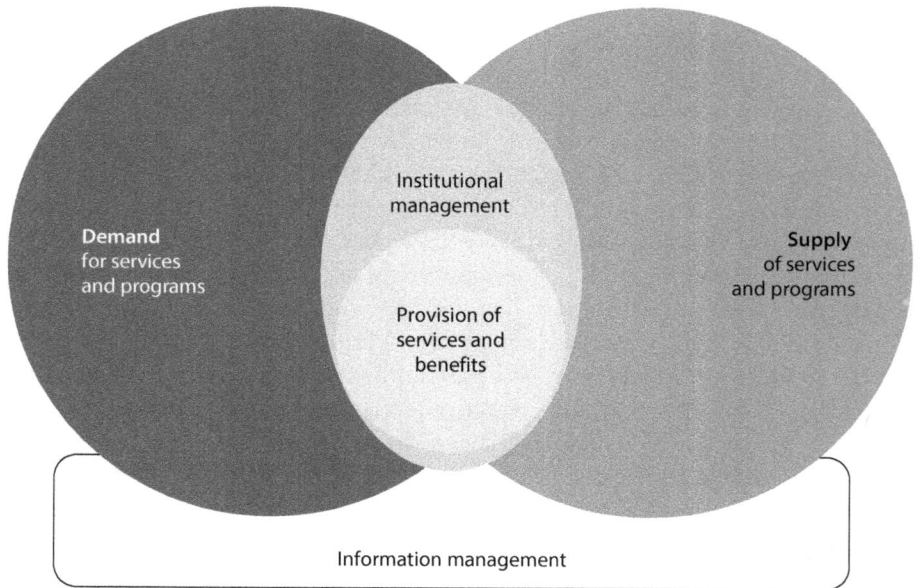

Demand
for services
and programs

Institutional
management

Provision of
services and
benefits

Supply
of services
and programs

Information management

Source: World Bank 2015.

Figure 10.2 Social and Work Risks over a Person's Life Cycle

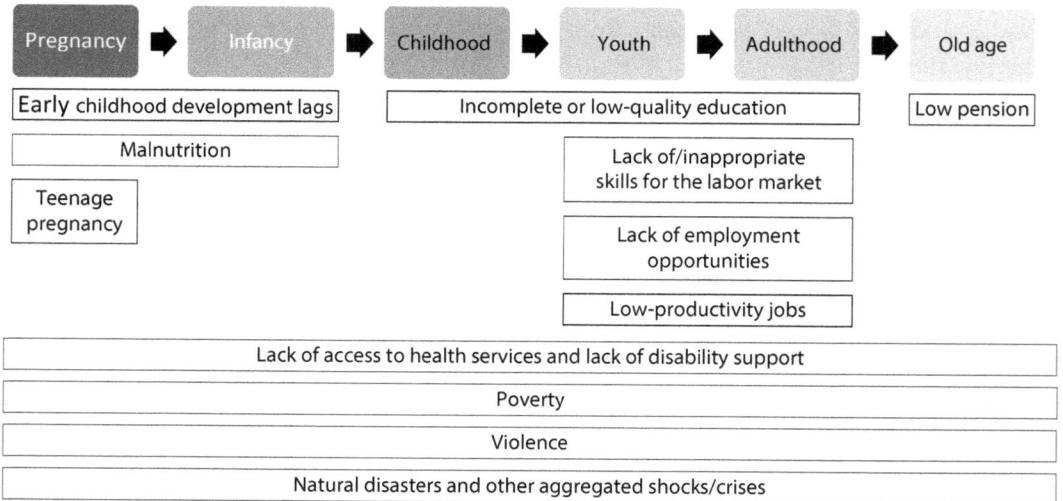

| Pregnancy | ➡ | Infancy | ➡ | Childhood | ➡ | Youth | ➡ | Adulthood | ➡ | Old age |

Early childhood development lags | Incomplete or low-quality education | Low pension

Malnutrition

Lack of/inappropriate
skills for the labor market

Teenage
pregnancy

Lack of employment
opportunities

Low-productivity jobs

Lack of access to health services and lack of disability support

Poverty

Violence

Natural disasters and other aggregated shocks/crises

Source: World Bank 2015.

interactions at different life stages. In this way a package of services and programs that is well articulated and coordinated can be developed.

The analysis of the demand can be done in three stages, from less to more complex matters. Figure 10.3 summarizes the steps of the analysis. It starts with a basic description of the overall risks, needs, and vulnerabilities of

Figure 10.3 Steps for the Analysis of Demand for Services

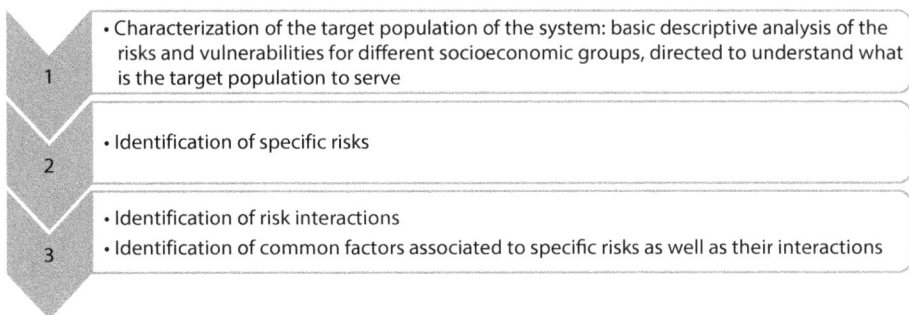

1
- Characterization of the target population of the system: basic descriptive analysis of the risks and vulnerabilities for different socioeconomic groups, directed to understand what is the target population to serve

2
- Identification of specific risks

3
- Identification of risk interactions
- Identification of common factors associated to specific risks as well as their interactions

Source: World Bank 2015.

different groups of the population. The objective is to understand the target population, which can be done using a combination of administrative and survey data. It continues with the analysis of the specific risks and the type of services and programs that could address each of them. This analysis uses a combination of quantitative and qualitative data to gain a deeper knowledge of the potential beneficiaries identified in stage one. The objective is to understand which groups should receive priority and what their needs and preferences are.

Next, the analysis centers on understanding the interactions of the different risks. Methodologies that allow this type of analysis include cluster analysis, examination of common risk factors, and qualitative data complements. The idea is to understand what the priority risks are, how frequently these risks occur to different population groups, and how risks overlap.

The analysis of the supply of services and programs aims to understand how the programs interact and complement each other to serve the target population in coping with the identified risks. It is important to understand whether there is duplication among benefits and functions and whether they apply equally to all the target population. It is critical to make efficient use of fiscal resources and to maximize the impact of social spending.

The analysis of the supply of services is done using the totality of the social programs registry. The first step is to take stock of all the programs and services that benefit the target population at all government levels. The sources of information include all the administrative data of all programs, including the cadaster registry. The stock-taking stage should gather the type of beneficiaries, the benefits, the eligibility rules, the ministry or agency in charge of the administration of the program, the budget (allocated and executed), the geographic distribution of the target population and beneficiaries, and so forth. This task might seem simplistic, but it is quite complex if it involves all levels of government.

The next stage is to understand the way the programs interact. Programs can have many elements in common—the targeting method (as in the case of the

Figure 10.4 Steps for the Analysis of Supply of Services

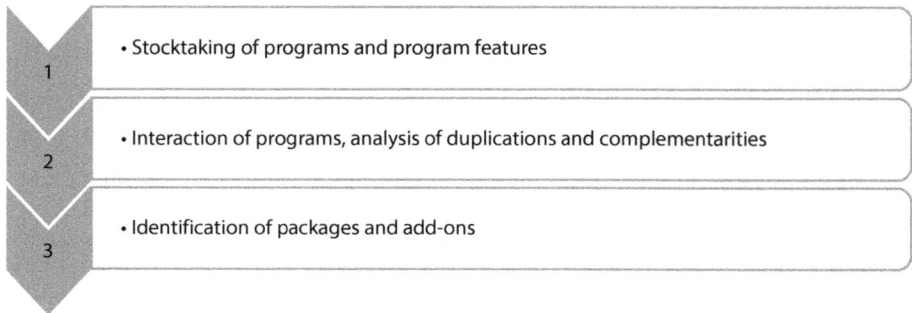

1 • Stocktaking of programs and program features

2 • Interaction of programs, analysis of duplications and complementarities

3 • Identification of packages and add-ons

Source: World Bank 2015.

TSA vulnerability score), common beneficiaries, programmatic goals that may serve the same objectives, and so forth.

The last stage of the analysis involves developing a systemic approach by identifying "packages" and "add-ons." The packages of programs can be implemented in sequence or in sync. Some programs can be bundled and combined for one of the following reasons: they mitigate the same risk, they are delivered by the same agency, or they imply monetary transfers. Bundling programs will result in efficiency gains by reducing administrative and implementation costs. On the other hand, there are programs that can be thought of as add-ons to provide complementary services. Part of the process is to redesign programs in order to facilitate coordination and complementarity. One example is the introduction of conditionality clauses to remain eligible to a program, especially for health and education, as exist in many conditional cash transfer programs. Figure 10.4 summarizes the three steps of the analysis of supply of programs.

Management of the System of Programs

To have a healthy social protection and labor system it is crucial to have fluid communication and information sharing among different line ministries and government agencies. Such coordination needs to be guided by an institutional framework that facilitates the communication. Nurturing the framework can be done in different ways depending on the complexity of the system, the monitoring of sector objectives, and the coordination of the cabinet. For example, in Colombia, the multidimensional poverty index is used mostly for coordination and monitoring of sector objectives, rather than for poverty tracking. In the same way, information sharing and linkage among administrative databases is fundamental for the coordination of programs.

To manage the system efficiently it is critical to develop a single social registry with an identity. Having a single targeting system accomplishes several objectives. First, it supports the analysis of the demand for and supply of programs as it facilitates tracking beneficiaries of all programs. Second, it is an efficient single tool for targeting beneficiaries of package programs and using add-ons for particular needs. Third, it levels the playing field by giving the same information and thus opportunities to all the population.

These unique social registries usually acquire an identity through communication and information campaigns. The identity is important if the system is to have transparency and public trust, and it also facilitates institutional arrangements that promote coordination among government agencies. As a by-product, information management can be simplified—a single, unique, personal identification number (most of the time the identity card) helps the sharing of information across administrative datasets. Moreover, the unique social registry will facilitate the implementation of outreach activities. As can be seen in Georgia, many households in the bottom quintile are not even applying to the TSA. Why is that? Governments with equity concerns implement outreach campaigns, via information but also active outreach, to give everybody in the target population the same opportunity to benefit from the programs.

Finally, a key part of this integration is linking social assistance to active labor market policies. Active labor market programs are in the works in Georgia. The employment support services agency is only now working to develop the first pool of training programs. High-income countries in Europe tend to have "rights-and-responsibilities" systems, in which social assistance beneficiaries are committed to actively search for jobs and to participate in retraining programs. This connection between social assistance and the labor market is important to minimize work disincentives. However, and given that these are already low in Georgia, it is critical to have dynamic labor markets before implementing this type of conditionality.

Notes

1. Benefits were raised in 2009 and 2013.
2. The results of the PMT revision were discussed on several occasions with the GoG and were widely presented in a workshop jointly organized by UNICEF and the WBG in December 2014.
3. This section draws heavily on the recommendations of Rawlings, Murthy, and Winder (2013).
4. The recommendations provided substantially reflect the principles outlined in the social protection and labor strategy of both institutions and summarized in Rawlings, Murthy, and Winder (2013).

References

Alkire, Sabina, and James Foster. 2011. "Counting and Multidimensional Poverty Measurement." *Journal of Public Economics* 95 (7): 476–87.

Christiaensen, Luc, Peter Lanjouw, Jill Luoto, and David Stifel. 2012. "Small Area Estimation-Based Prediction Methods to Track Poverty: Validation and Applications." *Journal of Economic Inequality* 10 (2): 267–97.

Ravallion, Martin. 2011. "On Multidimensional Indices of Poverty." *Journal of Economic Inequality* 9 (2): 235–48.

Rawlings, Laura, Sheila Murthy, and Natalia Winder. 2013. "Common Ground: UNICEF and World Bank Approaches to Building Social Protection Systems." Social Protection Study 78652, World Bank, Washington, DC.

World Bank. 2015. "Avanzando hacia sistemas de protección social y trabajo en América Latina y el Caribe." Social Protection and Labor Global Practice, Latin America and Caribbean Region, World Bank, Washington, DC.

APPENDIX A

Data

Table A.1 Sampling Frame and Deletions for Estimation and Validation Sample

Description	Observations
Sampling frame based on IHS 2013	3,700
Of which participated in Q3 and Q4 of IHS 2013	3,467
Of which responded to the additional module in spring 2014	3,262
Of which are Q3 2013	2,601

Note: Of the 205 households that are lost because they were not interviewed in February-March 2014, 166 correspond to the Q3 2013 (estimation sample). IHS = Integrated Household Survey; Q = quarter.

Figure A.1 Response Rate by Consumption PAE Decile

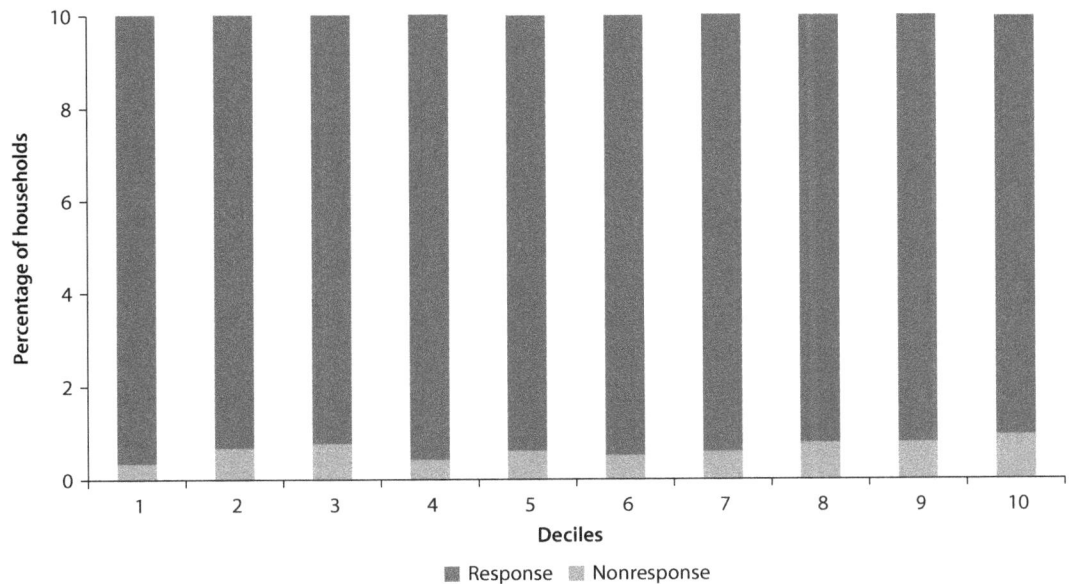

Note: The 166 households that were not interviewed in February-March 2014 are distributed across consumption deciles in the Integrated Household Survey (IHS) Q3 2013 (estimation sample). PAE = per adult equivalent; Q = quarter.

Table A.2 Distribution of New TSA and CBP Beneficiaries

	TSA only		CBP only		TSA+CBP	
Vulnerability score	Percent	Cumulative (%)	Percent	Cumulative (%)	Percent	Cumulative (%)
0–30,000	2.20	2.20	1.91	1.91	2.20	2.20
30,001–57,000	5.87	8.07	3.37	5.28	5.87	8.07
57,001–60,000	1.16	9.23	0.71	5.99	1.16	9.23
60,001–65,000	1.68	10.92	0.76	6.75	1.68	10.92
65,001–100,000	0	10.92	7.18	13.93	7.18	18.10
Over 100,000	0	10.92	0	13.93	0	18.10

Source: IHS 2013 estimation sample (additional module data).
Note: Households are sorted by TSA score. CBP = Child Benefit Program; TSA = Targeted Social Assistance.

Table A.3 Poverty Lines, UNICEF Absolute Poverty Line

Poverty line in GEL per month PAE	2009	2011	2013
Extreme poverty	61.1	71.7	71.2
Relative poverty	89.7	109.2	137.2
General poverty	122.2	143.4	142.4

Note: Monthly consumption PAE. GEL = Georgian lari; PAE = per adult equivalent.

Figure A.2 Poverty Incidence for Rural and Urban Areas: WBG Absolute Poverty and GeoStat Relative Poverty

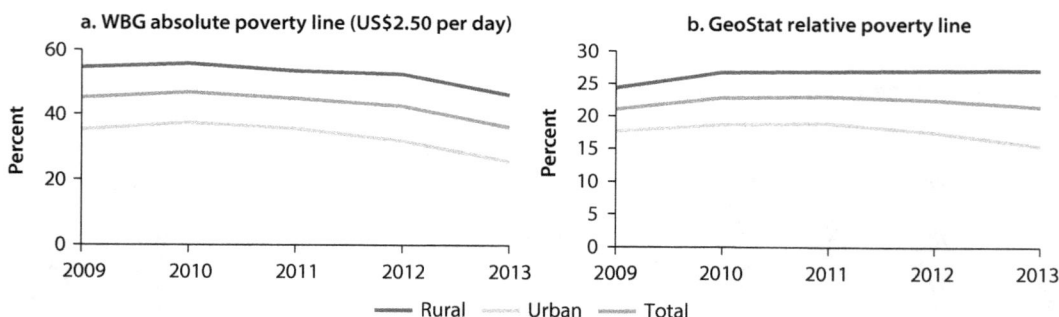

Source: World Bank 2014.
Note: GeoStat = National Statistics Office of Georgia; WBG = World Bank Group.

Table A.4 Coverage and Distribution of Beneficiaries for Status Quo, Models 2, 6, and 10 (15th Percentile Eligibility Threshold)

percent

Decile	Status quo model	Model 2	Model 6	Model 10
1	62.07	81.40	83.68	82.25
	41.43	*54.36*	*55.86*	*54.95*
2	22.98	35.94	32.60	36.18
	15.35	*24.03*	*21.79*	*24.19*
3	16.47	12.48	13.21	11.60
	11.00	*8.34*	*8.83*	*7.76*

table continues next page

**Table A.4 Coverage and Distribution of Beneficiaries for Status Quo, Models 2, 6, and 10
(15th Percentile Eligibility Threshold)** (continued)

percent

Decile	Status quo model	Model 2	Model 6	Model 10
4	10.15	6.29	6.08	5.49
	6.76	4.20	4.05	3.66
5	9.79	4.41	5.16	5.21
	6.52	2.94	3.44	3.48
6	7.81	4.10	4.08	2.72
	5.22	2.74	2.73	1.82
7	6.40	2.99	2.48	2.15
	4.27	2.00	1.65	1.43
8	6.81	0.86	0.51	0.86
	4.54	0.58	0.34	0.58
9	4.15	0.28	1.00	1.81
	2.77	0.19	0.67	1.21
10	3.23	0.96	0.96	1.40
	2.15	0.64	0.64	0.93
Total	14.99	14.98	14.99	14.98
	100.00	100.00	100.00	100.00

Note: The numbers in the first row of each decile correspond to coverage of the respective decile. The numbers in the second row of each decile (in italics) correspond to the distribution of beneficiaries.

**Table A.5 Coverage and Distribution of Beneficiaries for Status Quo, Models 2, 6, and 10
(30th Percentile Eligibility Threshold)**

percent

Decile	Status quo model	Model 2	Model 6	Model 10
1	79.50	95.67	94.70	94.08
	26.55	31.95	31.63	31.40
2	48.02	64.84	64.44	67.30
	16.05	21.68	21.54	22.48
3	38.39	44.14	43.74	44.30
	12.83	14.75	14.62	14.79
4	25.86	30.20	27.36	26.80
	8.62	10.07	9.12	8.92
5	27.31	21.95	22.47	23.20
	9.10	7.31	7.49	7.73
6	21.48	13.03	15.73	13.60
	7.18	4.35	5.26	4.54
7	18.67	13.81	13.38	12.24
	6.23	4.61	4.46	4.08
8	15.43	6.56	8.40	7.10
	5.15	2.19	2.80	2.37
9	16.07	4.90	6.58	6.55
	5.36	1.64	2.20	2.18
10	8.81	4.34	2.65	4.53
	2.94	1.45	0.88	1.51
Total	29.96	29.96	29.96	29.99
	100.00	100.00	100.00	100.00

Note: The numbers in the first row of each decile correspond to coverage of the respective decile. The numbers in the second row of each decile (in italics) correspond to the distribution of beneficiaries.

References

IHS (Integrated Household Survey). 2013. GeoStat, Tbilisi. http://www.geostat.ge/?action =meurneoba&mpid=1&lang=eng.

World Bank. 2014. *Georgia Public Expenditure Review: Diagnostics of Public Investment Management System*. Washington, DC. https://openknowledge.worldbank.org/handle /10986/19302.

Subcomponents of the Needs Index

Table B.1 Caloric Needs by Population Group

Group of the population	Kcal per day
All	
(0–3)	1,400
(4–6)	1,650
(7–12)	1,800
(13–17)	2,400
Male	
(18–29)	2,360
(30–39)	2,230
(40–59)	2,090
(60+)	1,890
Female	
(18–29)	1,860
(30–39)	1,800
(40–59)	1,750
(60+)	1,650
Child with disability	1,890
Person with disability group 1	1,890
Person with disability group 2	1,890
Refugee	1,890
Bedridden	1,750
Single pensioner	1,700
Pregnant	2,210
Breastfeeding woman	2,335
Single mother	1,890
Orphan	1,800

Source: Pkhakadze, Kvantaliani, and Tsakadze 2015, background paper for this report.

Table B.2 Coefficients of Caloric Needs, by Population Group

Status/age	All				Men				Women			
	(0–3)	(4–6)	(7–12)	(13–17)	(18–29)	(30–39)	(40–59)	(60+)	(18–29)	(30–39)	(40–59)	(60+)
Healthy	0.44	0.52	0.57	0.75	0.74	0.70	0.66	0.59	0.58	0.57	0.55	0.52
Child with disability	0.44	0.52	0.57	0.75	0.00	0.00	0.00	0.00	0.00	0.00	0.00	0.00
Person with disability group 1	0.00	0.00	0.00	0.00	0.74	0.70	0.66	0.59	0.59	0.59	0.59	0.59
Person with disability group 2	0.00	0.00	0.00	0.00	0.74	0.70	0.66	0.59	0.59	0.59	0.59	0.59
Refugee	0.59	0.59	0.59	0.75	0.74	0.70	0.66	0.59	0.59	0.59	0.59	0.59
Bedridden	0.55	0.55	0.57	0.75	0.74	0.70	0.66	0.59	0.58	0.57	0.55	0.55
Single pensioner	0.00	0.00	0.00	0.00	0.74	0.70	0.66	0.59	0.58	0.57	0.55	0.53
Pregnant	0.00	0.00	0.00	0.75	0.00	0.00	0.00	0.00	0.69	0.69	0.69	0.00
Breastfeeding woman	0.00	0.00	0.00	0.75	0.00	0.00	0.00	0.00	0.73	0.73	0.73	0.00
Single mother	0.00	0.00	0.00	0.75	0.00	0.00	0.00	0.00	0.59	0.59	0.59	0.00
Orphan	0.57	0.57	0.57	0.75	0.00	0.00	0.00	0.00	0.00	0.00	0.00	0.00

Source: Pkhakadze, Kvantaliani, and Tsakadze 2015, background paper for this report.

Table B.3 Caregiver Working Hours and Calories

Category	Working hours	Additional kcal	Coefficients
All			
(0–3)	8	667	0.21
(4–6)	6	500	0.16
(7–12)	4	333	0.10
(13–17)	2	167	0.05
Male			
(18–29)	0	0	0
(30–39)	0	0	0
(40–59)	0	0	0
(60+)	0	0	0
Female			
(18–29)	0	0	0
(30–39)	0	0	0
(40–59)	0	0	0
(60+)	0	0	0
Child with disability	3	250	0.08
Person with disability group 1	5	417	0.13
Person with disability group 2	3	250	0.08
Refugee	0	0	0
Bedridden	6	500	0.16
Single pensioners	1	83	0.03
Pregnant	0	0	0
Breastfeeding woman	0	0	0
Single mother	0	0	0
Orphan	1	83	0.03

Source: Pkhakadze, Kvantaliani, and Tsakadze 2015, background paper for this report.

Table B.4 Coefficients of Caregiver Needs (K_c)

Status/age	All				Male				Female			
	(0–3)	(4–6)	(7–12)	(13–17)	(18–29)	(30–39)	(40–59)	(60+)	(18–29)	(30–39)	(40–59)	(60+)
Healthy	0.21	0.16	0.10	0.05	0	0	0	0	0	0	0	0
Child with disability	0.21	0.16	0.10	0.08	0	0	0	0	0	0	0	0
Person with disability group 1	0	0	0	0	0.13	0.13	0.13	0.13	0.13	0.13	0.13	0.13
Person with disability group 2	0	0	0	0	0.08	0.08	0.08	0.08	0.08	0.08	0.08	0.08
Refugee	0.21	0.16	0.10	0.05	0	0	0	0	0	0	0	0
Bedridden	0.21	0.16	0.16	0.16	0.16	0.16	0.16	0.16	0.16	0.16	0.16	0.16
Single pensioner	0	0	0	0	0.03	0.03	0.03	0.03	0.03	0.03	0.03	0.03
Pregnant	0	0	0	0.05	0	0	0	0	0	0	0	0
Breastfeeding woman	0	0	0	0.05	0	0	0	0	0	0	0	0
Single mother	0	0	0	0.05	0	0	0	0	0	0	0	0
Orphan	0.21	0.16	0.10	0.05	0	0	0	0	0	0	0	0

Source: Pkhakadze, Kvantaliani, and Tsakadze 2015, background paper for this report.

Table B.5 Service Needs

Category	Transportation needs (GEL)	Other needs (GEL)	Medical services in subsistence minimum (GEL)	Service needs (GEL)
All				
(0–3)	0	24.68	11.22	35.90
(4–6)	0	24.68	11.22	35.90
(7–12)	8.98	24.68	11.22	44.88
(13–17)	8.98	24.68	11.22	44.88
Male				
(18–29)	8.98	24.68	11.22	44.88
(30–39)	8.98	24.68	11.22	44.88
(40–59)	8.98	24.68	11.22	44.88
(60+)	8.98	24.68	11.22	44.88
Female				
(18–29)	8.98	24.68	11.22	44.88
(30–39)	8.98	24.68	11.22	44.88
(40–59)	8.98	24.68	11.22	44.88
(60+)	8.98	24.68	11.22	44.88
Child with disability	8.98	24.68	11.22	44.88
Person with disability group 1	8.98	24.68	11.22	44.88
Person with disability group 2	8.98	24.68	11.22	44.88
Refugee	8.98	24.68	11.22	44.88
Bedridden	0	24.68	11.22	35.90
Single pensioner	8.98	24.68	11.22	44.88
Pregnant	8.98	24.68	11.22	44.88
Breastfeeding woman	8.98	24.68	11.22	44.88
Single mother	8.98	24.68	11.22	44.88
Orphan	8.98	24.68	11.22	44.88

Source: Pkhakadze, Kvantaliani, and Tsakadze 2015, background paper for this report.
Note: GEL = Georgian lari.

Table B.6 Service Needs Coefficients (K_s)

Status/age	All				Male				Female			
	(0–3)	(4–6)	(7–12)	(13–17)	(18–29)	(30–39)	(40–59)	(60+)	(18–29)	(30–39)	(40–59)	(60+)
Healthy	0.24	0.24	0.30	0.30	0.30	0.30	0.30	0.30	0.30	0.30	0.30	0.30
Child with disability	0.24	0.24	0.30	0.30	0	0	0	0	0	0	0	0
Person with disability group 1	0	0	0	0	0.30	0.30	0.30	0.30	0.30	0.30	0.30	0.30
Person with disability group 2	0	0	0	0	0.30	0.30	0.30	0.30	0.30	0.30	0.30	0.30
Refugee	0.24	0.24	0.30	0.30	0.30	0.30	0.30	0.30	0.30	0.30	0.30	0.30
Bedridden	0.24	0.24	0.24	0.24	0.24	0.24	0.24	0.24	0.24	0.24	0.24	0.24
Single pensioner	0	0	0	0	0.30	0.30	0.30	0.30	0.30	0.30	0.30	0.30
Pregnant	0	0	0	0.30	0	0	0	0	0.30	0.30	0.30	0
Breastfeeding woman	0	0	0	0.30	0	0	0	0	0.30	0.30	0.30	0
Single mother	0	0	0	0.30	0	0	0	0	0.30	0.30	0.30	0
Orphan	0.24	0.24	0.30	0.30	0	0	0	0	0	0	0	0

Source: Pkhakadze, Kvantaliani, and Tsakadze 2015, background paper for this report.

Table B.7 Special Means Needs

	Diapers	Walking pens	Playpens	Other equipment for ages 0–3	Kinder-garten	Text-books	Special notebooks	Note-books	Pens	Crayons	Special means for those with disabilities	Monthly expenditure (GEL)
Period in months	48	48	48	48	12	72	72	72	12	12	1	
All												
(0–3)	356	55	100	78	235	0	0	0	0	0	0	32
(4–6)	0	0	0	0	313	106	33	27	1	6	0	29
(7–12)	0	0	0	0	0	318	99	80	4	17	0	9
(13–17)	0	0	0	0	0	605	79	197	4	17	0	14
Male												
(18–29)	0	0	0	0	0	0	0	0	0	0	0	0
(30–39)	0	0	0	0	0	0	0	0	0	0	0	0
(40–59)	0	0	0	0	0	0	0	0	0	0	0	0
(60+)	0	0	0	0	0	0	0	0	0	0	0	0
Female												
(18–29)	0	0	0	0	0	0	0	0	0	0	0	0
(30–39)	0	0	0	0	0	0	0	0	0	0	0	0
(40–59)	0	0	0	0	0	0	0	0	0	0	0	0
(60+)	0	0	0	0	0	0	0	0	0	0	0	0
Healthy	0	0	0	0	0	0	0	0	0	0	0	0
Child with disability	0	0	0	0	0	0	0	0	0	0	2	2
Person with disability group 1	0	0	0	0	0	0	0	0	0	0	2	2
Person with disability group 2	0	0	0	0	0	0	0	0	0	0	2	2
Refugee	0	0	0	0	0	0	0	0	0	0	0	0
Bedridden	0	0	0	0	0	0	0	0	0	0	0	0
Single pensioner	0	0	0	0	0	0	0	0	0	0	0	0
Pregnant	0	0	0	0	0	0	0	0	0	0	0	0
Breastfeeding woman	0	0	0	0	0	0	0	0	0	0	0	0
Single mother	0	0	0	0	0	0	0	0	0	0	0	0
Orphan	0	0	0	0	0	0	0	0	0	0	0	0

Source: Pkhakadze, Kvantaliani, and Tsakadze 2015, background paper for this report.
Note: GEL = Georgian lari.

Table B.8 Special Means Needs Coefficients

Status/age	All				Male				Female			
	(0–3)	(4–6)	(7–12)	(13–17)	(18–29)	(30–39)	(40–59)	(60+)	(18–29)	(30–39)	(40–59)	(60+)
Healthy	0.21	0.19	0.06	0.09	0	0	0	0	0	0	0	0
Child with disability	0.22	0.20	0.07	0.10	0	0	0	0	0	0	0	0
Person with disability group 1	0	0	0	0	0.01	0.01	0.01	0.01	0.01	0.01	0.01	0.01
Person with disability group 2	0	0	0	0	0.01	0.01	0.01	0.01	0.01	0.01	0.01	0.01
Refugee	0.21	0.19	0.06	0.09	0	0	0	0	0	0	0	0
Bedridden	0.21	0.19	0.06	0.09	0	0	0	0	0	0	0	0
Single pensioner	0	0	0	0	0	0	0	0	0	0	0	0
Pregnant	0	0	0	0.09	0	0	0	0	0	0	0	0
Breastfeeding woman	0	0	0	0.09	0	0	0	0	0	0	0	0
Single mother	0	0	0	0.09	0	0	0	0	0	0	0	0
Orphan	0.21	0.19	0.06	0.09	0	0	0	0	0	0	0	0

Source: Pkhakadze, Kvantaliani, and Tsakadze 2015, background paper for this report.

Table B.9 Monitoring Needs Coefficients

Category	Initial estimate	Insurance losses estimate	Average	GEL 5.83 (52% of GEL 11.22) subtracted	Coefficient
All					
(0–3)	21.73	11.35	16.54	10.71	0.07
(4–6)	15.21	3.30	9.26	3.43	0.02
(7–12)	11.41	2.63	7.02	1.19	0.01
(13–17)	9.81	2.79	6.30	0.47	0
Male					
(18–29)	8.46	2.46	5.46	−0.37	0
(30–39)	8.30	3.36	5.83	0	0
(40–59)	17.90	6.22	12.06	6.23	0.04
(60+)	34.44	14.26	24.35	18.52	0.12
Female					
(18–29)	13.70	4.85	9.27	3.44	0.02
(30–39)	15.72	5.04	10.38	4.55	0.03
(40–59)	22.37	4.74	13.55	7.72	0.05
(60+)	38.25	8.42	23.33	17.50	0.12
Healthy	0	0	0	0	0
Child with disability	42.56	24.92	33.74	27.91	0.19
Person with disability group 1	31.92	19.14	25.53	19.70	0.13
Person with disability group 2	42.56	18.98	30.77	24.94	0.17
Refugee	14.90	11.90	13.40	7.57	0.05
Bedridden	31.92	20.8	26.36	20.53	0.14
Single pensioner	31.92	20.8	26.36	20.53	0.14
Pregnant	6.38	7.45	6.92	1.09	0.01
Breastfeeding woman	6.38	7.45	6.92	1.09	0.01
Single mother	29.79	19.69	24.74	18.91	0.13
Orphan	0	0	0	0	0

Source: Pkhakadze, Kvantaliani, and Tsakadze 2015, background paper for this report.
Note: GEL = Georgian lari.

Table B.10 Rehabilitation Needs

Category	GEL	Coefficient
Disability group 1	31.12	0.21
Disability group 2	15.56	0.10
Disabled child	15.56	0.10
Bedridden	25.93	0.17

Source: Pkhakadze, Kvantaliani, and Tsakadze 2015, background paper for this report.
Note: GEL = Georgian lari.

Table B.11 Final Medical Services Needs

Category	Monitoring (GEL)	Medicines (GEL)	Rehabilitation (GEL)	Total (GEL)	Coefficient
All					
(0–3)	11.17	10.31	0	21.47	0.14
(4–6)	3.66	3.38	0	7.04	0.05
(7–12)	1.29	1.19	0	2.49	0.02
(13–17)	0.52	0.48	0	1.00	0.01
Male					
(18–29)	−0.36	−0.34	0	−0.70	0
(30–39)	0	0	0	0	0
(40–59)	6.56	6.05	0	12.61	0.08
(60+)	19.41	17.91	0	37.32	0.25
Female					
(18–29)	3.63	3.35	0	6.97	0.05
(30–39)	4.80	4.43	0	9.23	0.06
(40–59)	8.20	7.57	0	15.77	0.11
(60+)	18.51	17.09	0	35.6	0.24
Healthy	0	0	0	0	0
Child with disability	29.59	27.32	15.56	72.48	0.48
Person with disability group 1	20.90	19.29	31.13	71.31	0.48
Person with disability group 2	26.63	24.58	15.56	66.77	0.45
Refugee	7.98	7.36	0	15.34	0.10
Bedridden	21.73	20.05	25.94	67.72	0.45
Single pensioner	21.73	20.05	0	41.78	0.28
Pregnant	16.81	1.02	0	17.82	0.12
Breastfeeding woman	1.10	1.02	0	2.12	0.01
Single mother	20.01	18.47	0	38.48	0.26
Orphan	0	0	0	0	0

Source: Pkhakadze, Kvantaliani, and Tsakadze 2015, background paper for this report.
Note: GEL = Georgian lari.

Table B.12 Medical Services Needs Coefficients (K_M)

	All				Male				Female			
Status/age	(0–3)	(4–6)	(7–12)	(13–17)	(18–29)	(30–39)	(40–59)	(60+)	(18–29)	(30–39)	(40–59)	(60+)
Healthy	0.14	0.04	0.02	0.01	0	0	0.08	0.24	0.04	0.06	0.10	0.22
Child with disability	0.46	0.46	0.46	0.46	0	0	0	0	0	0	0	0
Person with disability group 1	0	0	0	0	0.46	0.46	0.46	0.46	0.46	0.46	0.46	0.46
Person with disability group 2	0	0	0	0	0.42	0.42	0.42	0.42	0.42	0.42	0.42	0.42
Refugee	0.14	0.10	0.10	0.10	0.10	0.10	0.10	0.24	0.10	0.10	0.10	0.22
Bedridden	0.44	0.44	0.44	0.44	0.44	0.44	0.44	0.44	0.44	0.44	0.44	0.44
Single pensioner	0	0	0	0	0.26	0.26	0.26	0.26	0.26	0.26	0.26	0.26
Pregnant	0	0	0	0.12	0	0	0	0	0.12	0.12	0.12	0
Breastfeeding woman	0	0	0	0.01	0	0	0	0	0.04	0.06	0.10	0
Single mother	0	0	0	0.24	0	0	0	0	0.24	0.24	0.24	0
Orphan	0.14	0.04	0.02	0.01	0	0	0	0	0	0	0	0

Source: Pkhakadze, Kvantaliani, and Tsakadze 2015, background paper for this report.

Table B.13 Comparison to Old Coefficients

	All				Male				Female			
Status/age	(0–3)	(4–6)	(7–12)	(13–17)	(18–29)	(30–39)	(40–59)	(60+)	(18–29)	(30–39)	(40–59)	(60+)
Healthy	17	18	9	18	0	0	8	27	5	7	13	28
Child with disability	–7	1	–4	3	0	0	0	0	0	0	0	0
Person with disability group 1	0	0	0	0	–9	–10	–10	–11	–10	–9	–8	–7
Person with disability group 2	0	0	0	0	–9	–9	–9	–11	–9	–8	–7	–5
Refugee	4	11	–1	5	–10	–11	–11	1	–11	–10	–8	7
Bedridden	–8	–2	–10	0	–12	–12	–12	–12	–13	–13	–13	–12
Single pensioner	0	0	0	0	–10	–11	–11	–12	–12	–12	–12	–11
Pregnant	0	0	0	36	0	0	0	0	21	24	27	0
Breastfeeding woman	0	0	0	20	0	0	0	0	13	17	24	0
Single mother	0	0	0	37	0	0	0	0	14	16	19	0
Orphan	3	10	–4	5	0	0	0	0	0	0	0	0

Source: Pkhakadze, Kvantaliani, and Tsakadze 2015, background paper for this report.

Reference

Pkhakadze, Nikoloz, Varlam Kvantaliani, and Vasil Tsakadze. 2015. "Needs Index Revision—Project Report." International School of Economics at Tbilisi University.

Glossary

Attrition rate: Measure of the number of individuals or items moving out of a collective group over a specific period of time.

Bootstrapping: The statistical method through which the properties of an estimator like the variance are computed using a sample that was constructed by repeated draws (without replacement) of the current sample. This is usually done to increase precision of the estimator.

Child poverty: Share of children below the poverty line out of total number of child population.

Coverage: The share of beneficiaries in the total population. Unless explicitly stated otherwise, coverage figures consider both direct and indirect beneficiaries, that is, all members of beneficiary households.

Decile: A form of quantile. It is any of the 9 values that divide the sorted data into 10 equal parts, so that each part represents one-tenth of the sample population.

Extreme poverty: Threshold corresponding to US$1.25 per day consumption per adult equivalent (that is adjusted by the different needs of persons of different age and gender).

Leakage: The number of eligible households incorrectly included by the formula divided by the total number of eligible households.

Ordinary least squares (OLS): A method for estimating the unknown parameters in a linear regression model, with the goal of minimizing the differences between the observed response in some arbitrary dataset and the responses predicted by the linear approximation of the data.

Percentile: A measure used in statistics indicating the value below which fall a given percentage of observations in a group of observations.

Quantile: Values taken at regular intervals from the inverse function of the cumulative distribution function.

Salaried employment: Adults in formal, hired employment.

Seasonality: A characteristic of a time series in which the data experience regular and predictable changes that recur every calendar year. Any predictable change or pattern in a time series that recurs or repeats over a one-year period can be said to be seasonal.

Targeting: Selection of potential consumers. It involves segmenting the market, choosing which segments of the market are appropriate, and determining the products that will be offered in each segment.

Undercoverage: Defined as the number of poor households incorrectly excluded by the formula ("exclusion" or type 1 error) divided by the total number of poor in the sample.

Welfare aggregate: In this report, monthly household consumption before Targeted Social Assistance transfers.

Environmental Benefits Statement

The World Bank Group is committed to reducing its environmental footprint. In support of this commitment, World Bank Publications leverages electronic publishing options and print-on-demand technology, which is located in regional hubs worldwide. Together, these initiatives enable print runs to be lowered and shipping distances decreased, resulting in reduced paper consumption, chemical use, greenhouse gas emissions, and waste.

World Bank Publications follows the recommended standards for paper use set by the Green Press Initiative. The majority of our books are printed on Forest Stewardship Council (FSC)–certified paper, with nearly all containing 50–100 percent recycled content. The recycled fiber in our book paper is either unbleached or bleached using totally chlorine-free (TCF), processed chlorine-free (PCF), or enhanced elemental chlorine-free (EECF) processes.

More information about the Bank's environmental philosophy can be found at http://www.worldbank.org/corporateresponsibility.

green
press
INITIATIVE

www.ingramcontent.com/pod-product-compliance
Lightning Source LLC
Chambersburg PA
CBHW080423270326
41929CB00018B/3137